Psychoanalysis, Fatherhood, and the Modern Family

"At a time when cultural and academic discourse is overflowing with ideas about diversity and fluidity in gender and personal life, it is easy to overlook how Freud's concept of the Oedipus Complex continues to shape our most deeply held beliefs about fatherhood and the family. This fascinating book draws on a range of theoretical, clinical, and empirical perspectives to question, challenge, and highlight the relevance of Freud's work today. A wonderful collection of essays to stimulate debate and reflection for years to come."

—Tabitha Freeman, *Former Senior Research Associate at Centre for Family Research, University of Cambridge, UK*

"This is a first-rate collection of essays, which will revitalize the debate on one of the most important, influential, and controversial topics of psychoanalysis. All the essays are illuminating, learned, and engagingly written. It makes for an informative—as well as exciting and fun!—read."

—Mario Telò, *Professor of Classics and Comparative Literature, University of California, Berkeley*

"This volume takes us not only to Freud, his father, Oedipus, and *Oedipus*, but also to many of their interlocutors and critics from within the history of psychoanalysis as well as anthropology, feminism, and philosophy. Its lucid introduction and many splendid essays illuminate fatherhood from different angles even while making paternity itself uncanny. As a result, *Psychoanalysis, Fatherhood, and the Modern Family* will appeal to a wide range of readers—students, teachers, and the psychoanalytic community more generally—eager to learn all about fathers, past and present."

—Andrew Parker, *Professor of French and Comparative Literature, Rutgers University, USA*

Liliane Weissberg
Editor

Psychoanalysis, Fatherhood, and the Modern Family

palgrave
macmillan

Editor
Liliane Weissberg
Department of German and Program in Comparative
Literature and Literary Theory
University of Pennsylvania
Philadelphia, PA, USA

ISBN 978-3-030-82123-4 ISBN 978-3-030-82124-1 (eBook)
https://doi.org/10.1007/978-3-030-82124-1

Cover illustration: ARCHIVIO GBB / Alamy Stock Photo

This Palgrave Macmillan imprint is published by the registered company Springer Nature Switzerland AG.
The registered company address is: Gewerbestrasse 11, 6330 Cham, Switzerland

Acknowledgments

This book had its origin as a workshop, sponsored by the University of Pennsylvania in the context of the College's "Year of Health" program. David Fox from Penn's College Office suggested that I organize an event for that year, and taking him up on the idea, I set out to plan a collaboration with the Psychoanalytic Center of Pennsylvania (PCOP). As such, *Psychoanalysis, Fatherhood, and the Modern Family* became part of a series of lectures and colloquia that mark the cooperation between these institutions, organized to foster a wider appreciation of, and reflection on, psychoanalytic thought, and to sponsor conversations between practicing analysts and University faculty. This ongoing cooperation has led to new programs for the PCOP and to the creation of a psychoanalytic studies minor at Penn. I would like to thank David Fox, as well as Gregory Urban of Penn's Department of Anthropology, Lawrence Blum of the PCOP, and Richard Summers of Penn Psychiatry and PCOP, for their sponsorship and encouragement of, as well as participation in, the workshop. I would also like to thank German graduate students David Nelson and Alan Madin for their support. Martina Bale in German provided administrative help and Eduardo Glandt, then Dean of the School of Engineering, offered us the space for an event that quite literally engaged the University as a whole.

Some workshops do conclude at the end of the day. In this case, the discussions went on. Conversations about the role of fatherhood in Freud's work, as well as that of his successors and critics, continued, as did those regarding the role of the father in modern society. The participants of the workshop remained in touch and engaged, and new scholars and psychoanalytic practitioners joined the project as it expanded far beyond Philadelphia. The chapters collected in this book document the discussion. For me, at least, the book project evolved into a prime example of the kind of work a cooperation between a University and a Psychoanalytic Institute can and should promote.

As the project has evolved, I have been aided by various persons and institutions. In the psychoanalytic community, I would like to single out Beverly Stoute for special thanks. Penn's Research Council and the Dean's Office supplied funds for the preparation of the book. Philip Getz guided the project expertly at Palgrave Macmillan, and I am very grateful for his advice and support. I am also grateful for the constructive feedback that I received from the anonymous readers of the manuscript. And as always, I would also like to thank Jerry Singerman for his support.

Our group's project will embark into print, but our conversations will continue.

March 2021 Liliane Weissberg

Contents

Notes on Contributors

C. Jama Adams is Associate Professor of Psychology at the John Jay College of Criminal Justice, City University of New York, USA. He has written extensively on the role of fathers in Caribbean-American and African-American families and psychoanalytic perspectives on Blackness. His work has appeared in the *Caribbean Quarterly*, the *Journal of Infant, Child, and Adolescent Psychotherapy*, and other journals.

Richard H. Armstrong is Associate Professor of Classical Studies in the Department of Modern and Classical Languages at the University of Houston, USA. A scholar of the reception of classical culture, he is the author of *A Compulsion for Antiquity: Freud and the Ancient World* (2006) and *Theory and Theatricality: Classical Drama in the Age of Grand Hysteria* (2021), as well as co-editor with Alexandra Lianeri of the *Companion to the Translation of Classical Epic* (2022).

Harold Blum is a supervising and training analyst at the Psychoanalytic Association of New York, affiliated with New York University Medical School, USA, and the former Executive Director of the Sigmund Freud Archives. A former editor of the *Journal of the American Psychoanalytic Association*, he has written widely on many aspects of psychoanalysis, including Freud's life and works. He is an inaugural winner of the Sigourney Award, honoring his contribution to the advancement of psychoanalysis and psychoanalytic thought worldwide.

Adrian Daub is Professor of German and Comparative Literature, and Director of the Program in Sexuality and Gender Studies at Stanford

University, USA. His publications focus on German literature and culture from the late eighteenth century to the present, among them *Uncivil Unions: The Metaphysics of Marriage in German Idealism and Romanticism* (2012), *Tristan's Shadow: Sexuality and the Total Work of Art After Wagner* (2013), and *The Dynastic Imagination: Family and Modernity in Nineteenth-Century Germany* (2021). He is also a cultural critic and commentator whose essays have appeared in major American and German newspapers and journals.

John Frank is a child and adult psychiatrist and psychoanalyst. He is Clinical Professor of Psychiatry Emeritus at Drexel University College of Medicine, USA, and he is on the faculty of the Psychoanalytic Center of Philadelphia. He is working on a memoir about his relationship with his father, the author and ghostwriter Gerold Frank.

Patricia Gherovici is a psychoanalyst, supervisor, and recipient of the Sigourney Award. She is the author of more than seventy articles and book chapters. Her books include *The Puerto Rican Syndrome* (2003, Gradiva Award and Boyer Prize); *Transgender Psychoanalysis: A Lacanian Perspective on Sexual Difference* (2017); and, with Christopher Christian, the anthology *Psychoanalysis in the Barrios: Race, Class, and the Unconscious* (2019, Gradiva Award and American Board and Academy of Psychoanalysis Book Prize).

Dorothea Olkowski is Professor of Philosophy and Director of Humanities at the University of Colorado, Colorado Springs, USA. She has written widely on contemporary French philosophy and is the author most recently of *Deleuze and Guattari's Philosophy of Freedom: Freedom's Refrains* (2019) and *Deleuze, Bergson, Merleau-Ponty: The Logic and Pragmatics of Affect, Perception, and Creation* (2021).

Jean-Michel Rabaté is Professor of English and Comparative Literature at the University of Pennsylvania, USA. He is the co-editor of the *Journal of Modern Literature* and co-founder of Slought Foundation. He is the author or editor of more than forty books on modernism, psychoanalysis, philosophy, and literary theory. His most recent monographs include *Rust* (2018), *Kafka L.O.L.* (2018), *Rire au Soleil* (2019), *Beckett and Sade* (2020), and *Rires Prodigues* (2021); his most recent collections include *After Derrida* (2018), *New Beckett* (2019), *Understanding Derrida/Understanding Modernism* (2019), and *Knots: Post-Lacanian*

Psychoanalysis, Literature and Film (2020). Rabaté is a fellow of the American Academy of Arts and Sciences.

Laurence A. Rickels is Sigmund Freud Professor of Media and Philosophy at the European Graduate School, Saas-Fee, Switzerland, and Professor Emeritus at the University of California, Santa Barbara, USA. He is the author of many books on literary, cultural, and media criticism, among others: *Nazi Psychoanalysis*, 3 vols. (2002), *The Devil Notebooks* (2008), *I Think I Am: Philip K. Dick* (2010), *The Psycho Records* (2016), and *Critique of Fantasy*, 3 vols. (2020–2021).

Avital Ronell is Professor of German and Comparative Literature and University Professor of the Humanities at New York University, USA. She is the author of many books that bring together the fields of philosophy, the visual arts, and literary studies, among them *The Test Drive* (2005), *Loser Sons: Politics and Authority* (2012), and *Complaint: Grievance Among Friends* (2018). A selection of her work has been collected in *The ÜberReader: Selected Works of Avital Ronell*, ed. Diane Davis (2008).

Liliane Weissberg is Christopher H. Browne Distinguished Professor of Arts and Science at the University of Pennsylvania, USA. Among her recent book publications are *Münzen, Hände, Noten, Finger: Berliner Hofjuden und die Erfindung einer deutschen Musikkultur* (2018), the anthology *Nachträglich, grundlegend: Der Kommentar als Denkform in der jüdischen Moderne* (edited with Andreas Kilcher, 2018), and *Benjamin Veitel Ephraim: Kaufmann, Schriftsteller, Geheimagent* (2021). She has written widely on Sigmund Freud's life and work, and is an honorary member of the Psychoanalytic Center of Philadelphia. Among her awards are a Guggenheim Fellowship, a Fulbright-Freud Fellowship, the Berlin Prize of the American Academy, and the Alexander von Humboldt Research Award.

List of Figures

CHAPTER 1

Introduction: Psychoanalysis, Fatherhood, and the Work of Mourning

Liliane Weissberg

Full fathom five thy father lies;
Of his bones are coral made;
Those are pearls that were his eyes:
Nothing of him that doth fade,
But doth suffer a sea-change
Into something rich and strange.
—William Shakespeare, *The Tempest*

The Absent Father

At its origin, psychoanalysis was the work of mourning. Not any death was mourned, however, nor are we speaking about a random mourner. A father had died, and the mourner in question was his son Sigmund Freud.

Jacob Freud passed away on October 23, 1896. In July 1897, Freud embarked on a self-analysis during which he played the double role of analyst and patient, and focused on dreams rather than the free

L. Weissberg (✉)
University of Pennsylvania, Philadelphia, PA, USA
e-mail: lweissbe@sas.upenn.edu

L. Weissberg (ed.), *Psychoanalysis, Fatherhood, and the Modern Family*, https://doi.org/10.1007/978-3-030-82124-1_1

associations that he had encouraged in his earlier patients.[1] In the process, he would reflect on his relationship to his father, explore his own wishes and desires, but also formulate his ideas about the human psyche in general. The individual case study of Sigmund Freud led to Freud's writing of a book, the *Traumdeutung* [*The Interpretation of Dreams*], that would become his best-known work and the manifesto of a new discipline called psychoanalysis. It was published in 1899—but was postdated with 1900. After all, Freud had conceived it as the work of the new century.

While the *Interpretation of Dreams* was written by a son, this son was already a father himself. Freud's daughter Anna, who would later become a psychoanalyst too, was born a few months before Jacob Freud's death, in December 1895. She was the last of Freud's six children: three sons and three daughters all. But while Jacob Freud's death would send his son off on a road of discovery, the addressee of its account was very much alive. During the period of his self-analysis, Freud directed many letters to a fellow physician, Wilhelm Fliess, and kept him abreast of the analytical process and his insights.

Fliess was an otolaryngologist who lived and practiced in Berlin. He had met Freud in November 1887 in Vienna. Fliess had visited the city, and upon the advice of Freud's older mentor Josef Breuer, he had attended a scholarly lecture offered by Freud. After Fliess' return to Berlin, he and Freud engaged in a correspondence of which only Freud's letters survived. These letters offer insights into Freud's own family life as well as early psychoanalytic concepts. In a triangulation that involved a father, who had passed away, and a friend, who was geographically absent, Freud established himself as an author who was not only eager for self-exploration, but also for male friendship.[2] While there was no question about Freud's mourning, other questions soon arose. In his dreams and recollections, his father did not quite conform to then-current ideals of steadfast masculinity, and his behavior evoked the son's resentment. Once, when Jacob Freud was attacked by a stranger in the street just for being a Jew, the insulted man

[1] See Josef Breuer and Sigmund Freud, *Studies on Hysteria*, published as *Studien über Hysterie*, Leipzig: Franz Deuticke, 1895. The perhaps most famous case study in this volume was that of Bertha Pappenheim ("Anna O.") who coined a term that defined these free associations and the psychoanalytic process, "talking cure."

[2] Liliane Weissberg, "Was will der Mann? Gedanken zum Briefwechsel von Sigmund Freud und Wilhelm Fließ." In: Claudia Benthien and Inge Stephan (Eds.), *Männlichkeit als Maskerade. Kulturelle Inszenierungen vom Mittelalter bis zur Gegenwart.* (ser.) Literatur—Kultur—Geschichte (Kleine Reihe) 18 (Cologne: Böhlau, 2003), 81–99.

had not shown any pride. He had just picked up his hat from the gutter and remained silent.[3] No son should have to witness such embarrassingly submissive behavior. But as evidenced in his letters to Fliess, Jacob Freud's son did not quite conform to the ideals of masculinity either, albeit in a different way. In probing his relationship to his correspondent, and discovering his attraction to Fliess, Freud was exploring his own sexuality and desire. He had to face his feminine side.

Just like Freud, Fliess was both a practicing physician and a scientist and scholar. His research was biologically based and highly speculative. In 1897, he published a book entitled *Die Beziehungen zwischen Nase und weiblichen Geschlechtsorganen (in ihrer biologischen Bedeutung dargestellt)* [The Relationship Between the Nose and the Female Sex Organs (Depicted in Their Biological Significance)].[4] His theories led surgical experiments related to the nose by which he tried to reduce the complaints of female patients who were suffering from hysteric symptoms. One of these patients was Emma Eckstein. Fliess sent her to Freud after he had botched a medical procedure, and the incident takes center stage in one of Freud's dreams of 1895, and appears in the *Interpretation of Dreams* in the "Analysis of a Specimen Dream."[5] Fliess also focused on the importance of biorhythms for both women and men. He thought that these would be influential for the classification of mental illnesses and helpful for the treatment of hysterics. In *Der Ablauf des Lebens. Grundlagen zur exakten Biologie* [The Journey of Life. The Fundaments of Scientific Biology], he set out to describe human biology in terms of 23- or 28-day cycles.[6] This book was published in 1906, but already in his correspondence with Freud, he was focusing on collecting data for the study that Freud was eager to supply for his friend.[7] Most importantly, however, Fliess would be the first theorist to propose a general concept of human bisexuality. "Only someone who knows he is in possession of the truth writes as you do,"

[3] Daniel Boyarin, "Freud's Baby, Fliess' Maybe: Homophobia, Anti-Semitism, and the Invention of Oedipus" GLQ 2 (1995): 115–147.

[4] Wilhelm Fliess, *Die Beziehungen zwischen Nase und weiblichen Geschlechtsorganen (in ihrer biologischen Bedeutung dargestellt)*, Leipzig and Vienna: Franz Deuticke, 1897.

[5] Freud, *The Interpretation of Dreams: The Complete and Definite Text.* Ed. and tr. James Strachey (1955, New York: Basic Books, 2010), 130–145.

[6] Fliess, *Der Ablauf des Lebens. Grundlagen zur exakten Biologie.* Leipzig und Wien: Franz Deuticke, 1906.

[7] In regard to Freud's trust in biology at this time, see Frank J. Sulloway, *Freud: Biologist of the Mind*, Cambridge: Harvard University Press, 1992.

Freud wrote admiringly to his Berlin friend, and while he would consider Fliess' concept of bisexuality for his own work as well, his early analysis focuses on his development as a man, even though he could not deny his feelings for Fliess. Later, Fliess would blame Freud for having passed his ideas concerning bisexuality on to a third person, namely Otto Weininger, whose provocative study *Geschlecht und Charakter* [*Sex and Character*] was published in 1903, and gained immediate attention, thus sidelining Fliess' discovery.[8]

In terms of his own analysis, Freud stayed on course. One important scene from his childhood that he could recall relates to his mother. In a letter to Fliess from October 3, 1897, he recalls the family trip from Leipzig to Vienna, where the family was about to settle for good. In the train, the two-year-old child had an opportunity to spend the night with his mother,[9] "and there must have been an opportunity of seeing her *nudam*."[10] He continues to insert Latin terms that are perfectly suited for the scholarly and medical realm, and concludes by describing the effect of this scene, namely that his "libido toward *matrem* was awakened."[11]

"My self-analysis is in fact the most essential thing I have at present and promises to become of the greatest value to me if it reaches its end," Freud explains a couple of weeks later in a letter penned on October 15, 1897, in which he also mentions various of his dreams. "If the analysis fulfills what I expect of it," he writes,

> I shall work on it systematically and then put it before you. So far I have found nothing completely new, [just] all the complications to which I have become accustomed. It is by no means easy. Being totally honest with oneself is a good exercise. A single idea of general value dawned on me. I have found, in my own case too, [the phenomenon of] being in love with my mother and jealous of my father, and I now consider it a universal event

[8] Richard Pfennig, *Wilhelm Fliess und seine Nachentdecker, O. Weininger und H. Swoboda*. Berlin: Emil Goldschmidt, 1906.

[9] Freud describes himself here as two or two-and-a-half-year-old; he would later state that he was four-year-old. The family moved to Vienna in 1860. See José Brunner, "The Naked Mother or, Why Freud Did not Write about Railway Accidents." *Psychoanalysis and History* 9 (2007): 71–82.

[10] Freud, letter to Fliess, October 3, 1897. In: *The Complete Letters of Sigmund Freud to Wilhelm Fliess, 1887–1904*, ed. Jeffrey M. Masson (Cambridge, MA: The Belknap Press of Harvard University Press, 1985), 268.

[11] Freud, letter to Fliess, October 3, 1897. In: *The Complete Letters of Sigmund Freud to Wilhelm Fliess*, 268.

> in early childhood, even if not so early as in children who have been made hysterical. (Similar to the invention of parentage [family romance] in paranoia—heroes, founders of religion). If this is so, we can understand the gripping power of Oedipus Rex, in spite of all the objections that reason raises against the presupposition of fate; and we can understand why the later "drama of fate" was bound to fail so miserably. Our feelings rise against any arbitrary individual compulsion, such as is presupposed in *Die Ahnfrau* and the like; but the Greek legend seizes upon a compulsion which everyone recognizes because he senses its existence within himself. Everyone in the audience was once a budding Oedipus in fantasy and each recoils in horror from the dream fulfillment here transplanted into reality, with the full quantity of repression which separates his infantile state from his present one.[12]

Franz Grillparzer's *Die Ahnfrau* [*The Ancestress*], a drama first published in 1817, features a son who kills his father. In the letter cited above, Freud does not only place his reading of Sophocles in comparison to Grillparzer's work. Both plays are part of another triangulation as Freud refers to a third drama that would preoccupy him in the years to come. It is William Shakespeare's Hamlet.[13] With Shakespeare's work, he thought to have found a family drama similar to *Οἰδίπους Τύραννος* [*Oedipus the King* or *Oedipus Rex*], and superior to Grillparzer's *Ancestress.*[14] "How does Hamlet the hysteric justify his words, 'Thus conscience does make cowards of us all'?," Freud asks, "How does he explain his irresolution in avenging his father by the murder of his uncle—the same man who sends his courtiers to their death without a scruple and who is positively precipitate in murdering Laertes?"[15] While Sophocles' play puts the generational sequence into question, Freud quite curiously mistakes a father for his son in this passage, and replaces Polonius with the young Laertes.

Freud's letter of October 17, 1897, offers also his first consideration of Sophocles' play as a key text for understanding the human psyche. Once again, a father and son were on the road. But while Jacob Freud, the

[12] Freud, letter to Fliess, October 15, 1897; *The Complete Letters of Sigmund Freud to Wilhelm Fliess*, 272.

[13] See, for example, John Fletcher, "The Scenography of Trauma: A 'Copernican' Reading of Sophocles' Oedipus the King," *Textual Practice* 21 (2007): 17–41, here 21–24.

[14] Perhaps most prominently among Freud's students, Ernest Jones would late take up a comparison of both works in his *Hamlet and Oedipus*, London: V. Gollancz, 1949.

[15] Freud, letter to Fliess, October 15, 1897; *The Complete Letters of Sigmund Freud to Wilhelm Fliess*, 272–273.

father, met with insult, and remained passive, the same cannot be said about Oedipus, the son, who was quick to respond, and to get his way. We never learn about the identity of the stranger whom Jacob Freud encountered, but the stranger to whom Oedipus responded, and with a violent act, turned out to be his father.[16] That story would now gain special significance, and carried forth from his letter to Fliess to the *Interpretation of Dreams*. There, he would reformulate his argument as follows, while providing a renewed reference to Grillparzer's play:

> If *Oedipus Rex* moves a modern audience no less than it did the contemporary Greek one, the explanation can only be that its effect does not lie in the contrast between destiny and human will, but is to be looked for in the particular nature of the material on which the contrast is exemplified. There must be something which makes a voice within us ready to recognize the compelling force of destiny in the *Oedipus*, while we can dismiss as merely arbitrary such dispositions as are laid down in *Die Ahnfrau* or other modern tragedies of destiny. And a factor of this kind is in fact involved in the story of *King Oedipus*.[17]

It is Freud's first mention of a phenomenon that he would name the Oedipus complex. Here, however, Freud no longer refers to his own personal experience. And as he moves from writing a personal letter to Fliess to writing a book for a general public, he no longer simply recognizes Fliess' truth, as he once claimed, or his very own, as Oedipus did in Sophocles' play. Instead, the story of Oedipus achieves a universal truth and provides a general key to the human psyche:

> His destiny moves us only because it might have been ours—because the oracle laid the same curse upon us before our birth as upon him. It is the fate of all of us, perhaps, to direct our first sexual impulse towards our mother and our first hatred and our first murderous wish against our father. Our dreams convince us that that is so. King Oedipus, who slew his father Laïus and married his mother Jocasta, merely shows us the fulfilment of our own

[16] No doubt, this turn of events in the Greek drama would also be attractive for Freud's later contemplation on the notion of the "uncanny." In regard to Sophocles and the uncanny, see John Gould, "The Language of Oedipus." In: Harold Bloom (Ed.), Sophocles' Oedipus Rex. (ser.) Modern Critical Interpretations (New York: Chelsea House Publishers, 1988), 143–160, esp. 153.

[17] Freud, *The Interpretation of Dreams*, ed. and tr. James Strachey. Complete and definite Text (1955; New York: Basic Books, 2010), 279–280.

> childhood wishes. But, more fortunate than he, we have meanwhile succeeded, in so far we have not become psychoneurotics, in detaching our sexual impulses from our mothers and in forgetting our jealousy of our fathers. Here is one in whom these primaeval wishes of our childhood have been fulfilled, and we shrink back from him with the whole force of the repression by which those wishes have since that time been held down within us. While the poet, as he unravels the past, brings to light the guilt of Oedipus, he is at the same time compelling us to recognize our own inner minds, in which those same impulses, though suppressed, are still to be found.[18]

His own case study provided Freud with a new understanding of Sophocles' drama. Freud had already treated hysteric patients for several years by then, and had been hopeful to be able to cure them. Together with Breuer, he had published the *Studien über Hysterie* [*Studies in Hysteria*] in 1895. In October of that same year, he wrote to Fliess:

> I am almost certain that I have solved the riddles of hysteria and obsessional neurosis with the formulas of infantile sexual shock and sexual pleasure, and I am equally certain that both neuroses are, in general, curable—not just individual symptoms but the neurotic disposition itself. This gives me a kind of faint joy—for having lived some forty years not quite in vain—and yet no genuine satisfaction because the psychological gap in the new knowledge claims my entire interest.[19]

But Freud also explained the "shock" in question as an early sexual incident in the female patient's life that has caused trauma, and he urged the patient to remember her relationship with her father or perhaps other older men in her family circle. In his treatment of patients, Freud had set out to find those incidents that were seemingly forgotten by his patients, but curiously remembered as hysteric symptoms still.

With the discovery of the Oedipus story as a universal template, Freud moved away from the so-called seduction theory of his earlier work. Trauma could not only be caused by an actual incident, it seemed, but by an imagined one as well. Further, Freud was able to assume a different temporal concept of *Nachträglichkeit* (afterwardness, belatedness, or

[18] Freud, *The Interpretation of Dreams*, 280.

[19] Freud, letter to Fliess, October 16, 1895; *The Complete Letters of Sigmund Freud to Wilhelm Fliess*, 145.

après-coup), in which the event was established in memory only.[20] For this discovery, Fliess' former patient Eckstein, now in Freud's care, was important as well. In 1895, he offers Fliess an "Entwurf einer Psychologie" ["Project for a Scientific Psychology"],[21] and offers the following glimpse from her case study:

> Emma is subject at the present time under a compulsion of not being able to go into shops *alone*. As a reason for this, [she produced] a memory from the time when she was twelve years old (shortly after puberty). She went into a shop to buy something, saw the two shop-assistants (one of whom she can remember) laughing together, and ran away in some kind of *affect of fright*. In connection with this, she was led to recall that the two of them were laughing at her clothes and that one of them had pleased her sexually.[22]

The story is seemingly trivial, and young woman's "affect of fright" is difficult to understand. Why was she so eager to leave the store? Freud has to refer to Eckstein's associations and her earlier memories to find an explanation:

> Further investigation now revealed a second memory, which she denies having had in mind at the moment of Scene I. Nor is there anything to prove this. On two occasions when she was a child of eight she had gone into a small shop to buy some sweets, and the shopkeeper had grabbed her genitals through her clothes. In spite of the first experience she had gone there a second time; after the second time she stopped away. She now reproached herself for having gone there a second time, as though she had wanted in that way to provoke the assault. In fact a state of 'oppressive bad conscience' is to be traced back to this experience.

[20] The English translation of the term "Nachträglichkeit" has been much discussed, see also Jean Laplanche and Jean-Bertrand Pontalis, *The Language of Psycho-analysis*, tr. Donald Nicholson-Smith. New York, Norton, 1973. For a discussion of the various translations of the term and its history, see also Jonathan House and Julie Slotnick, "Après-coup in French Psychoanalysis: The Long Afterlife of Nachträglichkeit: The First Hundred Years, 1893–1993." *The Psychoanalytic Review* 102 (2015): 683–708.

[21] The "Entwurf einer Psychologie" (Project for a Scientific Psychology, 1895) was first published in 1950. In regard to the context and the late publication of the "Project," see Zvi Lothane, "Freud's 1895 *Project*. From Mind to Brain and Back Again." *Annals New York Academy of Sciences* 843 (1998): 43–65.

[22] Freud, "Project for a Scientific Psychology." In: Freud, *The Standard Edition of the Complete Psychological Works*, tr. James Strachey, ed. Anna Freud et al., 24 vols. (London: The Hogarth Press, 1953–1974), I: 282–397; here 353 (edition will be abbreviated *SE*).

> We now understand Scene I (shop-assistants) if we take Scene II (shopkeeper) along with it.[23]

In the first and in the second narrative, Freud relies on Eckstein's memories, not dreams. Curiously, however, the second experience as an eight-year-old girl is able to comment on the later experience of the twelve-year old, and both of them reflect on the behavior of the grown woman in Freud's treatment. The temporal direction is reversed; Freud has to forge his way into Eckstein's past to find an explanation. When the eight-year-old girl is being molested by a man, would she already know about his sexual desire? As the twelve-year-old encounters the laughing salesmen, Freud discovers the opposite; the girl seems to take a liking to one of them. Here, Eckstein is already past puberty. Only later, after passing puberty, the young girl will realize what had happened before; only when encountering her own sexual desire, was she able to understand the earlier man's intention toward the younger girl. As Freud realized, memories do not simply recall the past. They take place in the present and orient themselves according to the knowledge that one has in present time. Because of this afterwardness or *Nachträglichkeit*, nothing can be attributed to the past that could not be changed later on as well. Even trauma forms itself only belatedly, in seeming repetition of past experience. For the trauma itself, it is irrelevant whether the earlier incident existed or not; it is the memory that bears importance.

Sophocles' drama did not only serve Freud to discover an old myth, but to rediscover it; to realize a truth that he must have known already. Later critics like Jeffrey M. Masson would famously criticize Freud's abandonment of the seduction theory.[24] In turning away from it, Masson argued, Freud consciously turned away from social reality and the large numbers of cases of child molestation in fin-de-siècle Vienna. Was Freud so conservative a family father himself that he chose to remain blind vis-à-vis the behavior of other fathers toward their young daughters? But in rejecting the seduction theory, and privileging the imaginary versus the real, Freud also set the framework for psychoanalysis proper. Even a son's

[23] Freud, "Project for a Scientific Psychology," *SE* I: 353–354.

[24] Masson, *The Assault on Truth: Freud's Suppression of the Seduction Theory*. New York: Farrar, Straus and Giroux, 1984. See also the discussion in Lawrence Birken, "From Seduction Theory to Oedipus Complex: A Historical Analysis." *New German Critique* 43 (1988). Special Issue on Austria: 83–96.

relationship to his father no longer had to be real, but could be imagined. The Oedipus complex moved to become psychoanalysis' core.[25]

The Drama of *Oedipus the King*

Perhaps it was not too far-fetched for Freud to focus on a literary work when arguing for the power of imagination, although the abandonment of the seduction theory also replaces the reality of an event in social life with that of a biologically based sexual development—as well as the shift from the girl as hysteric patient to the boy as the focus of the Oedipal complex. But Freud did not see Sophocles as the author of the story of Oedipus. The Greek author had not freely invented a plot; instead, he was a dramatist who transformed a myth for the stage. The myth's significance reached beyond a single author's achievement, and transcended classical Greek drama. In viewing *Oedipus the King*, Sophocles' audience realized the story's truth; they could recognize themselves. Still, it was the drama that taught Freud about the myth and thus, the drama's greater truth. Sophocles' work offered Freud insight, just as the figure of Oedipus in the play would gain his insights from the account of a truthsayer who, like the Sphinx, offered a riddle. "Do you know?" asks the blind seer Tiresias, for example,

> All unknowing
> you are the scourge of your own flesh and blood,
> the dead below the earth and the living here above,
> and the double lash of your mother and your father's curse
> will whip you from this land one day, their footfall
> treading you down in terror, darkness shrouding
> your eyes that now can see the light![26]

Oedipus seems to know enough to solve the Sphinx's riddle—"What walks on four feet in the morning, two in the afternoon and three at night?"—as he answers: man. But while he would know about the nature of man in general, he knows little about himself—at least, he does not

[25] See also the survey by Lowell Edmunds and Richard Ingber, "Psychoanalytical Writings on the Oedipus Legend: A Bibliography," *American Imago* 34 (1977): 374–386.

[26] Sophocles, *Oedipus the King*, 473–479; in: Sophocles, *The Three Theban Plays: Antigone—Oedipus the King—Oedipus at Colonus*, tr. Robert Fagles (London: Penguin Press, 1984), 183.

know his true identity and history. He does not realize who his father is, or that he had killed his father at a crossing of country roads. He views himself as a stranger who had vanquished the evil Sphinx and has become King of Thebes as a reward; he does not know that he is not a stranger at all, but a Prince of Thebes; or that woman whom he would marry, the Queen, is his mother. Again, and again, the blind seer Tiresias would offer him hints and point him to the direction of his self-discovery, but it takes time until Oedipus is able to understand. Once he gains this knowledge, he blinds himself. His blindness will meet that of Tiresias. But did Oedipus learn something new in this process, or had he somehow known everything already?

Unlike Freud's patients, Sophocles' hero bears the physical mark of a swollen foot that is not a hysteric symptom. His tragedy is that he is unable to draw any conclusions from that which Tiresias offers. It is the audience of this play who knows, as it listens to Tiresias' words. The problem of afterwardness becomes one of staging here, as Oedipus enters belatedly, only to miss part of Tiresias' speech:

> A stranger,
> You may think, who lives among you,
> He will soon be revealed a native Theban
> But he will take no joy in the revelation.
> Blind who now has eyes, beggar who now is rich,
> He will grope his way towards a foreign soil,
> A stick tapping before him step by step.
> [Oedipus *enters the palace*]
> Revealed at last, brother and father both
> To the children he embraces, to his mother
> Son and husband both—he sowed the loins
> His father sowed, he spilled his father's blood![27]

As in all true Greek drama, the last revelation comes to Oedipus as a surprise. Freud would introduce the idea of such a revelation or *katharsis* in his terminology of treating patients. Thus, he follows a Greek tradition where dramatic and medical professions come together. The classicist Jacob Bernays, an uncle of Freud's wife Martha, had already pointed out

[27] Sophocles, *Oedipus the King*, 513–523; *The Three Theban Plays*, 185.

the rich meaning of the word.[28] But there is a difference between a surprising revelation, and a revelation that equals recognition, or the recall of something that one already knew.

And unlike Sophocles' hero, Freud's Oedipus seems to act knowingly. He falls in love with his mother and kills his father with the purpose of removing a rival for his mother's affection. In Sophocles, Oedipus does not even know that the man whom he kills was married—and married to his own mother; and Oedipus does not marry out of love, but political considerations and dynastic obligations. We do not know whom he desires. At the same time, Sophocles' character is not just engaged in incest, but troubles the logic of generations that is crucial for the polis as well: His children are his siblings, too.

In the *Interpretation of Dreams*, Freud writes: "Being in love with one parent and hating the other are among the essential constituents of the stock of psychical impulses which is formed at that time and which is of such importance in determining the symptoms of the later neurosis."[29] Freud's version of the Oedipus story not only privileges private feelings over a political agenda while offering his own interpretation of what Oedipus may have known, but also focuses on mother, father, and son while neglecting other relations that are important to the Greek story. No siblings appear, for example. And Oedipus' story is significant as that of a son only, although he is the father of children as well.

Laius, moreover, is not Oedipus' only father. Indeed, Oedipus would look at Polybus, the King who raised him, as his father, while Laius believed his son to be dead. Even Zeus is called upon in the drama as yet another father by the chorus: "O lord of the stormcloud, you who twirl the lightning, Zeus, Father, thunder Death to nothing!"[30] And far from driving the plot by his own desire, Oedipus' fate in *Oedipus the King* is already set by his own father's actions, and a story that takes place before his birth. Laius had raped Chrysippus, a young man whom he carried off to Thebes before marrying Jocasta. The oracle of Delphi had warned him not to have a child; if he had a son, this son would kill him. Nevertheless, Laius fathered a child with Jocasta. When Oedipus was born, Laius tried

[28] Jacob Bernays, "Zur Katharsis-Frage." *Rheinisches Museum für Philologie*. Neue Folge 15 (1860): 606–607. In regard to the issue of katharsis as "recognition" in Freud's reading of the Oedipus story, see Rachel Bowlby, "Family Realisms: Freud and Greek Tragedy," *Essays in Criticism* 56 (2006): 111–138.

[29] Freud, *The Interpretations of Dreams*, pp. 260–261.

[30] Sophocles, *Oedipus the King*, 229; *The Three Theban Plays*, 170.

to prevent what was predicted to happen, and thus to ensure his life. But the servant charged with killing the child merely abandoned him instead, after first injuring its foot: This child could perhaps survive, but was not to return.

Oedipus presents this injury, which results in a swollen foot—*oid* and *podos*—in his very name,[31] but as Bernard Knox points out, the Greek word for swollen, *oidi*, retains an acoustic resemblance to *oida*, I know.[32] With his name, the adult Oedipus acknowledges his father's guilt without seeming to know of the deed. Much has been written on the topic of sacrifice in regard to Oedipus' story. While the Biblical Abraham was asked to sacrifice his son and wants to follow God's command, Laius attempts to sacrifice his son to avoid the Gods' judgment.[33] Isaac was saved; Oedipus was only seemingly saved. Unbeknownst to Laius, he stayed alive. But when the adult Oedipus kills his father, he is not just acting on his own, nor does he realize the Gods' plans for his own destiny only. He fulfills an oracle offered to his father, and becomes the Gods' instrument in sealing Laius' fate. It is Laius' guilt that brings about Oedipus' actions; Oedipus' fate is not simply triggered by what he himself knows and does not know, but by his father's actions and the Gods' judgment. Oedipus may not know enough, but Laius does not either.

Is Oedipus' story thus the tragedy of a son, or that of a father? This question has been posed by literary critics including Silke-Maria Weineck who have returned to the Classical texts, and who have shifted their attention to Laius,[34] by folklorists who have collected versions of the myth,[35] as well as psychoanalysts, who have pointed at different versions of

[31] ποδός translates as foot οἴδημα; as edema, lump, swell.

[32] Bernard Knox, "Sophocles' Oedipus." In: Bloom (Ed.), *Sophocles' Oedipus Rex*, 5–22, here 9.

[33] See Moshe Shamir, "Oedipus and Abraham," *Hebrew Studies* 47 (2006): 275–279.

[34] Silke-Maria Weineck, "Heteros Autos: Freud's Fatherhood." In: Catherine Liu, John Mowitt, Thomas Pepper and Jakki Spicer (Eds.), *The Dreams of Interpretation: A Century down the Royal Road* (Minnesota: University of Minnesota Press, 2007), 97–114; and Weineck, *The Tragedy of Fatherhood: King Laius and the Politics of Paternity in the West*. New York, NY: Bloomsbury Academic, 2014.

[35] See, for example, Edmunds and Alan Dundes (Eds.), *Oedipus: A Folklore Casebook*, Madison, WI: University of Wisconsin Press, 1995, and Allen Johnson and Douglass Price-Williams, *Oedipus Ubiquitous: The Family Complex in World Folk Literature*. Palo Alto, CA: Stanford University Press, 1996.

the story.[36] And this question has been posed by critics who have been eager to distinguish between Sophocles' story and that told by Freud,[37] who brought it into tune with Shakespeare, Grillparzer, or—elsewhere—Friedrich Schiller, a poet whom, as Freud would discover with the help of his student Otto Rank, had already theorized about the human unconscious.[38] Freud offers a reading of *Oedipus the King* that is not thoroughly faithful to Sophocles, but that is in conversation with other literary texts that posit a tradition of sorts. He wanted to be an original thinker, but also a thinker in good company and who had solidified his reputation by establishing his own lineage of thought: not necessarily slaying intellectual fathers, but adopting them. Perhaps, his reading of drama was to follow quite simply a logic of recall that Freud had sketched elsewhere: not so much as an example of *Nachträglichkeit*, as that of a *Deckerinnerung*, foregrounding one remembered detail or event while hiding, veiling, others.

Reaching for Universal Truth

In 1913, only a few months before the start of WWI, Freud published *Totem und Tabu: Einige Übereinstimmungen im Seelenleben der Wilden und der Neurotiker* [*Totem and Taboo: Some Points of Agreement between the Mental Lives of Savages and Neurotics*].[39] It is a work that would reflect

[36] Patrick Mullahy, *Oedipus: Myth and Complex; a Review of Psychoanalytic Theory*, intr. Erich Fromm. New York: Hermitage Press, 1948.

[37] Edmunds, "Freud and the Father: Oedipus Complex and Oedipus Myth," *Psychoanalysis and Contemporary Thought* 8 (1985): 87–103; Richard Armstrong, *A Compulsion for Antiquity: Freud and the Ancient World*. Ithaca, N.Y.: Cornell University Press, 2005; Jean-Pierre Vernant, "Ambiguity and Reversal: On the Enigmatic Structure of *Oedipus Rex*," tr. Janet Lloyd. In: Bloom (Ed.), *Sophocles' Oedipus Rex*, 103–126. This translation appeared before in *Tragedy and Myth in Ancient Greece*, Atlantic Highlands, NJ: The Humanities Press, 1981; Jean Bollack, "Le fils de homme: Le mythe freudienne d'Œdipe." In: Bollack, *La naissance d'Œdipe: Traduction et commentaires d'Œdipe roi* (Paris: Gallimard, 1995), 282–321; Bollack, Ödipus: Von der Tragödie zum Komplex und vice-versa." *Maske und Kothurn* 52 (1955): 9–16; Jan N. Bremmer, "Oedipus and the Greek Oedipus Complex." In: Bremmer (Ed.), *Interpretations of Greek Mythology* (New York: Routledge, 1987), 41–59. See also Cynthia Chase, "Oedipal Textuality: Reading Freud's Reading of Oedipus," *Diacritics* 9,1 (1979): 53–68.

[38] Weissberg, "Freuds Schiller." *Friedrich Schiller and the Path to Modernity*, ed. Walter Hinderer (Würzburg: Königshausen & Neumann, 2006), 421–434.

[39] The book appeared first with a different subtitle, see: *Totem and Taboo: Resemblances Between the Psychic Lives of Savages and Neurotics*. New York: Moffat, Yard and Company, 1918 (and in London with G. Routledge).

on his psychoanalytic experience, but would apply this to a sketch of cultural history that charted the development of society and the distinction between so-called primitive men and civilization. The book was informed by Freud's extensive study of anthropological literature. In psychoanalytical practice, he asked his patients to remember childhood events,[40] so that by reaching back into their past, they would move forward. What they told was their very personal and private history. Freud, however, was interested in a larger picture. In sketching an outline for a history of civilization, Freud proposed to study the childhood of mankind. Vienna's neurotic patients were to illuminate the course of human history, for it was by reaching back to the "savages" that Freud now wanted to offer new insights into their neurotic illnesses, while, at the same time, offering psychoanalysis as a tool to understand the course of history. The once absent father, murdered on some country road, turned into an omnipresent one. Freud cites the spirit Ariel from Shakespeare's *The Tempest*: "Nothing of him that doth fade."[41]

Freud discusses incest and its early prohibition, which led to more complex social structures while focusing largely on his readings about Australian Aborigines. He tried to show that civilization, and cultural development, rested on prohibitions such as that. Most strikingly, however, is his introduction of the Oedipus story, which as the consideration of the Oedipus complex had become a center point of his psychoanalytic treatment. "At the conclusion, then, of this exceedingly condensed inquiry, I should like to insist that its outcome shows that the beginnings of religion, morals, society and art converge in the Oedipus complex." Freud writes, "This is in complete agreement with the psychoanalytic finding that the same complex constitutes the nucleus of all neuroses, so far as our present knowledge goes. It seems to me a most surprising discovery that the problems of social psychology, too, should prove soluble on the basis of one single concrete point—man's relation to his father" (156–157).

If the *Interpretation of Dreams* established the importance of the Oedipus complex for psychoanalytic theory and practice, *Totem and Taboo* tried to do the same for social anthropology. Freud wanted to establish a

[40] See Taylor Schey, "Ritual Remembrance: Freud's Primal Theory of Collective Memory," *SubStance* 42 (2013): 102–119.

[41] Freud, *Totem and Taboo: Some Points of Agreement Between the Mental Lives of Savages and Neurotics*, *SE* XIII: vii-162; here 155.

close connection between the psychoanalytic discoveries of an individual's development and possible neurotic suffering, and the development of societies. Psychoanalysis was not just a field of medical investigation or philosophical speculation, but of social analysis as well. In the process, the Oedipus complex would become the focus point in the relationship between psychoanalysis and anthropology that it remains today. Two questions seem to structure this encounter already early on. First, Freud's insistence on the universal truth of his discovery rested on a description of a nuclear family—father, mother, son—and did not include the consideration of differently structured families: either families with different membership constellations or different father roles. Second, and this is related to the first, there is the issue of gender. Freud's early concept of the Oedipus complex was largely sketched along the lines of the development of boys. Only in 1923, in his *Das Ich und das Es* [*The Ego and the Id*], did he consider a fuller treatment, and a description of the "complete" Oedipus complex that included the development of a girl.[42]

The British William Halse Rivers Rivers and Charles Gabriel Seligman, anthropologists who were also physicians, were interested in Freud's writings early on, hoping that they would provide support for the treatment of soldiers returning from the WWI battle fields with war traumas. Both were critical of Freud's theses, and tried to test them with ethnographic material. The English translation of *Totem and Taboo* was published in 1918, just as WWI ended, and a more thorough international reception of the work ensued. As Eric Smadja points out, Bronisław Malinowski's engagement with Freud's work occurred after the publication of his monograph, *Argonauts of the Western Pacific* (1922), the result of his field work in Oceania.[43] In a sequence of essays, "Psychoanalysis and anthropology" (1923), "Psychoanalysis and anthropology" (1924), and "Complex and myth in mother-right" (1925), and finally in *Sex and Repression in Savage Society* (1927), he argued against Freud's model of human development as a universal one. "The complex exclusively known to the Freudian School," Malinowski states there,

[42] In regard to the extended elaboration on the model, see the discussion in Eric Smadja, "The Oedipus complex, crystallizer of the debate between psychoanalysis and anthropology." *The International Journal of Psychoanalysis* 92 (2011): 985–1007; here 987. Smadja's essay offers an account of the early anthropologists' reactions to Freudian theory.

[43] Smadja, "The Oedipus complex," 988.

> and assumed by them to be universal, I mean the Oedipus complex, corresponds essentially to our patrilineal Aryan family with the developed *patria potestas*, buttressed by Roman law and Christian morals, and accentuated by the modern economic conditions of the well-to-do bourgeoisie. Yet this complex is assumed to exist in every savage or barbarous society. This can certainly not be correct.[44]

According to Malinowski, the Oedipus complex was absent in the matrilineal societies that he studied. In such societies, a boy's desire was not directed toward his mother, but his sister. Ernest Jones tried to refute Malinowski's findings already early on,[45] and with the financial support of Freud's former student, the psychoanalyst Marie Bonaparte, Géza Róheim departed for Australia and Melanesia to test Malinowski's thesis. In 1932, Róheim published *Psychoanalysis and Anthropology*, in which he described repressed oedipal impulses among the members of a matrilineal society.[46] In 1982, the anthropologist Melford Spiro refuted Malinowski's claim by reviewing Malinowski's data, with *Oedipus in the Trobriands*.[47]

But questions regarding the universal validity of the Oedipus complex continued to haunt anthropological research in regard to family formation, matrilineal versus patrilineal societies, and the role of women within society. Indeed, it seems that the disciplines of anthropology and psychoanalysis found points of contact, but have diverged in regard to their goals. Psychoanalysts have sought to theorize about human nature in general, while anthropologists have been eager to insist on their subject's specificity, and on the differences among the peoples. There were also concerns in regard to Freud's approach. Claude Lévi-Strauss questioned Freud's description of desire by posing the model of an unconscious of devoid of content, initiating a structural understanding of the psyche. The motif of incest, for example, was not to mean anything in itself, and gain meaning only in the relationship to the other motifs.[48] "If a myth is made

[44] Bronisław Malinowski, *Sex and Repression in Savage Society* (New York: Harcourt, Brace, and Co., 1927), 5.

[45] See Ernest Jones, "Mother-right and sexual ignorance of savages," *International Journal of Psychoanalysis* 6 (1925): 109–130.

[46] Géza Róheim, *Psychoanalysis and Anthropology: Culture, Personality and the Unconscious.* New York, International Universities Press, 1950.

[47] Melford Spiro, *Oedipus in the Trobriands.* Chicago: University of Chicago Press, 1982.

[48] Claude Lévi-Strauss, *Les structures élémentaires de la parenté* (ser.): Bibliothèque de philosophie contemporaine. Psychologie et sociologie. Paris: Presses universitaires de France, 1949. A translation of the revised edition appeared as: *The elementary structures of kinship*, tr.

up of all its variants," Lévi-Strauss writes in his study on "The Structural Study of Myth," moreover, "structural analysis should take all of them into account."[49] Elements can be rearranged, and further versions of a myth can be added. For Lévi-Strauss, Freud's comments on Oedipus, his formulation of the Oedipus complex, becomes part of this collection, and takes his place next to Sophocles.[50]

Gilles Deleuze and Félix Guattari published *Anti-Oedipe: Capitalisme et Schizophrénie* (*Anti-Oedipus: Capitalism and Schizophrenia*) in 1972, and followed up with a second volume of *Capitalisme et Schizophrénie*: *Mille Plateaux* (*A Thousand Plateaus*). They built on a structural understanding of desire while providing a Marxist framework.[51] Family relationships as well as the repression of desires—important for Freud's idea of civilization—should be understood within a model of capitalism, rather than severed from any economic context, they argued. Deleuze and Guattari do not make any distinction between the "savages" and a "civilized" Western culture, but between capitalist societies and possible alternatives.

Deleuze and Guattari were able to return to the anthropological insights that were formed in Australia or Oceania to Western Europe and Freud's Vienna, and they did it in different ways than Freud in *Totem and Taboo*. While Freud (or Jones, or Malinowski) wrote about "savages," Deleuze and Guattari were hesitant to distinguish between primitive and civilized populations, and to claim Western superiority. They wanted to consider class, for example, a category that Freud, treating primarily private patients from well-to-do households, for the most part neglected.[52] With the fading influence of its aristocracy, Vienna was largely a bourgeois

and ed. James Harle Bell, John Richard von Sturmer and Rodney Needham. London, Eyre & Spottiswoode, 1969.

[49] Claude Lévi-Strauss, "The Structural Study of Myth." *The Journal of American Folklore* 68 (1955):428–444, here 435.

[50] Lévi-Strauss, "The Structural Study of Myth," 435.

[51] Gilles Deleuze and Félix Guattari, *L'anti-œdipe: capitalism et schizophrénie* I (ser.) Collection Critique. Paris: Éditions de Minuit, 1972; English as: *Anti-Oedipus: Capitalism and Schizophrenia* I, tr. Robert Hurley, Mark Seem and Helen R. Lane. London and New York: Continuum, 2004. The second volume of *Capitalism and Schizophrenia* appeared as *Mille plateaux*. Paris: Les Editions de Minuit, 1980; English as: *A Thousand Plateaus*, tr. Brian Massumi. London and New York: Continuum, 2004.

[52] An exception here is perhaps Freud's call for free psychoanalytic clinics, see Elisabeth Ann Danto, *Freud's Free Clinics: Psychoanalysis and Social Justice, 1918–1938*. Columbia: Columbia University Press, 2007.

city; by 1918, it was a Republic. But Freud, whose family had belonged to the immigrants of Vienna's Leopoldstadt or second district, must have known about the great poverty of many of the city's inhabitants as well; their tight housing quarters that brought together members of an extended family. Between the World Wars, social movements in the city were strong, and tried to alleviate the situation with new housing projects and social institutions.[53] Perhaps ironically, Freud acquired his traditional *Bildung*, and read the Greek texts first, in the Leopoldstädter Gymnasium, the high school located in this center of immigration, with a student body largely drawn from Jewish families of modest means.[54] In Vienna as elsewhere, abandoned wives and mothers, as well as abandoned children, were common among the poor. While many men had to struggle to make a living, women tried to get positions as domestics, saleswomen, lower-level factory workers—or turned to prostitution.[55] In his critique of Freud's rejection of the seduction theory, Masson stressed occurrences of criminal and even violent behavior in many households that were, perhaps, just better hidden in bourgeois homes.

Freud's Vienna was not an ethnically homogeneous society, moreover, but increasingly diverse. The city's population had grown rapidly since 1848. With the destruction of the city walls, Vienna's territory was extended to include many new districts. New immigration laws made it possible for people from all parts of the Empire to settle there. As a Jew, Freud belonged to such a minority of new settlers, and was very aware of social prejudices and exclusions. But wondering about his father's reaction toward discrimination, he did not consider his father's father figures—or even ones of his own who might be in competition with Jacob Freud. In contrast to the Ashkenazi-Jewish tradition, for example, Freud did not choose names of his ancestors for his sons, but named them after his teachers Jean-Martin Charcot, Ernst Brücke, and even after one of the historical figures he admired, Oliver Cromwell.

[53] See Anson *Rabinbach, The Crisis of Austrian Socialism: From Red Vienna to Civil War, 1927–1934. Chicago: University of Chicago Press, 1983*, and Sheldon Gardner, *Red Vienna and the Golden Age of Psychology, 1918–1938*. Santa Barbara, CA: Praeger Publishers, 1992.

[54] See Jacques Le Rider, *Freud, de l'Acropole au Sinaï: Le retour à l'Antique des Modernes viennois*. Paris: Presses Universitaires de France, 2002.

[55] See, for example, Helmut Gruber, "Sexuality in 'Red Vienna': Socialist Party Conceptions and Programs and Working-Class Life, 1920–34," *International Labor and Working-Class History* (1987): 37–68.

This neglect has marked the profession of psychoanalysis deeply. The question of a "white" and bourgeois standard in regard to psychoanalytic theory has moved to the forefront in recent years, both in regard to the treatment of Black, Native, and Latino families in the United States, and in the resulting theorizing.[56] It has also had an effect on the choice of profession: Very few black students enter training to become psychoanalysts, a field that many regard as simply "white" or one of privilege.[57] In the United States, moreover, the history of slavery continues to mark the role of Black males within society, as family members, and on their own self-perception.[58]

While anthropologists have taken issue with Freud's concept of the family, early feminist theorists began to counter Freud with their distinction between sex and gender. Sex was linked to biology and defined the body as male or female, whereas gender was defined as socially bound. Freud had at least begun to relate a girl's development to the model of the Oedipus complex by altering the model of attraction—a girl would move to desire her father and develop a hostility toward her mother. He referred to the Oedipus complex in his analysis of the development of boys and girls. Carl Gustav Jung coined a different term for the girl's development altogether around 1913, namely the "Electra complex."[59] Beginning in the 1970s, Freud's description of female sexuality was criticized by French analysts such as Hélène Cixous and Luce Irigaray. In his larger description of the Oedipus complex and human development, Freud had described a boy's castration anxiety after realizing a girl's absent penis, and on the other hand, a girl's penis envy. For Cixious and Irigaray, female sexuality

[56] See, for example, Jaipaul L. Roopnarine (Ed.), *Fathers Across Cultures. The Importance, Roles, and Diverse Practices of Dads*. Santa Barbara, CA: Praeger, 2015.

[57] See the series of interviews, Black *Psychoanalysts Speak*, directed by Basia Winograd, https://www.pep-web.org/document.php?id=pepgrantvs.001.0001a (access August 2021).

[58] Just as one early example of a study on absent fathers, see Marion Burger, "The Oedipal Experience: Effects on Development of an Absent Father," *International Journal of Psycho-Analysis* 66 (1985): 311–320; studies of the effect of absent fathers in Black minority communities are usually conducted by sociologists, see for example the work by Elijah Anderson, *Streetwise: Race, Class, and Change in an Urban Community*. Chicago: University of Chicago Press, 1990.

[59] Carl Gustav Jung's essay, published in the *Jahrbuch für psychoanalytische und psychopathologische Forschungen* in 1913, appeared in a series of English lectures as "The Content of the Unconscious," in: *The Theory of Psychoanalysis* (ser.) Nervous and Mental Disease Publishing Series 19 (New York: The Journal of Nervous and Mental Disease Publishing Company, 1915), 67–71.

should not be defined by a lack. They countered Freud's concept with their own description of the female human body, and female sexual development, rejecting "penis envy," and redefining female desire.[60] "And man, are you still going to bank on everyone's blindness and passivity, afraid lest the child make a father, and consequently, that in having a kid the woman land herself more than one bad deal by engendering all at once child—mother—father—family?" Cixous asks in "The Laugh of the Medusa": "Let us demater-paternalize rather than deny woman in an effort to avoid the co-optation of procreation, a thrilling era of the body. Let us defetishize. Let's get away from the dialectic which has it that the only good father is a dead one, or that the child is the death of his parents."[61] Irigaray in turn redefined desire, as her woman could please herself. Woman is no longer defined by the lack of a sex organ, but "*woman has sex organs more or less everywhere*. She finds pleasure almost anywhere."[62]

The American analyst Nancy Chodorow chose another route to critique Freud. She did not focus as much on his perception of the female body, but rejected the complementary role of a female Oedipus complex. "For Freud and the early analysts, the major oedipal task was preparation for heterosexual adult relationships," she writes: "In the traditional paradigm, a girl must change her love object from mother to father, her libidinal mode from active to passive, and finally her libidinal organ and eroticism from clitoris to vagina. A boy has to make no such parallel changes."[63] If Masson thought that Freud turned away from fin-de-siècle Viennese reality, Chodorow argues that he is too much in tune with it, favoring a heterosexual, nuclear family in which the man assumes a dominant role. If Malinowski questioned the validity of Freud's concept in matrilineal

[60] Hélène Cixous, "Le Rire de la Meduse," *L'Arc* 17 (1975): 39–54. A revised English version appeared as Cixous, "The Laugh of the Medusa," tr. Keith Cohen and Paula Cohen, *Signs* 1 (1976): 875–893; Luce Irigaray, *This Sex Which is Not One*, tr. Catherine Porter with Carolyn Burke. Ithaca, NY: Cornell University Press, 1985 (*Sexe qui n'en pas un*, Paris: Éditions de minuit, 1977). Further critique came from analysts Julia Kristeva and Maria Torok. See also Nicholas Rand, "Did Women Threaten the Oedipus Complex Between 1922 and 1933? Freud's Battle with Universality and Its Aftermath in the Work of K. Horney and M. Torok," *Angelaki: Journal of the Theoretical Humanities* 9 (2004): 53–66. While Maria Torok was working in Paris, Karen Horney was a German psychoanalyst who had moved to the United States.

[61] Cixous, "The Laugh of the Medusa," 890.

[62] Irigaray, *This Sex Which is Not One*, 28.

[63] Nancy Chodorow, "Mothering, Object-Relations, and the Female Oedipal Configuration." Feminist Studies 4 (1978): 137–158; here 137–138.

societies in Oceania, Chodorow wanted to make room for more than heterosexual models in the very Western culture itself. She is, moreover, less interested in the position of the father, but in the role of fathering; and even more so, in the woman's role in any family. For Chodorow, the central issue is a woman's ability to bear a child, and the fact that she could assume the role of a mother:

> [I]n a new interpretation of the feminine Oedipus complex, I suggest that because women mother, the Oedipus complex is as much a mother-daughter issue as it is one of the father and daughter, and that it is as much concerned with the structure and composition of the feminine relational ego as it is with the genesis of sexual object choice.[64]

In insisting on the mother as a more active presence for the girl, Chodorow redefines the role of the father as well, and finally questions the heterosexual relationship as a universal template.

Freud's attention to female sexuality came belatedly, and so did his attention toward non-heterosexual desire. Would the Oedipus complex work the same with boys or girls who do not desire the opposite sex? Freud may have shown tolerance toward homosexuality, as critics who follow Jacques Lacan's attentive readings of Freud's work are eager to argue.[65] But Freud displayed blindness as well, as most famously exposed in his case study of Ida Bauer ("Dora") called "Bruchstück einer Hysterie-Analyse" [Fragment of a Case Fragment of an Analysis of a Case of Hysteria]. Only in a couple of footnotes would he consider his patient's attraction to another woman, an attraction that, however, would put most of his argument in the main text at rest.[66]

While questioning Freud's description of female sexuality or desire, Cixous, Irigaray, or Chodorow still operated with a stable definition of women for whom they sought to gain more rights, not the least that of pleasure. By the 1990s, however, this sense of stability began to crumble. Already in 1929, Freud's student Joan Riviere published a case study of a female patient who would alternate between a more resolute behavior, and

[64] Chodorow, "Mothering," 137.

[65] See Deborah Luepnitz, "Accentuate the Negative: Two Contributions to a Non-Normative Oedipal Theory," *Psychoanalysis, Culture & Society* 12 (2007): 44–49.

[66] Freud, "Fragment of an Analysis of a Case of Hysteria (1905 [1901])," *SE* VII: 2–122. See also Weissberg, "Exit Dora: Freud's Patient Takes Leave." *Psychoanalytic Inquiry* 25. Special issue, *Freud and Dora: 100 Years Later* (2005): 5–26.

one that could be traditionally defined as feminine, and wonder whether womanliness could be understood as a masquerade.[67] Lacan referred to Riviere in a paper he presented in 1958,[68] and Judith Butler has expanded on Riviere's insight in *Gender Trouble: Feminism and the Subversion of Identity* (1990).[69] If biological sex seemed fixed at first, gender could, however, be performed. In the context of performance, fatherhood becomes differently relational as well. But to what degree does the role of a father change for a person who performs as a woman at one point and as a man at another time?

"Integral to Freud's oedipal story is the inevitability of patriarchy, a bias that has long served to justify the suppression of women, but I would also add has been detrimental to individuals who identify as male," writes Cathy Siebold,[70] placing Freud's work firmly within the context of patriarchal thought, and moving his interpretation of Oedipus firmly into the realm of myth. But could he also be read differently, as critics Juliet Mitchell and Jacqueline Rose would like to suggest, for example with the help of Lacan's re-readings of Freud's work?[71] Or does one have to reformulate the Oedipus complex?[72] And how does one, with or without Freud, conceive of the role of the father today?

The twenty-first century has not only offered additional work on the performance of gender roles, but biological sex has been increasingly been recognized as unstable, and not just because of the rejection of simple binaries. Biological sex cannot always be assigned simply one way or the

[67] Joan Riviere, "Womanliness as Masquerade." *International Journal of Psycho-Analysis* 9 (1929): 303–313.

[68] See Jacques Lacan's "Guiding Remarks for a Congress on Feminine Sexuality (1958) [Presented in Amsterdam, 5th September 1960]"; see Jacqueline Rose, "Introduction II," in: Juliet Mitchell and Rose (Eds.), *Feminine Sexuality: Jacques Lacan and the École Freudienne* (London: Macmillan, 1982), 27. See also Lacan, *Seminar* VI: *Desire and Its Interpretation 1958–1959*, ed. Jacques-Alain Miller, tr. Bruce Fink (Cambridge: Polity, 219): 159. The book appeared first as Lacan, *Séminaire*, livre VI: *Le désir et son interpretation*, ed. Miller (ser.) Le champ freudien (Paris: Éditions de la Martinière, 2013). See also Judith Butler, Gender Trouble: Feminism and the Subversion of Identity (New York: Routledge, 1990): 55–73.

[69] Judith Butler, *Gender Trouble*. See also Weissberg (Ed.), *Weiblichkeit als Maskerade* (Frankfurt/M: Fischer Verlag, 1994).

[70] Cathy Siebold, "Is Patriarchy Inevitable? Rethinking the Freudian Myth," *Psychoanalytic Social Work* 27 (2020): 42–60; here 43.

[71] Mitchell and Rose (Eds.), *Feminine Sexuality: Jacques Lacan and the École Freudienne*.

[72] Catherine Chabert, "Incertitudes œdipiennes," *Revue française de psychoanalyse* 76 (2012/5): 1623 à 1631.

other, and intersex persons have been subject to increased scholarly attention.[73] And sex assignment can change. A man who acts like a woman or wants to desire like a woman does not necessarily want to be a woman. People who are transgender, however, are not considering the questions of social gender roles, but of changes to the body. Often, persons who pursue a change of sex describe themselves as feeling misplaced in their body, of trying to correct a biological error. A psychological identity does not agree with the physical one. This feeling of mis-alignment between a body and one's felt identity may occur in a son or in a daughter. But it can occur in a father, too. Does a child view his or her father who comes out as transgender as a father still? Television shows like *Transparent* move this question into the realm of popular culture, and at times even of a comedy of mistaken identities of a special kind.[74]

There is not only the question of determining gender or sex, however, but an increased awareness of the split between a biological father and the father who assumes the role of a male parent. While this has always existed in cases of adoption, it assumes new importance when traditional family structures are no longer in place. Same-sex couples who raise a child may assume traditional gender roles, or not. When a biological or surrogate parent is openly introduced into the family, fathers, just as mothers, can double. Fathers can assume the role of nurturing care givers, a role traditionally assigned to women, while mothers pursue careers outside the home. "By allowing for the positive presence of the 'real father'—and increasingly, of a plurality of 'real fathers'—within the child development, contemporary psychoanalytic discussions of involved fatherhood present a significant challenge to Freudian notions of the father as an absent authority," social psychologist Tabitha Freeman writes.[75] Adding to a discussion of changed family constellations, Freeman has provided data for cases in which artificial insemination was at play, the biological father

[73] See, for example, recent work such as Renée Bergland and Gary Williams (Eds.), *Philosophies of Sex: Critical Essays on The Hermaphrodite*. Columbus: Ohio State University Press, 2012.

[74] The American television comedy series Transparent was created by Joey Soloway for Amazon Studios and debuted in February 2014 and ended after season five in 2019 after Jeffrey Tambor, who played the transgender father, was let go.

[75] Tabitha Freeman, "Psychoanalytic Concepts of Fatherhood: Patriarchal Paradoxes and the Presence of an Absent Authority," *Studies in Gender and Sexuality* 9 (2008): 113–139, here 131.

absent, and no real replacement in sight.[76] Here too, social models evolved that question Freud's assumption of a family structure that proves to be a specifically bourgeois one, informed by his place and time and personal experience.

The Father, Today

In her work on the treatment of children, the Freud student and British psychoanalyst Melanie Klein tried to change Freud's time frame for the Oedipal complex, but she reflected on the role of the mother as well. Klein asked simply for a "good enough mother."[77] Chodorow's response to Freud's concept of the Oedipus complex is an increased stress on the female role of mothering. But while child bearing is and has remained a biological woman's role, the task of raising children has very much changed since Freud's time, and has increasingly become a father's purview as well. It may be time to ask what a good enough father should be like.

Unlike in Freud's time, marriage is no longer necessarily a desired condition if not a requirement for the formation of families, and at the same time, the concept of marriage has changed as well. Privileged women today may choose to have children out of wedlock and without male life partners, and suffer little discrimination. Professional women may choose belated parenthood, and rely on reproductive medical interventions. Other women may raise their children alone, but not out of choice. Children may know their biological father or not, or rely on a non-biological father. "Increased divorced rates and the inexorable rise in single-parent families have contributed to a social climate in which fathers, as consistent and stable role models, are increasingly unavailable to the next generation," Anton Oberholzer writes, "Even unstable fathering role models are in short supply."[78] But father roles were always unstable, as Sophocles' drama shows. Fathers, in turn, may opt for parental leaves to

[76] Vasanti Jadva, Freeman, Wendy Kramer, and Susan Golombok, "The Experiences of Adolescents and Adults Conceived by Sperm Donation: Comparisons by Age of Disclosure and Family Type," *Human Reproduction* 24 (2009): 1909–1919.

[77] See, for example, Melanie Klein, "Early Stages of the Oedipus Conflict," *International Journal of Psycho-Analysis* 9 (1928): 167–180, and Klein, "The Oedipus Complex in the Light of Early Anxieties," *International Journal of Psycho-Analysis* 26 (1945): 11–33.

[78] Anton Oberholzer, "Foreword." In: Judith Trowell and Alicia Etchegoyan (Eds.), *The Importance of Fathers: A Psychoanalytic Re-evaluation* (ser.) The New Library of Psychoanalysis 42 (New York: Brunner-Routledge, 2002), xv.

spend more time with child rearing, or even choose to raise children on their own. Open adoptions offer their own parental constellations. Children are raised in households with two fathers or two mothers.

The traditional father, it seems, has not only been killed by Oedipus, but he is dead in some psychoanalytic theory as well.[79] In an article published in the *New York Times*, journalist Sarah Boxer states that "Oedipus Is Losing His Complex":

> [I]s it really possible in the late 20th century to read Sophocles' "Oedipus Tyrannus" so that the central point of the drama is not Oedipus' terrible discovery that in killing his father and sleeping with his mother he surrendered to his unconscious wishes? Sure, if you listen to the latest generation of theorists, who suggest that Oedipus' shame about his crimes masked the real point of the story: the violence of fathers, the inevitable perversity of nature, the authoritarianism of the state and the patriarchal roots of society.[80]

The present volume tries to put attention on the father once again, and test Freud's model in the context of more recent psychoanalytic work, new sociological data, and theoretical reflection. *Psychoanalysis, Fatherhood, and the Modern Family* brings together scholars from different fields, as well as medical practitioners, approaching questions of texts and their sources, but also with psychoanalytic patients in mind. The book's goal is not to provide a unified answer, but case studies in theory and practice in hope of inspiring a new consideration of the subject.

The chapters in Part I explore the work of Freud himself, and the early development of his concept of the Oedipus complex. Richard H. Armstrong is a trained classicist who has already considered Freud's classic sources in his book, *A Compulsion for Antiquity: Freud and the Ancient World*. This time, he will not write about Freud's reading of Greek drama or his collection of antiquities, but of his relationship to Jean-Martin Charcot. Freud had spent a semester in Paris October 1885 to February 1886, and he was impressed with Charcot's work with hysteric patients at the Salpêtrière hospital; he translated Charcot's writings into German as well. In Chap. 2, Armstrong takes us back to Freud's training in Paris with

[79] See Lila J. Kalinich and Stuart W. Taylor (Eds.), *The Dead Father: A Psychoanalytic Inquiry*. London: Routledge, 2009.

[80] Sarah Boxer, "How Oedipus Is Losing His Complex," *The New York Times*, December 6, 1997, Section B, Page 7.

Jean-Martin Charcot, to map out the influence of "retrospective medicine" on Freud. While Freud's later work in Vienna and his conception of psychoanalytic theory has often been viewed as a break with Charcot's practices that relied on hypnotizing the female patients, and on visually documenting their hysteric fits, Armstrong gives evidence of a more enduring influence of Charcot's work on Freud. Chapter 3 by Harold Blum, a psychoanalyst and scholar of Freud's work and the former Director of the Freud Archives, takes us back to Freud's early correspondence. Blum focuses on two of Freud's letters, and in his close reading, he is able to sketch the development of Freud's ideas of the Oedipus complex in more detail.

The book's Part II focuses on Freud's students, and on their reception of the Oedipus complex. It begins with a reconsideration of Jacques Lacan's work. Was Jacques Lacan really a Freudian? That is the question that guides Mikkel Borch-Jacobson and Douglas Brick's study of Lacan. They write:

> Essentially, Lacan's debate with Freud pivots on the Oedipus question, and this question, more than any other, supplies the key to the apparently heterodox reconstructions brought by the disciple to his predecessor's doctrine. Indeed, Lacan's reformulation of the Oedipus complex corresponds with a desire to solve a *problem* that, as can be shown, Freud was already obsessed with but that Lacan was undoubtedly the first to have deliberately confronted (note that I avoid saying *solved*). That problem is *identification*, as both the beginning and end of the Oedipus complex.[81]

In Chap. 4, Jean Michel Rabaté takes up the challenge of considering the Freudian legacy in Lacan's thought in regard to the Oedipus complex. While Lacan had claimed to be a faithful reader of Freud, Rabaté's summary can point at the agreement as well as critical difference between these two analysts' concepts.

Dorothea Olkowski in Chap. 5 turns to Félix Guattari and Gilles Deleuze. As mentioned before, their *Anti-Oedipe* had tried to rewrite psychoanalytic theory within a context of Marxist materialism. They question Freud's concept of the Oedipus complex, but Olkowski is able to sketch the traces of classical Freudian theory in their work. The last chapter in this part deals with the work of two other students of Freud, Jung and

[81] Mikkel Borch-Jacobsen and Douglas Brick, "The Oedipus Problem in Freud and Lacan," *Critical Inquiry* 20 (1994): 267–282; here 268.

Léopold Szondi. At one point, Freud had designated Jung as his successor, to lead the International Psychoanalytic Association. But differences between Freud and Jung led to Jung's final departure from the IPA in 1913, just the year of the publication of *Totem and Taboo*; Jung founded his own association in Zurich in Spring 1914. Léopold Szondi, a Hungarian psychoanalyst who would practice in Switzerland after WWII, conceived of his own brand of psychoanalysis, fate analysis, which was influenced by both the classical Freudian theory and Jung's insistence on the importance of myths and archetypes. Chapter 6 by Adrian Daub deals with the reception of Freud's thought by Jung, Szondi, and Anna Freud, and he is primarily interested in exploring the idea of generation within the familial as well as the institutional context.

Part III of chapters focuses on contemporary case studies that deal with "fatherhood" in the light of social as well as analytic theory, as well as those that concern the history of the psychoanalytic institutions. The psychologist C. Jama Adams studies Caribbean immigrant and African-American families, and he is particularly concerned with the role of the father in these families. Chapter 7 cites examples from his work with minority students and patients in New York City. Adams is observing a doubling of sorts of fatherhood, and suggests to theorize about concurrent Black and white father figures in Black families. Patricia Gherovici is a Lacanian psychoanalyst who has worked extensively with Latino families in Philadelphia. She, too, has been concerned with minority families and underprivileged patients.[82] She has been increasingly concerned with transgender patients in these communities, and her experiences entered her theoretical studies.[83] In Chap. 8, Gherovici offers case studies of transgender patients, and she asks: "Does a father need to be a man?" She theorizes about the relevance of the Oedipus complex, and the position of the father, in the context of transgender patients and families.

Fatherhood is not simply an issue within families, and the home, but also for public institutions. Freud himself was aware of his role as a father figure within the psychoanalytic association. With his establishment of a "Secret Society" of loyal students, Freud had even openly formed a family

[82] See Patricia Gherovici, *The Puerto Rican Syndrome*. New York: The Other Press, 2003; Gherovici and Christopher Christian (Eds.), *Psychoanalysis in the Barrios: Race, Class, and the* Unconscious. New York: Routledge, 2018.

[83] Gherovici, *Please Select Your Gender: From the Invention of Hysteria to the Democratizing of Transgenderism*. New York: Routledge, 2010, and Gherovici, *Transgender Psychoanalysis: A Lacanian Perspective on Sexual Difference*. New York: Routledge, 2017.

structure which was to compete against others, but also nurtured rivalry within.[84] Membership in local or international psychoanalytical associations has traditionally reflected a society largely dominated by white males, and questions of scholarly influence or administrative succession have often been dealt with within a context not dissimilar to Oedipal strife. Howard B. Levine has remarked upon this in regard to the role of psychoanalysts and the implication of such strife for the psychoanalytic profession.[85] The last two chapters in this part focus on the "fatherhood" in the context of the professional institution. John Frank's question does not only refer to his experience in treating gay patients, but also to the status of homosexual patients within the psychoanalytic institute(s); he sketches a history of the institutional blindness (at best) vis-à-vis homosexuality in Chap. 9. In Chap. 10, I offer an institutional example of another kind that leads the reader back to post-war Germany and the re-establishment of the psychoanalytic associations there after WWII. The popular German psychoanalyst Alexander Mitscherlich defined the post-war German nation as one that had lost its father, Adolf Hitler, whose death it is unable to mourn. His bestselling book coined popular phrases like "a society without a father" and "the inability to mourn." In turning post-war Germans into psychoanalytic patients, Mitscherlich was able to put any distinction between victims and perpetrators aside.

The final two chapters in this volume deal with the discussion of the role of fathers in film and literature. Laurence A. Rickels in Chap. 11 reorients the discussion of the Oedipal constellation in the light of current media theory, citing examples from popular literature as well as film, and he brings his examples in conversation with texts by Freud as well as Walter Benjamin's study of allegory and the Baroque mourning play. Avital Ronell in Chap. 12 selects Franz Kafka as the subject of her study, and focuses on his well-known letter to his father. The letter exemplifies a son's reckoning with a parent who seems both distant and omnipresent. If Freud may have regarded his father as too weak, Kafka thought of his as too strong. Did Kafka plan to mail his letter? Or was it simply a work of fiction? This is a question that has preoccupied literary critics for many

[84] See Phyllis Grosskurt, *The Secret Ring: Freud's Inner Circle and the Politics of Psychoanalysis*, Reading, MA: Addison-Wesley Publishing Co., 1991.

[85] Howard B. Levine, "The Sins of the Fathers: Freud. Narcissistic Boundary Violations, and Their Effects on the Politics of Psychoanalysis," *International Forum of Psychoanalysis* 19 (2010): 43–50.

years.[86] Ronell gives evidence that a single letter can contribute much to our understanding of the human psyche. But in writing about Kafka, she has also chosen an author of Freud's own time, who has been an interested reader of Freud's text.

The present book begins with a discussion of letters (Freud writes to his friend Fliess), and ends with a discussion of a letter (Kafka writes to his father Hermann Kafka). Freud and Kafka were sons trying to come to terms with their fathers. Freud's letters can be viewed as the origin of psychoanalysis. Kafka's letter did not even reach its addressee, but today, it has simply become world literature.

[86] Weissberg, "Der Familienbrief als Genre: Franz Kafkas nie abgesandter Brief an den Vater." In: *Die Familie. Ein Archiv. MarbacherKatalog* 70 (Marbach: DLA, 2017): 224–225.

PART I

Freud Discovers Oedipus

CHAPTER 2

The Road to Thebes: Freud and French Retrospective Medicine

Richard H. Armstrong

The Scholar's Lament

Freud has many detractors and critics, but Jean-Pierre Vernant's critique of the Oedipus complex has had an unusually long shelf life. This has to do with the fact that as one of the pre-eminent classicists of the twentieth century, Vernant (1914–2007) held a position from which to deliver a particularly serious criticism of Freud's recourse to myth. Myth is, after all, the bread and butter of classicists, and when someone as learned as Vernant tells you that it is time to stop Freudianizing Sophocles, you feel compelled to obey—particularly if you are a budding scholar looking for the proper way to think about Greek culture. Since its first publication in 1967 in the journal *Raison Présente*, Vernant's piquant essay "*Oedipe sans complexe*" has served a kind of gatekeeper function, encouraging scholars to close the door on Freudian interpretation as unfit for duty in the serious

R. H. Armstrong (✉)
Department of Modern and Classical Languages, University of Houston, Houston, TX, USA
e-mail: richarda@Central.UH.Edu

L. Weissberg (ed.), *Psychoanalysis, Fatherhood, and the Modern Family*, https://doi.org/10.1007/978-3-030-82124-1_2

world of scholarship.[1] In Vernant's view, Freud made a superficial appropriation of Sophocles' incomparable drama in a manner that shows a deplorable lack of respect for the alterity of ancient culture.

> But in what respects is it possible that a literary work belonging to the culture of fifth-century Athens ... should confirm the observations of a doctor on the patients who throng his consulting rooms at the beginning of the twentieth century? From Freud's point of view the question needs no answer because it is one that there is no point in asking. As he sees it the interpretation of the Greek myth and drama poses no problems of any kind. It is not necessary to decode them using the appropriate analytical methods. To the psychiatrist, they are immediately comprehensible, perfectly transparent, and at once yield up a meaning that guarantees universal validity to the doctor's psychological theories. But where is this "meaning" to be found—the meaning that is supposed to be immediately revealed in this way to Freud, and after him, to all psychoanalysts as if they were latter-day Tiresiases with a gift of second sight enabling them to reach beyond mythical or literary forms of expression to grasp a truth invisible to the profane? It is not the meaning sought by the Greek scholar or the historian, the meaning present within the work, contained in its structures, a meaning that must be painstakingly reconstructed through a study at every level of the message that a legendary tale or a tragic fiction constitutes. (85–86)

On the surface, Vernant's critique constitutes a kind of special pleading for historical expertise, mobilized against the methodological imperialism of a psychology that is pillaging classical studies. No doubt, this is the basis of its appeal, which still manages to strike classicists as somehow profoundly important. While writing this essay, in fact, I reviewed a submission to a prominent American philological journal that cited Vernant gleefully as the point of departure for what the author felt was a thorough and definitive demolition of Freud's take on Oedipus.

I must of course be on my guard about coming to the aid of one dead white male against another (what belated obedience would lie behind *that*?), particularly on so fraught a topic as the Oedipus complex. But as one who spans the worlds of psychoanalysis and classical studies, I can't help but feel drawn to the role of mediator. The truth is, Vernant's essay

[1] Jean-Pierre Vernant, "Oedipe sans complexe," *Raison présente* 4 (1967): 3–20; published in English as "Oedipus without the Complex". In: Vernant and Pierre Vidal-Naquet, *Myth and Tragedy in Ancient Greece*, tr. Janet Lloyd (New York: Zone Books, 1990), 85–111. Further page references in text.

shows an appalling lack of understanding of psychoanalysis—one needs to go no further than his astonishing statement that with mythic texts the psychoanalyst feels no need "to decode them using the appropriate analytical methods"—as if the whole tension between the latent and manifest that infuses the Freudian theory of dreams, myths, and textuality generally didn't exist. Vernant, truth be told, reads Freud neither historically nor well, so his criticism seems far more a kind of drive-by shooting than a serious attack. But it costs us little and gains us even less to make that point *tout court*. My real purpose here is to outline some larger historical ironies than to say Vernant never truly grappled with the challenge of Freud's thinking about Greek myth.

To frame my approach here, let's situate Vernant for a moment. First, it bears mentioning that he was both an active combatant of the French Resistance and a member, until 1969, of the French Communist Party. This certainly suggests he knew what a unique historical moment was, and was deeply committed to collective action. His work on Greek tragedy in particular is ostensibly concerned with respecting Greek culture in its historical uniqueness, with especial focus on the cultural politics of the emerging city-state. In fact, he went so far in arguing for the distinctive nature of the Greeks that he has been accused of purposefully "othering" them.[2] This effort represents a strain of post-modern critical humanism that was divorcing itself from early European philhellenism—think of Shelley's old liberal canard, "We are all Greeks."[3] More often than not in his work on Greek tragedy, Vernant is attempting to highlight the particular historical tensions in Greek culture, defending it against the sort of bourgeois universalism that simply wants to reinstate or appropriate the Greeks' archetypal character under some new guise. So Vernant's fundamental objection to Freud's approach is that his "point of departure is an intimate experience undergone by the public, which is historically unlocated [*qui n'est pas historiquement situé*]" (87). By this he means an emotional conflict in modern bourgeois subjects (ambivalence toward parents)

[2] On Vernant's "othering," see Nicole Loraux, "Back to the Greeks? Chronique d'une expédition lointaine en terre commune." In: Jacques Revel and Nathan Wachtel (Eds.), *Une école pour les sciences sociales: de la VI ième section à l'École des Hautes Études en Sciences Sociales*, (Paris: Éditions du CERF, 1996), 275–294; and Miriam Leonard, *Athens in Paris: Ancient Greece and the Political in Post-War French Thought* (Oxford: Oxford UP, 2005), 40, 228–229.

[3] Percy Bysshe Shelley, *Hellas* (1922). In: *Shelley's Poetry and Prose: Authoritative Texts, Criticism*, ed. Donald H. Reiman and Sharon Powers (New York: Norton, 1977), 409.

for which Freud wished to provide a universal genealogy by referencing Greek myth. Against what he feels is a historically "unlocated" psychology, Vernant insists upon a *historical* psychology, one subject to the rigors of historical and philological research on the one hand, and respectful of the unrepeatable special circumstances of historical cultures on the other.

The task I have set myself here is to *relocate* the historical nature of Freud's particular deployment of theory in the Oedipus complex, not simply to point out the frailty of Vernant's criticism. This relocation will reveal two things of importance: first, that Vernant is misguided in assuming only the Greeks are historically *situés*. The explosion of reception studies since Vernant's day has heightened the awareness that how an author invites "the Greeks" into his work can be very symptomatic of a particular historical horizon, of particular needs for consolation, self-definition, or convenient alliance.[4] Vernant denies Freud the same historical specificity he allows for the Greeks, preferring to make him a straw man instead. Second, relocating Freud in this instance means putting his thinking back in the context of *French* history, which will go a long way to explaining Freud's assumptions about the historical nature of psychological phenomena. So in essence, Vernant's critique of Freud isn't so much a case of French classical studies rejecting Viennese psychoanalysis as it is a conflict between two eras in the French deployment of psychology in the study of history. Vernant's resistance to Freud in that respect begins to look like the return of the repressed—namely, the repressed "retrospective medicine" of Paris in the *fin-de-siècle*.

My argument is that Freud came to develop his approach to the historical application of psychoanalysis in large part in response to the school of Jean-Martin Charcot (1825–1893). While it is generally agreed that Freud's months in Paris at the Salpêtrière during 1885–1886 were quite crucial in veering his interests toward hysteria and other psychological phenomena, the fuller implications of this remain to be traced in the cultural realm. I'm thinking specifically of the wider deployment of medicine for cultural and historical analysis—the very thing that piques Vernant. My aim is to introduce a different "French Freud" in this discussion: a French Freud of the exuberantly positivistic Third Republic, not the skeptical Fourth; a Freud energized by the broad applicability of medical science,

[4] I attempted to give a full accounting of Freud's own reception of classical antiquity in: Richard Armstrong, *A Compulsion for Antiquity: Freud and the Ancient World*. Ithaca: Cornell UP, 2005.

which arrives on the scene to unlock perennial mysteries. To restore Freud's indebtedness to a French context in this way does not detract from Freud's originality, in my view. In fact, I find this French interlude helps us to better trace the exact arc of his divergence from Charcot as he shifts toward an approach we can begin to recognize as properly psychoanalytic. And this in turn will return us to considerations of what Vernant has missed in Freud's approach to the Oedipal myth.

Medical Republicanism and Retrospective Medicine at the Salpêtrière

To see what Freud picked up in Paris, we can start with a passage from an article on hysteria he wrote for the *Handwörterbuch der gesamten Medizin* in 1888—some two years after his return from Paris, but before the properly "psychoanalytic Freud" emerges. This is just a reference work, and it is not one of Freud's memorable contributions. But it is all the more important, to my mind, in that it shows Freud's championing of Charcot in a manner that quite accurately reflects the tenor of the Salpêtrière's overall approach. This approach is as much historical as it is purely diagnostic—or rather, it used historical data to confirm the diagnosis.

> The name 'hysteria' originates form the earliest times of medicine and is a precipitate of the prejudice, overcome only in our own days, which links neuroses with diseases of the female sexual apparatus. In the Middle Ages neuroses played a significant part in the history of civilization, they appeared in epidemics as a result of psychical contagion, and were at the root of what was factual in the history of possession and of witchcraft. Documents from that period prove that their symptomatology has undergone no change up to the present day. A proper assessment of and a better understanding of disease only began with works of Charcot and of the school of the Salpêtrière inspired by him. Up to that time hysteria had been the *bête noire* of medicine. The poor hysterics, who in earlier centuries had been burnt or exorcized, were only subjected, in recent, enlightened times, to the curse of ridicule; their states were judged unworthy of clinical observation, as being simulation and exaggerations.[5]

[5] Sigmund Freud, "Hysteria" (1888). In: Freud, *The Standard Edition of the Complete Psychological Works*, tr. James Strachey, ed. Anna Freud et al., 24 vols. (London: The Hogarth Press, 1953–1974), I: 41. (edition will be abbreviated *SE*).

The historical structure of this passage is not dictated by its function as a reference article, but by Freud's desire to champion the "latest advances" in medicine. Freud first alludes to the etymology of hysteria from the Greek ὑστέρα "womb" as a product of perennial *prejudice*, an error in effect that has only recently been overcome with the modern understanding of neurosis. He then traces a new historical link that is rooted not in Greek antiquity but in the Middle Ages, an era whose documentation supposedly provides a stable symptomatology for the neurosis, which he insists "has undergone no change up to the present day." Why would such a statement even be necessary, after we have granted the premise that only the modern understanding of neurosis has come to the root of the problem? Why bring in witches and medieval psychical epidemics at all?

The simple answer is revealed in what follows: the true understanding of hysteria "only began with works of Charcot and of the school of the Salpêtrière inspired by him," and their construction of hysteria relied very much on two things: the performance of symptoms by hysterical patients in their keeping (their "medical muses" as Asti Hustvedt calls them)[6] and a broad historical project to uncover these same symptoms in accounts of religious ecstasy, demonic possession, and witchcraft. The live performance of symptoms was supposed to reveal them in their rich and complex reality, but the historical project established their enduring nature and stability. In Freud's characterization, then, we see how clearly Charcot's clinical expertise in identifying the true nature of hysteria is inseparable from the historical dimension of his argument: hysteria has *always* been with us and is a stable disease entity identifiable through time; thus the histrionic nature of the disease should not blind us to its underlying and enduring reality. In this way, Charcot emerges as the historic liberator of the wretched hysterical masses. The combination of historical vision, diagnostic acuity, and social liberation makes up the distinctive blend of "medical republicanism" that characterized the Salpêtrière in Charcot's heyday. Nowhere else, I contend, would Freud have encountered such a powerful enterprise of retrospective medicine, one which takes the emerging truths of medical science to new importance through historical investigation. It was a heady brew from which Freud never fully recovered; it must have appealed to his broadly synthetic mind, as much intrigued by cultural questions as by clinical problems.

[6]Asti Hustvedt, *Medical Muses: Hysteria in Nineteenth-Century Paris* (New York: Norton, 2011), passim.

We are used to seeing by now various indictments of Charcot's "invention of hysteria" through his problematic use of hypnosis to elicit symptoms, the coaching of the female inmates by subalterns, and the disturbing photographic record left by the *Iconographie Photographique de la Salpêtrière* (1876–1880), whose main purpose was to "fix" the image of the florid hysteric.[7] Charcot, the grand *visuel* that Freud admired,[8] all too easily represents Foucault's "clinical gaze" gone awry, and the deplorable parlor tricks his patients were subject to are hardly defensible. But his investment in visual epistemology was profound: his famous clinical lectures were all about *seeing*, not just reading about diseases. As he brought out four women suffering from chorea, he told his audience on March 13, 1888, at the beginning of his lecture,

> I have often told you it is better to see than to read. Reading is good, but seeing is even better; one can learn a good deal more in a quarter of an hour spent seeing patients than in reading the descriptions of the diseases with which they are afflicted in books. I'm talking about the *best* books, because ultimately our accounts are never but a pale image of the reality of things.[9]

The paradox of course is that Charcot's need to produce reliable visual evidence through clinical demonstrations only increased the suspicion of histrionic performance, not the certainty of organic symptoms. So this superiority of the seen over the read was never fully upheld even by Charcot, who was quick to enlist the *written* historical record at the same time.

We can return to that same clinical lecture hall to see a strident example of this interplay between the seen and the read. Just a few months before in January of 1888, he quite polemically defended his characterization of *hysteria major* (*la grande hystérie*) with this two-pronged approach. First he brought in a 22-year-old patient who seemed to have the classic 3-phase grand attacks—yet she was *not* an inmate of the Salpêtrière, nor had she ever witnessed any such attack other than her own. While he did not induce a hysterical attack in her for the audience, Charcot questioned her

[7] See Hustvedt, and Georges Didi-Huberman, *Invention of Hysteria*, tr. by Alisa Hartz, Cambridge: MIT Press, 2003.

[8] Freud, "Charcot" (1893), *SE* III: 11–23, here 12.

[9] Jean-Martin Charcot, *Leçons du mardi à la Salpêtrière: Policlinique 1887–1888, Notes de cours de MM. Blin, Charcot et H. Colin*. 2nd edition, vol. I. (Paris, Progrès Médical, 1892), 170.

and her mother long enough to convince himself that she conformed true to type. He therefore proudly proclaimed this case as the necessary counter to his critics, who alleged that the elaborate seizure disorder he defined was a creation of the Salpêtrière occurring nowhere else—that is, a *hystérie de culture*, a product of suggestion, and not a naturally occurring disease. If it is suggestion, Charcot insisted, it is a vast one spanning centuries and continents, as the evidence compiled by his student Paul Richer shows,[10] whose book contains "200 pages of genuine documents to which we refer the skeptics."[11] Charcot concludes defiantly,

> The truth is that the grand attack for which I've formulated the characteristics is definitely a natural type of disease; it is not an artificial creation, it belongs to all eras, all races, all countries. I would add that without a deep familiarity with the type, one will never understand well what hysteria is; a large part of its history is made up of the transformations it can undergo. (105)

For hysteria to be an organic disease, it must be proven to exist in all eras, in all races, in all countries—which is to say, hysteria must be *historical* to be natural. By coming to know the pure "type," one then sees the local inflections, and grasps the stable essence beyond the fluctuating appearances of this most notorious illness.

For all its avowed empiricism, then, there is at the heart of Charcot's method a stealthy Platonism, a desire to locate the pure type from which the individual instances diverge in imperfect participation with their source. The metaphor behind this use of *type* is not just epistemological, but also numismatic: there is the clear image, the "original," and then there are the abraded *formes frustes,* which like well-worn coins only hint at their original image.[12] As Freud described Charcot's "practicing nosography" in a retrospective article after the Frenchman's death, "the complete and extreme cases, the 'types,' could be brought into prominence with the help of *a certain schematic planning*, and, with these types as a point of departure, the eye could travel over the long series of ill-defined

[10] Paul Richer, *Études cliniques sur la grande hystérie ou hystéro-épilepsie*. 2nd revised edition (Paris, Delahaye & Lecrosnier Éditeurs, 1885).

[11] Charcot, *Leçons du mardi*, 105. Further reference in text.

[12] The word τύπος in fact had served Plato in the *Republic* for the types or models of myth (377b) that are impressed on the mind. The word originally means a blow, then came to refer to an image impressed on wax or on a coin, then a kind or type in our sense. Its medical use for disease type can be found in the works of Galen.

cases—the *formes frustes*—which, branching off from one or other characteristic feature of the type, melt away into indistinctness."[13] So in light of this dialectic of type and *formes frustes*, I would argue it is not the case that Charcot simply retrojected his diagnosis into the past, but rather that he deployed the past in the construction of his diagnosis "with a certain schematic planning," particularly in the case of hysteria.[14]

As Charcot's reference to Paul Richer's 1885 book shows, he relied more on his colleagues and students to plumb the fuller depths of the historical record for this evidence. Richer's monograph, *Études cliniques sur la grande hystérie ou hystero-epilepsie*, particularly in the second revised edition, is as masterful a presentation of grand hysteria à la Charcot as anyone could want. There the visual evidence (in the form of Richer's oft-reproduced drawings—he was a gifted medical illustrator) is as vital as the clinical case studies in establishing the "type," whose essence is best expressed in an elaborate visual menu disclosing the full panoply of the grand attack (Fig. 2.1).

The long historical appendices then round out the argument, as Charcot alludes in his lecture.[15] But in addition to the evidence compiled by the diligent and gifted Richer, another Charcot acolyte, Désiré-Magloire Bourneville (1840–1909), opened a whole collection of historical materials, which he published in a series called the *Bibliothèque Diabolique* from 1882 to 1902.[16] The volumes were edited accounts of witches' Sabbaths, demonic possessions, and exorcisms. Bourneville was a powerful proponent of the medical republicanism of the time, active as much as a writer and publisher for the cause as he was as a working psychiatrist.[17] He had

[13] Freud, "Charcot," 12; my emphasis.

[14] Freud comments on how different Charcot's method of type and *formes frustes* was from the German physiological mindset in the preface to his translation of Charcot's *Leçons du mardi*. In: Freud, *SE* I: 134–135.

[15] Richer alludes to a tradition of retrospective medicine toward the end of his long book: "It's not one of the least merits of this new conception of hysteria that it can find its justification in the study of the past, and that it can link by a common thread a certain number of seemingly disparate facts, whose true meaning it allows us to grasp by a series of legitimate comparisons. Some authoritative writers have already undertaken these studies of retrospective medicine on certain points—I would cite here Calmeil, Littré, Valentiner, and Charcot." See Richer, *Études cliniques*, 797.

[16] Désiré-Magloire Bourneville and Paul Regnard, *Iconographie photographique de la Salpêtrière (Service de M. Charcot)*. 3 vols. Paris, Adrien Delahaye, 1876–1880.

[17] Galanopoulos, Philippe. 2011. "La *Bibliotèque diabolique du docteur Bourneville*." *Vesalius* 17.2 (2011): 89–98.

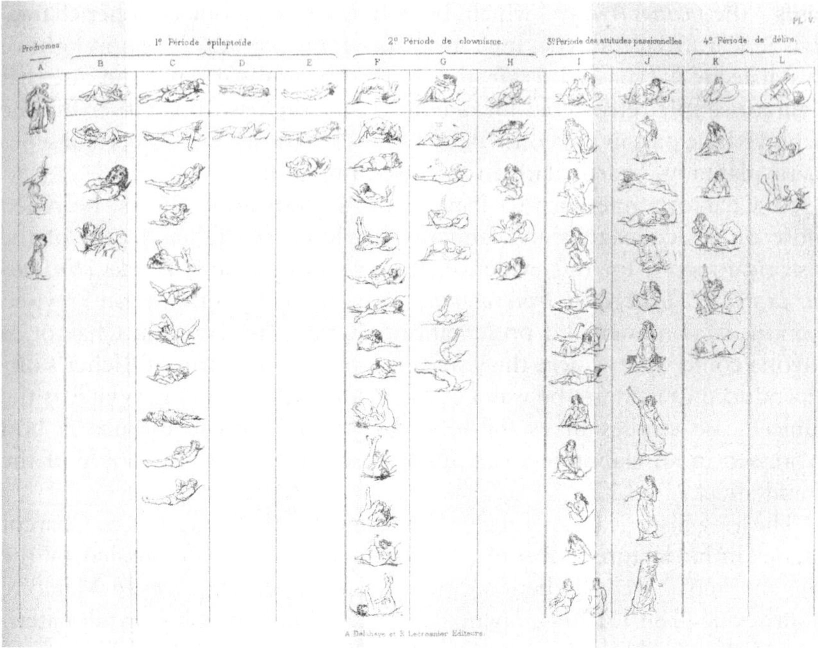

Fig. 2.1 Stages of the hysterical grand attack. From: Paul Richer, *Études cliniques sur la grande hystérie ou hystero-epilepsie*, 2nd edition (1885). (Image courtesy of Blocker History of Medicine Collections, UTMB, Galveston)

even entered into a strident polemic concerning the contemporary Belgian mystic and stigmatic Louise Lateau, whom he saw as a hysteric put to shameful use by clerical forces: "Louise Lateau is afflicted by a serious illness which ignorance and fanaticism have prohibited her from fighting, having let it advance with total freedom."[18]

All this is to say, there is a profoundly constructed nature to the visual, performative moments of grand hysteria so proudly paraded at the Salpêtrière, mobilized in complicated ways to vindicate the female hysteric while simultaneously casting her as an enduring type—the witch, the mystic, the demoniac (Fig. 2.2), tragically misunderstood until liberated from shame by secular medicine through appropriate diagnosis (treatment or cure, however, are a different matter).

[18] Bourneville, *Louise Lateau ou la stigmatisée belge*. (Paris: Progrès Médical, 1875), 61.

Fig. 2.2 A demoniac attack. From: Paul Richer, *Études cliniques sur la grande hystérie ou hystero-epilepsie*, 2nd edition (1885). (Image courtesy of Blocker History of Medicine Collections, UTMB, Galveston)

Part of the fervor of the Salpêtrière school stems, in fact, from their dogmatic conviction that hysteria *is* historically locatable, allowing them to reoccupy the former positions of exorcist and inquisitor, thus outmaneuvering the Catholic Church's power by returning the supernatural to the natural world.

As Charcot's translator and former intern, Freud initially played his part in communicating the Salpêtrière school's ideas to a German-speaking audience, and his library still reveals a strong connection to the school's approach. He owned not only copies of Charcot's clinical lectures—some of which he translated himself—but also a copy of Richer's 1885 monograph,[19] which he deemed "in more than one respect a noteworthy volume."[20] He also possessed all three volumes of Bourneville's *Iconographie Photographique*,[21] whose images of carefully posed hysterical patients were clearly staged to reflect the conventions of religious iconography (Figs. 2.3 and 2.4).

Volume 3 also contained a full account of a witches' Sabbath, which Bourneville appended to the clinical studies, a clear anticipation of his later *Bibliothèque Diabolique*. As we have seen from Freud's reference article, the historical dimension of the Salpêtrière was thoroughly imparted to him in his initial understanding of hysteria.

However, it did not take long for Freud to diverge from Charcot, shifting away from a nosographical interest in symptoms toward a therapeutic and scientific preference for causes. Freud's particular focus on "antithetic" or "pathogenic" ideas steered him deeper into the phantasmagoric content of the hysteric's mental world. As he put it some 20 years after his time with Charcot, "Anyone who studies hysteria … soon finds his interest turned away from its symptoms to the phantasies from which they proceed. The technique of psychoanalysis enables us in the first place to infer from the symptoms what those unconscious phantasies are and then to make them conscious to the patient."[22] The dynamic agency of pernicious ideas fits very well with the background of demonic possession already in place thanks to Charcot. A paper of 1892–1893, "A Case of Successful Treatment by Hypnotism," written with the evident influence of Josef Breuer, shows how quickly Freud has run ahead with the idea. "This emergence of a counter-will is chiefly responsible for the daemonic characteristic which hysteria so often exhibits—the characteristic, that is, of the patients' not being able to do something precisely when and where they

[19] Richer, *Études cliniques*, Freud catalogue 2967.

[20] Freud, "Preface to the Translation of Charcot's *Lectures on the Diseases of the Nervous System*" (1886) *SE*, I: 21–22, here 22.

[21] Bourneville and Regnard, *Iconographie Photographique*, Freud library catalogue 332. For catalogue references, see also note 29.

[22] Freud, "Hysterical Phantasies and Their Relation to Bisexuality," (1908), *SE* IX: 159–166, here 162.

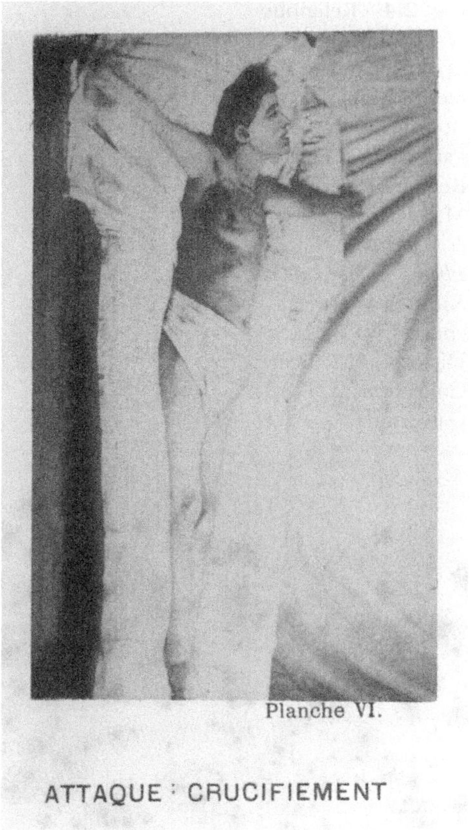

Fig. 2.3 Crucifixion pose during a hysterical attack. From: Désiré-Magloire Bourneville and Paul-Marie-Léon Regnard (Service de M. Charcot), *Iconographie Photographique de la Salpêtrière*. (Image courtesy of Blocker History of Medicine Collections, UTMB, Galveston)

want to most passionately, of doing the exact opposite of what they have been asked to do, and of being obliged to cover everything they most value with abuse and suspicion." Thus, inhibited intentions retain a certain force of their own, lurking in "a sort of shadow kingdom, till they emerge like bad spirits and take control of the body, which is as a rule under the orders of the predominant ego-consciousness."[23] Freud's shift in interest toward the psychological conflicts of the individual patient led him seriously to question Charcot's dogged insistence on heredity as a

[23] Freud, "A Case of Successful Treatment by Hypnotism" (1892–1893), *SE* I 117–128, here 126–127.

Fig. 2.4 Religious ecstasy during an hysterical attack. From: Désiré-Magloire Bourneville and Paul-Marie-Léon Regnard (Service de M. Charcot), *Iconographie Photographique de la Salpêtrière*. (Image courtesy of Blocker History of Medicine Collections, UTMB, Galveston)

root cause in hysteria, a resistance that his obituary tribute to Charcot already manifests.[24]

Clearly it is important not simply to trace Freud's retention of the Salpêtrière's interests over time, but also his transformation of them. A case in point would be an iconic image of the Salpêtrière hysterics: the *arc de cercle*, a spectacular upward arching of the back while in the throes of the grand attack (Figs. 2.5 and 2.6).

This position was to the Salpêtrière hysteric what the can-can was to the Parisian cabaret dancer. Twenty-three years on, we see Freud still pondering

[24] Freud, "Charcot," *SE* III: 11–23, here 23.

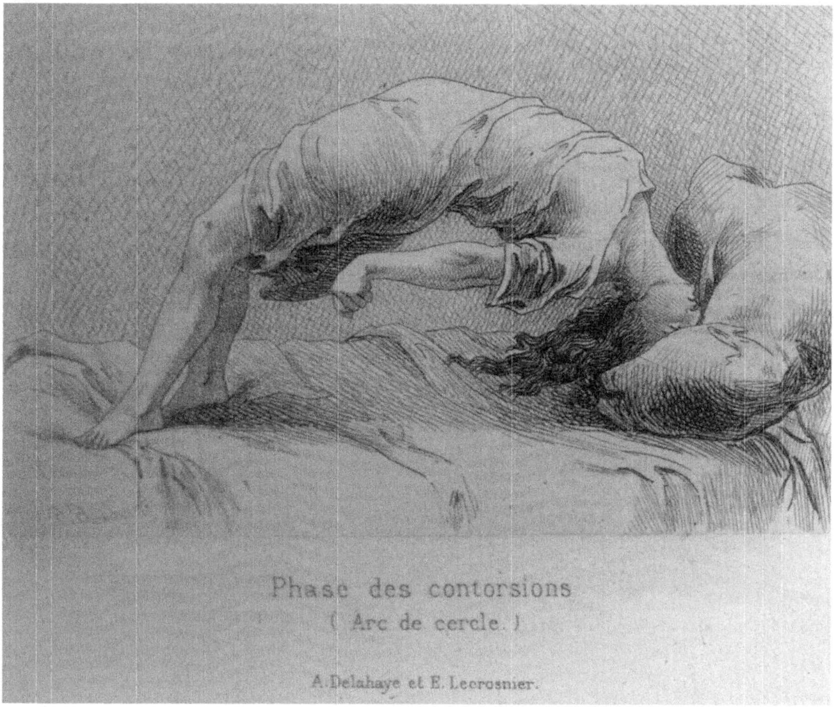

Fig. 2.5 L'arc de cercle. From: Paul Richer, *Études cliniques sur la grande hystérie ou hystero-epilepsie,* 2nd edition (1885). (Image courtesy of Blocker History of Medicine Collections, UTMB, Galveston)

this wonder, but now within the context of psychoanalytic ideas: the *arc de cercle* is an "antagonistic inversion" of a physical gesture into its opposite, a transformation analogous to what can happen in dream-work.

> For instance, an embrace may be represented in the attack by drawing back the arms convulsively till the hands meet over the spinal column. It is possible that the well-known *arc de cercle* which occurs during attacks in major hysteria is nothing else than an energetic repudiation like this, through antagonistic innervation, of a posture of the body that is suitable for sexual intercourse.[25]

[25] Freud, "Some General Remarks on Hysterical Attacks," (1909[1908]) *SE* IX: 229–234, here 230. Further reference in text.

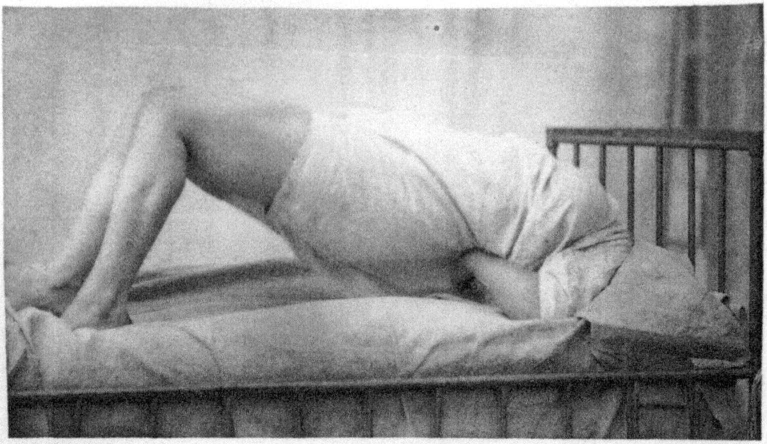

Fig. 2.6 L'arc de cercle. From: Désiré-Magloire Bourneville and Paul-Marie-Léon Regnard (Service de M. Charcot), *Iconographie Photographique de la Salpêtrière*. (Image courtesy of Blocker History of Medicine Collections, UTMB, Galveston)

Thus, the posture that once stood as evidence of a neurological enormity now stands as proof of a powerful hysterical counter-will, a kind of anti-hug whose intensity is a physical manifestation of a powerful *idea*. This example is taken from an article in which Freud is recasting features of Charcot's grand attack in the service of psychoanalysis, making them tractable to interpretation analogously to dreams. Freud's view is that the intense theatricality of the grand attack is a kind of unconscious mummery: "these attacks are nothing else but phantasies translated into the motor sphere, projected on to motility and portrayed in pantomime" (229).

As late as 1923, we still see Freud taking an interest in demonic possession, this time making use of the journal *Imago* to publish a historical study of the seventeenth-century painter Christoph Haizmann. Again, we find both credit and critique for Charcot in his introduction: Charcot was right to identify demonic possession and religious ecstasy as hysterical phenomena, but wrong in not diving deeper into the discovery of causes. Psychoanalysis, he argues, can now do this with its more robust, psychodynamic approach. "In our eyes, the demons are bad and reprehensible wishes, derivatives of instinctual impulses that have been repudiated and repressed. We merely eliminate the projection of these mental entities into the external world which the Middle Ages carried out; instead, we regard them as having arisen in the patient's internal life, where they have their abode."[26]

With the use of projection, Freud shows his hand here as a devotee of Ludwig Feuerbach (1804–1872), the great nineteenth-century philosopher whose work Freud devoured as a young student. Indeed, we might see in this moment the best angle on Freud's thinking about religion: on the one hand, marked by the Salpêtrière's identification of religious experience with neurosis, and on the other, powered by the Feuerbachian psychodynamics of projection and wish-fulfillment. It was from such a synthetic position, in the end, that Freud launched his own salvo of untimely medical republicanism: *The Future of An Illusion* (1927).[27]

Enter Oedipus

We have seen Freud marked and motivated by the Salpêtrière's historical interests, still arguing with Charcot some forty years after he met him; but we must return now to consider where Oedipus fits into this. Oedipus, after all, was not a figure in whom Charcot took interest. The "discovery of the Oedipus complex" as we rehearse it in the standard narrative of psychoanalysis means the shift from a psychology of trauma derived from sexual molestation to a psychology of fantasy, of "events" that take place in the child's vivid imagination without rising to the level of juridical "facts." Interestingly, there is clear evidence that Freud was deep into the Salpêtrière's witchery when he was in the throes of working out his "seduction theory,"

[26] Freud, "A Seventeenth-Century Demonological Neurosis" (1923 [1924]), *SE* XIX: 72–105, here 72.

[27] See Armstrong, Richard. 2013. "Myth, Religion, Illusion: How Freud Got His Fire Back." In: Ellen O'Gorman and Vanda Zajko (Eds.), *Classical Myth and Psychoanalysis: Ancient and Modern Stories of the Self* (Oxford: Oxford University Press), 59–74.

though he changed direction once his interpretation of *Oedipus the King* and Hamlet began to realign the import of recovered sexual fantasies. In letters of January 17 and 24, 1897, to Wilhelm Fliess, he exults that his new "prehistory of hysteria" coincides exactly with medieval accounts of possession: "Do you remember that I always said that the medieval theory of possession held by the ecclesiastical courts was identical with our theory of a foreign body and the splitting of consciousness?"[28] He seems obsessed with the links between diabolical possession and sexual perversion. A week later, he is on about witches again: "Details are beginning to abound. Their 'flying' is explained: the broomstick they ride probably is the great Lord Penis" (227). He is eager to turn to the historical and cultural now to shed light on the link between repressed memories of sexual abuse and fantasy formations. "I have ordered the *Malleus maleficarum*, and now that I have put the final touch on the infantile paralyses I shall study it diligently. The story of the devil, the vocabulary of popular swear-words, the songs and customs of the nursery—all these are now gaining significance for me" (227).[29]

By September 1897 his fervent interest had cooled considerably and he was stepping away from the idea that such elaborate fantasy formations are screens built over traumatic events. This was in part, as he confessed to Fliess, because this required that "the *father*, not excluding my own, had to be accused of being perverse," and in part because "there are no indications of reality in the unconscious, so that one cannot distinguish between truth and fiction that has been cathected with affect" (264). By October 15, then, he has hit upon a new configuration: the fantasy *was* the event. Far from being unlocatable in history, the Oedipus complex is specifically located by Freud as an oft-recurring event, *ein allgemeines Ereignis früher Kindheit* ("a universal event in early childhood," 272). And the eruption of Oedipal catharsis in the play occurs precisely at the intersection of *two* events: the repressed childhood memory of deeply ambivalent feelings

[28] Freud, *The Complete Letters of Sigmund Freud to Wilhelm Fliess 1887–1904*, tr. and ed. Jeffrey Masson (Cambridge: Belknap Press, 1985), 224. Further references in the text. German edition: *Sigmund Freud: Briefe an Wilhelm Fliess 1897–1904*, ed. Jeffrey Masson and Michael Schröter (Frankfurt am Main: S. Fischer Verlag, 1986).

[29] Freud's library does contain a German edition of the *Malleus maleficarum* (Freud Library cat. 3323), but note that it is an edition of 1906—that is, from nine years later than the letter to Fliess. This does point to his continued interest, however, as does a two-volume history of witch trials (Freud Library cat. 3304). See J. Keith Davies and Gerhard Fichtner, *Freud's Library: A Comprehensive Catalogue*, London: Freud Museum/Tübingen: edition discord, 2006.

awakened by the *performance* of the Sophoclean script. I emphasize below in the German text how the "reality" of the performance calls back the traumatic "fantasy" of childhood.

> Everyone in the audience was once a budding Oedipus in fantasy and each recoils in horror from the dream fulfillment here transplanted into reality, with the full quantity of repression which separates his infantile state from his present one. (272)
>
> *Jeder der Hörer war einmal im Keime und in der Phantasie ein solcher Ödipus, und vor der hier in die Realität gezogenen Traumerfüllung schaudert jeder zurück mit dem ganzen Betrag der Verdrängung, der seinen infantilen Zustand von seinem heutigen trennt.* (293)

Freud not only accounts for the psychological situation of the audience in historical (as he would say, ontogenetic) terms, but treats the Sophoclean play not as a script, but as a performance, as a virtual reality that powerfully confronts an audience with the fulfillment of its unconscious wishes. Freud's argument explicitly assumes that the only reason this ancient play—so remote from modern ideas in its manifest content—can have a powerful effect on the modern audience is that it dredges up their lived experience through the realization of now-repressed desires. Similarly, Freud expands this reading of the psychic conflict by adjoining a reading of Hamlet, in which again "a real event stimulated the poet to his representation" (*eine reale Begebenheit den Dichter zur Darstellung reizte*, 293).

The Oedipus complex was always a bifocal vision, an Oedipus-Hamlet Complex; yet the implication is not drawn often enough that this is proof of the *historical nature* of Freud's theory. While a Vernant will see only the ham handed application of a theory to two texts, we should see the matter in higher resolution. Oedipus shocks the audience as a figure who has fulfilled the unfulfilled desires of childhood, but Hamlet represents the more typically "modern" situation of neurotic inaction, occasioned by "the secular advance of repression in in the emotional life of mankind" (282). Freud situates, in other words, the two works in their historical periods as differentiated by the force of historically conditioned repression. One can certainly disagree with this "repressive hypothesis," but at the same time, one has to see it for what it truly is: a historical thesis, roughly hewn though it might be. Having hit upon his type in Oedipus, Freud could array the *formes frustes* along a historical axis now explained through the emerging psychodynamics of repression, a psycho-social force embedded in culture but originating in the family.

Back to Vernant

Vernant's brief against psychological "ahistoricism" also comes from a place. It was inspired by another Eastern-European Jewish psychologist trained at the Salpêtrière: Ignace Meyerson (1888–1983), founder of a historical and "objective" psychology in France that influenced Vernant in his formative years.[30] Vernant had even dedicated his *Mythe et pensée chez les Grecs* to Meyerson in 1965. Vernant was effectively trying to bridge the waning school of historical psychology begun by Meyerson and inspired by thinkers like Émile Durkheim and Marcel Mauss to the rising vogue of structuralism, all while retaining a humanism that did not give way to the current skepticism on the subject of man as seen in the work of Michel Foucault. In works such as *The Origins of Greek Thought* (1962), he continued the argument for a collective political consciousness, concluding that the emergence of "Greek reason" was a product of the *polis*, not an attitude born of contemplating the nature of things. "Greek reason is that reason which makes it possible to act practically, deliberately, and systematically on human beings, not to transform nature. In its limitations as in its innovations, it is a creature of the city."[31]

So Vernant, the "nuanced rationalist," in publishing a critique of Freud's Oedipal interpretation in *Raison Présente*, was trying to shift the focus away from the isolation of individual psychological conflict (so bourgeois and self-indulgent, one senses from his disdain), to an awareness of the crucial moment in the collective elaboration of the human will in the Athenian polis, which broke from the archaic traditions of divine causality. The real questions being probed by Greek tragedy, for Vernant, lie in this emergent conception of the will:

> To what extent is man really the source of his actions? Even when he seems to be taking the initiative and bearing the responsibility for them does not their true origin lie elsewhere? Does not their significance remain to large extent hidden even from the one who performs them, so that it is not so

[30] Françoise Parot, "Psychology in the Human Sciences in France, 1920–1940: Ignace Meyerson's Historical Psychology." *History of Psychology* 3.2 (2000):104–21, and Frédéric Fruteau de Laclos, "Vernant et Meyerson le mental, le social et le structural." *Cahier philosophiques* 112 (2007): 9–25.

[31] Vernant, *The Origins of Greek Thought*, tr. NN. (Ithaca: Cornell University Press, 1982), 132.

much the agent that explains the action, rather the action that, by revealing its real meaning after the event, reflects light upon the agent's nature, revealing what he is and what in actual fact he has unwittingly done.[32]

So focused as he is on the unique moment of secular reason's emergence in his polemic, Vernant doesn't fully appreciate that these same questions are preeminently psychoanalytic concerns. We can also say for the same reason he ironically doesn't always savor the *tragic* sense of reason's limitations, unlike Freud. Freud's unconscious collects the asymmetries of human action under a new conceptual domain of a counter-will, another scene, an Other in human action that lies within, yet is tied very much to human interaction without. Freud, in other words, sees the human psyche far more dynamically shaped by conflict, not just by structure, and by what lies *beyond* language, what lingers in the Tartarus of the unspoken and unspeakable. This has a lot to do, I would argue, from his initial point of departure: disease and disorder, not discourse and order. Such a point of departure introduces a very different dynamic in what interpretation is accounting for.

Vernant's Marxist and structuralist impulses, pushing him always to see the *polis* emerging in tragedy and myth, occlude his vision of something equally central to both tragic plot and Greek society: the family. It's telling that his one look at the family in *Myth and Society in Ancient Greece* is at the institution of marriage,[33] predictably seen as a system of exchanging females. He goes as far as considering endogamy—but not incest, the shadow union that for Freud historically necessitated exogamy as a final solution. But how can one construct a historical psychology without adequate consideration of the family, not just as a "social structure" but also a locus of wounds? It is a common problem of any anthropology of ancient Greece conducted on a set of literary texts that enormities get ignored. The particularity and specificity of tragic conflict don't fit neatly into large generalizations of social systems. But the view from the couch at Berggasse 19 was always this: human life is made up of very specific and particular conflicts, informed to be sure by social structures and mores, but energized by individual personalities, trajectories, and desires. The social, for Freud, can only emerge after the *tragedy* of the personal has been

[32] Vernant and Vidal-Naquet, *Myth and Tragedy in Ancient Greece*, 89.

[33] See Vernant, *Myth and Society in Ancient Greece*, chapter 3.

written—the individual child renounces his/her love object, and defers to the greater power of the other parent.

In this regard, Freud's focus on *Oedipus the King* is highly appropriate. For Oedipus, unlike so many other instances of people misled by the Delphic oracle, suffers from a tragedy of extreme and literal specificity. He will *literally* and not figuratively sleep with this mother, and he will *literally* kill the man who very specifically is his biological father. What is revealed in Oedipus' fate is not an ambiguity as to what will happen, only an ambiguity of reference as to who the people in question truly are. It seems telling that Vernant misses this point, as do so many interpreters of Sophocles' play, who wish to explain away incest and patricide as somehow standing in for something else—in Vernant's case, for "the form of a purely operational schema of reversal, a rule of ambiguous logic."[34] To reduce Oedipus' familial conflict to a mere crisis of signification reflects, as Vincenzo di Benedetto commented in relation to another of Vernant's readings, "an attitude ... that, more than the Athenian spectator of the fifth century BC, seems to characterize certain intellectuals of today, always in crisis, or better, perpetually in search of new cultural models (or fashions)."[35]

History cannot vaguely be invoked as something epistemologically superior to psychology in the study of culture simply because the past has been claimed as the domain of historians. In his conclusion, we find Vernant too eager to refute Freud with such thinking to his own detriment. He chides Freud for his assertion that when Jocasta raises the question of incestuous dreams, this is a clear indication of the link between this common dream type and this ancient myth. As his parting shot, Vernant explains that incest dreams in Greek culture often mean something nonliteral, such as taking possession of one's homeland. There is therefore nothing inherently distressing about incest dreams, and Freud's ahistorical dream theory is wide of the mark. "The meanings of dreams themselves, inasmuch as they are symbolic, appear as a cultural fact that can be discovered by means of a study of historical psychology."[36] But this objection completely ignores the dramatic context. Vernant seems tone-deaf here to something the psychoanalyst is *keenly* attuned to: irony. The one person

[34] Vernant and Vidal-Naquet, *Myth and Tragedy in Ancient Greece*, 139.

[35] Vincenzo di Benedetto, "La tragedia greca di Jean-Pierre Vernant," *Balfagor* 32 (1977): 461–468; here 468.

[36] Vernant and Vidal-Naquet, *Myth and Tragedy in Ancient Greece*, 111.

who tells Oedipus not to worry about incest is the one who soon realizes she has, indeed, committed incest—and the Greek audience knew this full well. Her cavalier suggestion that one should live unconcerned about such things (*Oedipus Tyrannus* 977–983) clearly points to the opposite truth. Sophocles brilliantly waves this ghastly false-consolation at the audience on purpose, moments before Jocasta self-destructs—and a Freudian can certainly be allowed to see it not just as a dramatic irony, but as a defensive denial on her part. She is, after all, a woman who has knowingly gone to bed *many, many times* with a vigorous young hero her son's age—what fantasies lie in *her* cougar's heart, the modern method actor might inquire.

Vernant's interest in the emergence of reason and the secular political order oddly did not extend far enough to his own times; he did not see the clear links between a nineteenth-century secular historical psychology (the retrospective medicine of Paris) and the twentieth-century version he professed. To say psychoanalysis must be supplanted by a historical psychology is to ignore the historical argument embedded in psychoanalysis. One can critique the *kind* of history Freud's doing, but to say it is ahistorical is an error; and there can be no historical psychology that ignores the actual history of psychology.

CHAPTER 3

The Dawn of the Oedipus Complex: A Tale of Two Letters

Harold Blum

Freud's formulation of the Oedipus complex in 1897 was a landmark in the history of ideas, as well as in psychoanalytic theory. In two letters, dated October 3 and October 15, 1897, written from Vienna to his quasi-analyst, confidant, and sounding board, Wilhelm Fliess in Berlin, Freud outlined the basic ideas of the Oedipus complex. Nodal points in a creative correspondence, these letters were preceded and followed by other significant letters. This formulation was the coalescence of ideas from a variety of sources, including Freud's self-analysis, work with patients, and interpretations of literature. In an almost circular process, Freud discusses the Oedipal themes in *Oedipus Rex* and Hamlet, attesting to the universality of the Oedipus complex across time and cultures.

The specific term "Oedipus complex," however, was not introduced in the psychoanalytic literature until Freud's 1910 paper on the psychology

H. Blum (✉)
Psychoanalytic Association of New York, New York University Medical School, New York, NY, USA

L. Weissberg (ed.), *Psychoanalysis, Fatherhood, and the Modern Family*, https://doi.org/10.1007/978-3-030-82124-1_3

of love.[1] In its original formulation, the Oedipus complex is a set of triangular relationships between child, mother, and father, with conflicting thoughts, feelings, and attitudes. It is typically an unconscious fantasy system, because of the subject's anxiety, shame, and guilt. The Oedipus complex emerged in a self-analytic analog of clinical psychoanalysis, and in the application of psychoanalytic thought to enduring masterpieces of literature. These communications are masterworks of understatement, discovery, and integration. Discovering the Oedipus complex and later its pre-Oedipal antecedents became cornerstones of psychoanalytic theory.

In the first letter, Freud casually wrote that he had nothing new to report, and the letters were nearly lost to posterity. They were preserved, however, by Princess Marie Bonaparte, Freud's grateful patient and friend, who bought them from Fliess's widow. She refused Freud's request to destroy the correspondence. Freud could not have imagined that his mail would be permanently preserved at the United States Library of Congress. Fliess's letters to Freud so far have never been found. Many authors have contributed to our appreciation of the importance of these letters and I have greatly profited from their scholarship and research, for example, Ernest Jones, Max Schur, Marianne Krull, William J. McGrath, Peter Rudnitsky, and Eugene J. Mahon.[2] Fliess was important to Freud not only as a correspondent whom he met occasionally in what they called a Congress, but as a prominent figure in Freud's self-analysis and in the discovery of the Oedipus complex. Freud for a long time idealized Fliess, but inwardly grew ambivalent toward Fliess in his real but also in his transference relationship. He wrote "you altogether ruin my critical faculties, and I truly believe you in everything."[3]

[1] Sigmund Freud, "A Special Type of Choice of Object Made by Men." In: Freud, *The Standard Edition of the Complete Psychological Works*, tr. James Strachey, ed. Anna Freud et al. 24 vols. (London: The Hogarth Press, 1953–1974), XI: 165–175 (edition will be abbreviated *SE*).

[2] Ernest Jones, *The Life and Work of Sigmund Freud*. 3 vols. New York: Basic Books, 1953–1957; Max Schur, *Freud Living and Dying*, New York: International Universities Press, 1979; Marianne Krull, *Freud and His Father*, New York: Norton, 1986; William J. McGrath, *Freud's Discovery of Psychoanalysis: The Politics of Hysteria*, New York: Cornell University Press, 1986; Peter Rudnitsky, *Freud and Oedipus*, New York: Columbia University Press, 1987; Eugene J. Mahon, *A Psychoanalytic Odyssey*, London: Karnac Books, 2014.

[3] Freud, letter to Wilhelm Fliess, September 29, 1893. In: Freud, *The Complete Letters of Sigmund Freud to Wilhelm Fliess, 1887–1904*, ed. Jeffrey Moussaieff Masson (Cambridge: Harvard University Press, 1985), 56. See also Harold Blum, "Freud, Fliess and the Parenthood of Psychoanalysis," *Psychoanalytic Quarterly*, 59 (1990): 21–39.

Freud had also been inspired by his earlier mentor, Josef Breuer, who had informed Freud of his treatment of "Anna O" by hypnosis. Freud had earlier observed Jean-Martin Charcot removing, inducing, and substituting symptoms by hypnosis, indicating unconscious mental processes.[4] Prior to the 1897 letters, Freud and Breuer had co-authored "Studies on Hysteria."[5] In their book the new "talking cure" emphasized an etiology of trauma with therapeutic recovery of suppressed and repressed tormenting memories with their accompanying painful affects, for example, fright, shame, guilt, and rage. A precursor of the Oedipus complex was present in Freud's letter to Fliess of May 31, 1897, in which Freud noted: "The death wish is directed in sons against the father and in daughters against their mother."[6] Fliess replaced earlier idealized figures such as Ernst Brücke, Charcot, and Breuer.

Freud's self-analysis was an entirely new creation, largely progressing through the interpretation of his own dreams and associations. Although his analytic work with patients was also helpful, his self-analytic dream interpretation was crucial to the discovery of the Oedipus complex. His writing of his dreams and his communication with Fliess also had significant psychological ramifications. Instead of becoming fleeting memories, his dreams were recorded in a more permanent form for study, and analyzed in the process of writing and reading. During his self-analysis Freud developed and overcame a writing block related to Oedipal inhibition. Many years later he wrote, "as soon as writing which entails making a liquid flow out of a tube onto a piece of white paper assumes the significance of copulation, writing is stopped because it represents a forbidden sexual act."[7] This interpretation likely had relevance to his writing block.

Freud repudiated his earlier proposition of "seduction trauma," sexual abuse of a child in modern terminology, as an exclusive cause of adult neurosis in September 1897, just before his October formulation of the Oedipus complex. He had previously even assumed that his own father had traumatically abused his siblings. The expression "seduction trauma" was a euphemism for the experience of a traumatized child as an innocent victim of an adult pedophile. Following this repudiation of seduction

[4] Freud [section on Paris], "Report on My Studies in Paris and Berlin" (1886), *SE* I: 5–15.

[5] Freud and Josef Breuer, *Studies on Hysteria* (1895), *SE* II.

[6] Freud, "Draft N," enclosed in letter to Fliess, May 31, 1897. In: Freud, *Complete Letters to Fliess*, 254.

[7] Freud, "Inhibitions, Symptoms, and Anxiety," (1926 [1925]), *SE* XX: 77–178, here 90.

trauma as the exclusive theory of pathogenesis in September 1897, Freud stated in October 1897 that his father played no role, but the prime originator of his own seduction trauma was an ugly, elderly, clever nursemaid.[8] In contrast, however, he further wrote that she instilled in him a high opinion of his capacities. In the same letter Freud wrote of seeing his mother nude with awakened libido on a train journey from Leipzig to Vienna which he mistakenly dated as between two and two and a half years of age (268). Did Freud unconsciously experience seduction by his mother? Was he not also sexually aroused, and masturbating at other times?

The notion of endogenous Oedipal erotic excitement during masturbation was consistent with Freud's observations of infantile sexuality. This idea that it was biologically based was later incorporated in libido theory (unless externally restricted, infants spontaneously engage in masturbation with apparent pleasurable sexual arousal). Immediately following his reference to incestuous arousal Freud wrote of his jealous rivalry with his new brother. Oedipal and pre-Oedipal themes were juxtaposed. Julius was born when Freud was approximately eighteen months old and died when Freud was about two years old. Julius's birth and his death in April 1858 occurred during the anal phase of libidinal development and the rapprochement phase of separation-individuation.[9]

The earlier repudiated seduction theory, however, had again re-emerged in the immediately succeeding letter of October 3–4, 1897. There, Freud referred to his nursemaid washing him in reddish water in which she washed herself, insinuating that it contained her menstrual blood.[10] The old trauma theory and the new endogenous incestuous arousal virtually coexisted side by side. The author was at first seemingly aware and unaware of the contrast between incestuous wishes of childhood, and acting out of incest fantasy in the adult's traumatic sexual abuse of children.

In the letter begun on October 3, Freud used the Latin terms "matrum" and "nudam" instead of colloquial German.[11] Choosing antiquated Latin indicates both concealing and revealing the emotionally highly charged prohibited incestuous desires. On this trip from Leipzig to Vienna, when he was little more than four years old, Freud was alone with his pregnant

[8] Freud, Letter to Fliess, October 3, 1897. In: Freud, *Complete Letters to Fliess*, 268.

[9] Blum, "The Prototype of pre-Oedipal Reconstruction," *Journal of the American Psychoanalytic Association* (*JAPA*). 25 (1977): 757–785.

[10] Freud, letter to Fliess, October 4 (c'd October 3), 1897. In: Freud, *Complete Letters* to Fliess, 263.

[11] Freud, letter to Fliess, October 3, 1897. In: Freud, *Complete Letters to Fliess*, 268.

mother without the protective and inhibiting presence of his father. Was Freud seeing and reacting to his mother nude for the first time? More likely he condensed observations of his mother in varied stages of undress in the one small room the family shared during his first three and a half years in Příbor.

On a preceding train trip, confusingly referred to in a later letter to Fliess,[12] the Freud family was moving away from Příbor to Leipzig. En route to Leipzig, Freud's train stopped at Breslau where little Sigmund had observed burning gas jets in the train station. He thought of souls burning in hell, which he connected with his travel anxiety. By separating "burning in hell" from the later trip (from Leipzig to Vienna) where he was aroused seeing his nude mother, he would have avoided Oedipal guilt.[13] His travel phobia apparently encompassed both Oedipal conflict and antecedent separation anxiety. Actually, Freud did not completely overcome his anxiety concerning train travel which persisted through his life.

In the October 15 letter Freud referred to what became the prototype analysis of a screen memory. Freud saw his mother emerge slender and beautiful from a cabinet in which she had been "boxed up."[14] Aware of her body on the train trip during her pregnancy, Freud was evidently also aware of the change in her body after the birth of Julius. As a toddler Freud was exposed to his mother's pregnant body and to her own physical and mental reactions to her pregnancy. He conjectured that his older half-brother, about the same age as his mother, had somehow impregnated her. Freud's analysis of his screen memory was not recognized as autobiographical until its true nature was uncovered by Siegfried Bernfeld in 1949.[15] He had contemplated the complexities of pregnancy, and the birth and death of his first sibling.

Freud remarked later in the same famed letter of October 15 that he had found nothing completely new, and being totally honest with oneself is a good exercise. He then announced the Oedipus complex: "A single idea of general value dawned on me. I have found, in my own case too, the phenomenon of being in love with my mother and jealous of my father,

[12] Freud, letter to Fliess, December 12, 1897. In: Freud, *Complete Letters* to Fliess, 285–286.

[13] Freud, letter to Fliess, December 12, 1897. In: Freud, *Complete Letters to Fliess*, 286.

[14] Freud, letter to Fliess, October 15, 1897. In: Freud, *Complete Letters to Fliess*, 272.

[15] Siegfried Bernfeld, "An Unknown Autobiographical Fragment by Freud," *American Imago* 4 (1946): 3–19.

and I now consider it a universal event in early childhood."[16] This brief statement spoke volumes; it was followed by the analysis of *Oedipus Rex* and of Hamlet, illustrating the Oedipus complex in world myth and literature. As a repressed universal fantasy, Freud's inquiry did not encompass Oedipus as an abused, abandoned, and adopted child.[17]

In their one room in Příbor Freud would have been exposed to the primal scene as well as to his mother holding, nursing, and generally attending to his infant brother Julius. Early psychoanalytic focus on the primal scene can blind observation of the very intimate non-verbal and verbal affective interaction of Freud with his mother and father and the interaction of his parents with each other. He would have observed their affection, antagonism, laughter, tears, comfort or tension, and so on. His parents would have conversed in Yiddish. The intimacy of private communication in the one small room isolated from the external Czech society may foreshadow the psychoanalytic situation. Freud's interest in language may have been stimulated by his pre-Oedipal experience of the manifold nuances of communication.

Freud's unconscious ambivalent relation to his mother was related to the explicitly ambivalent relationship he reported about his nursemaid. Current research has revealed that there were three nursemaids, with implications of different styles of child rearing and varied responsibility as nanny or maid.[18] Freud telescoped the three into the one nursemaid who sexually abused and paradoxically supported and comforted him. Only one was present with Amalia when she was pregnant with Julius in the Roznau Spa, away from Freud's father and brothers. The relationship of Amalia to that nursemaid is unknown. One nursemaid was listed as a wet nurse, but it is not known whether she had or lost her own infant and at any time nursed Sigmund. We do not know the relationships of the nursemaids to each other or to Freud's parents. Nor do we know how much time each spent with Sigmund, compared with other duties. It is not clear which nursemaid took him to church or outdoors to play with his nephew and niece. I am doubtful that a nursemaid, compared to his mother, was his primary caregiver who provided support when he was in an anxious or

[16] Freud, letter to Fliess, October 15, 1897. In: Freud, *Complete Letters to Fliess*, 272.

[17] John Munder Ross, "Oedipus revisited. Laius and the Laius Complex," *Psychoanalytic Study of the Child* 37 (1982): 169–200.

[18] Blum, "Reconstructing Freud's Prototype Reconstructions," *International Forum of Psychoanalysis* 24 (2015):47–56; and Vaclav Burianek, "Paradise Lost and Trauma Mastered: New Findings on Little Sigmund. *International Forum of Psychoanalysis* 24 (2015): 22–28.

depressive state. Nor do I regard, as Freud proposed, that his relationship with his nephew John rather than his parents was a prototype for his later ambivalent relationships, particularly to male colleagues.[19] In unconscious rage at his mother for her divided love for his father and new brother, he split off her bad object representation to preserve the good object. She then represented the caring nanny who gave him the strength to live and go on being, dissociated from the nursemaid who washed him in reddish water with her menstrual blood, instructed him in sexual matters, that is, who sexually abused him.

Freud referred to fantasies of play with John and inferred sex play with John's younger sister, Pauline. They snatched flowers from her in a disguised adolescent fantasy of deflowering a girl, projected backward in time to early childhood (268). Did Freud and John also engage in sex play with each other? An Oedipal incestuous configuration emerges from the adolescent erotic fantasy, which has been modified from the childhood scenes in the screen memory.[20] Freud was confused in childhood about the children and grandchildren of his father. His perplexity was related to the great riddles of childhood: Where do babies come from and how are babies born? These perplexities were linked to the riddles of the Sphinx, the riddles of femininity, and of the father's role in reproduction.

Why did the Oedipus complex occur to Freud at that particular time, in that familial, cultural, and historical context? What were the motives for self-analysis, for interpreting dreams, for the analytic method of free association to his dreams, daydreams, and the retrieval of buried memories? What impelled Freud at age 40–41 to reconstruct Oedipal development and its formative antecedents? As Shakespeare said, nothing comes of nothing, and an array of determinants fostered and facilitated the creation of psychoanalysis and the construction of the Oedipus complex.

The dawn of the Oedipus complex in October 1897 may be related to the anniversary of Freud's father's death in October 1896, and the unnoted death of his maternal grandfather in October 1865. His father and grandfather were both named Jacob, a figure of great significance in the Bible, the father of Joseph, the interpreter of the Pharaoh's dreams. His mother had married a man old enough to be her own father, with the same name as her father, perhaps later contributing to Freud's incestuous fantasies.

[19] Freud, letter to Fliess, October 3, 1897. In: Freud, *Complete Letters to Fliess*, 268.

[20] Blum, "Adolescent Trauma and the Oedipus Complex," *Psychoanalytic Inquiry* 30 (2010): 548–566.

Freud annotated the 1908 edition of the *Interpretation of Dreams*, stating that the work had been instigated by mourning his father's death.[21] He then described a father's death as the most poignant experience of any man's life. The experience of the death of one's mother was not addressed nor was the very important experience of Freud's own fatherhood. The births of Freud's six children within the first ten years of marriage altered his familial relationships and renewed his direct exposure to infant and child development. His large family might also have been associated with a mid-life crisis.

Freud's ambivalent relationship with Fliess was another significant determinant of Freud's becoming his own patient. His idealization of Fliess actually began almost immediately after their meeting in 1887, soon after Freud had become a father. Feeling displaced in the mother figure's affection and attention by his first child, Freud then turned to Fliess as a father figure. Freud's observations and reactions as a father would likely have facilitated the October 1897 reconstructions of his own infancy and early childhood. Freud had been partly replaced by the children in Martha's hitherto individual marital devotion. Freud's sibling rivalry and jealousy of brother Julius in Příbor had been unconsciously revived. Fliess was two years younger than Freud, both a parent and brother figure. In the aftermath of the birth and death of Julius, Freud experienced his mother's successive pregnancies and the arrival of six more siblings, a sorority of five sisters and then his brother Alexander. While idealizing Fliess as a colleague, Freud had completed his biological fatherhood, replaced his own father, and was similarly the head of a large family with six of his own children. Freud's relationship to Martha had been altered in the complexity and conflicts of family life. In my view these circumstances, the onset of the devaluation of Fliess, and the reactivation of the unresolved conflicts of Freud's first three and a half years of life in Příbor were major determinants of later psychoanalytic theory.

I believe the increasing disillusionment and divergence from Fliess was propelled by the nearly lethal surgery Fliess performed on Emma Eckstein about January–February, 1895, to cure her masturbation and neurasthenia. Freud was guilty having recommended the surgery to his own patient for an unnecessary operation during which Fliess left half a meter of gauze in her nose. She is represented in the composite figure of Irma in "The

[21] Freud, *The Interpretation of Dreams* (1900), *SE* IV: xxvi.

Specimen Dream" of July 1895 in the *Interpretation of Dreams*.[22] Freud displaced blame of Fliess onto Emma for "hysterical bleeding,"[23] with Freud exonerating Fliess as he would soon exonerate his father of seduction trauma. Freud had been vulnerable to psychological seduction trauma by Fliess and was initially unaware of his ambivalence.[24]

In Freud's adolescent intellectual development, we can also discern precursors of the formulation of the Oedipus complex. Freud was interested in *Oedipus Rex* in his adolescence as were many well-known authors of the day.[25] First in his class in the gymnasium, what did Freud choose to read in advance of his final exam for graduation? Two letters attest to Freud's adolescent psychological journey from classical Greece to contemporary Vienna. He wrote to his friend Emil Fluss on March 17, 1873: "I have done a great deal of reading on my own account from the Greek and Latin classics, among them Sophocles' 'Oedipus Rex.' You deprive yourself of much that is edifying if you can't read all of this."[26] Freud followed with another letter to Fluss on June 16, 1873, about his "Matura" (high school graduation) exam, in which he decided on the formidable task of translating Sophocles from the ancient Greek. Freud wrote: "The Greek paper, consisting of a thirty-three-verse passage from 'Oedipus Rex' came off better."[27] Continuing to be inspired by the great literary masterpieces, Freud identified with Sophocles, Shakespeare, Cervantes, and Goethe, among his favorite authors. He sought "men whom I could respect and take as my models."[28] Freud had learned Spanish to read Cervantes, English to read Shakespeare, and French to study with, and translate, Charcot. At the time of his "Matura" he was rapidly maturing and avidly reading and absorbing new ideas and pondering different cultures. In the first known destruction of his documents in 1885, Freud stated that

[22] Freud, "The Specimen Dream," *The Interpretation of Dreams* (1900 [1899]), *SE* IV: 96–121.

[23] Freud, letter to Fliess, April 26, 1896. In: Freud, *Complete Letters to Fliess*, 183: "I shall be able to prove to you that you were right, that her episodes of bleeding were hysterical."

[24] Masson, *The Assault on Truth, Freud's Suppression of the Seduction Theory*, New York: Farrar, Straus, and Giroux, 1984; and Blum, "The Irma Dream: Self-Analysis and Self-Supervision," *JAPA* 44 (1996): 511–552.

[25] See Rudnitsky, *Freud and Oedipus*.

[26] Freud, letter to Emil Fluss, March 17, 1873. In: Ernst L. Freud (Ed.), "Some Early Unpublished Letters of Freud," *The International Journal of Psychoanalysis* 50 (1969):419–427, here 423.

[27] Freud, letter to Fluss, June 16, 1873. In: Freud, "Some Early Unpublished Letters," 425.

[28] Freud, "An Autobiographical Study" (1935), *SE* XX: 7–76, here 9.

otherwise he would have suffocated from the stuff settling around him, like sand drifts around the Sphinx, already a reference to *Oedipus Rex*.[29] Freud later wrote to his betrothed, Martha Bernays, from Paris in February 1886: "In my youth I was never young."[30] He had also then written to Minna Bernays, Martha's sister, comparing Paris to a vast Sphinx who gobbles up every foreigner unable to solve her riddle. Drawn to the Paris theater, Freud was impressed by the performance of *Oedipus Rex*. Upon his return to Vienna in 1886, he attended an acclaimed *Oedipus Rex* and went to another performance of the drama in 1887. He had elaborated on the play in *The Interpretation of Dreams*, comparing the cunning disguise and gradual revelation to the psychoanalytic process.[31] Freud added "disguised dreams of sexual intercourse with the dreamer's mother are many times more frequent than straight-forward ones."[32] Freud continued to see the play as he mentioned in a letter to Jung, written October 12, 1911; he wrote that he dismissed Alfred Adler, viewed as an Oedipal rival after seeing a performance of *Oedipus Rex*.[33] Sandor Ferenczi added that the name "Oedipus" or swollen foot symbolized an erection and his blinding symbolized castration.[34] Castration anxiety was later considered part of the male Oedipus complex. Oedipus's determination to penetrate the obscure riddles of *Oedipus Rex* contrasted with his biological mother's, Jocasta's, denial of the significance of dreams and other evidence indicative of incest.

Freud's psychological journey during his inwardly turbulent adolescence was concurrently fostered by his external travel experience. He had registered in the University of Vienna's medical school in the Fall of 1873 and in the same year he visited his birthplace, Příbor (at Freud's time still Freiberg), a remote small town in what is now the Czech Republic. There he experienced his first adolescent love for Gisela Fluss, his friend's brother,

[29] Richard Armstrong, *A Compulsion for Antiquity*, Ithaca: Cornell University Press, 2005; and Janine Burke, *The Sphinx on the Table*, New York: Walker & Company, 2006.

[30] Freud, letter to Martha Bernays, February 2, 1886. In: Freud, *Letters of Sigmund Freud*, ed. Ernst L. Freud, tr. Tania and James Stern (New York: Basic Books, 1960), 202.

[31] Freud, "The Material and Sources of Dreams," *The Interpretation of* Dreams," *SE* IV: 264–265.

[32] Freud, "The Dream-Work," *The Interpretation of Dreams*, *SE* IV, 398.

[33] Carl Gustav Jung, letter to Freud, October 12, 1911. In: *The Freud/Jung letters: The Correspondence between Sigmund Freud and C.G. Jung*, ed. William McGuire, tr. Ralph Manheim and R.F.C. Hull (Princeton: Princeton University Press, 1974), 447.

[34] Sandor Ferenczi, "The Symbolic Representation of the Pleasure and Reality Principles in the Oedipus Myth" (1912). In: Ferenczi, *Sex in Psychoanalysis* (New York: Dover, 2014), 214–227.

then thirteen years old. The Fluss family had also resided in Příbor and were friends with the Freud family. Freud, the youthful Oedipus, recognized his thinly disguised erotized attraction to Gisela's idealized mother. As a youthful budding psychoanalyst, seventeen years of age, he wrote to his friend Eduard Silberstein, September 4, 1872: "I have transferred my esteem for the mother to friendship for daughter,"[35] anticipating the psychoanalytic concept of "transference." Freud had urged Silberstein, the epistolary precursor of his addressees Martha and Fliess, to destroy their correspondence, which he did not do. Were not all his "auto da fés," his destructions of his documents, related to concealment of wishful erotic interests?

Having conceptualized the Oedipus complex in the two letters of October 1897, Freud considered and modified his ideas throughout his life. After publication of *The Interpretation of Dreams* in 1900 (1899),[36] Freud became ever more confident of the importance of the Oedipus complex in normal development and psychopathology. Clinical experience with his patients continued to be synergistic with Freud's analysis of myth and literature. Writing to Fliess about an intriguing patient in December 1899, Freud inferred: "Beneath his fantasies was a scene ... where the remaining puzzle converged. It is as if Schliemann had once more excavated Troy ... providing the solution which I had overlooked to my former railroad phobia. For this piece of work I made him a present of a picture of Oedipus and the Sphinx."[37] Freud's gift is a very early example of a counter-transference enactment. The unconscious meaning of analyst and/or patient giving gifts to each other had not yet been elucidated.

In 1905, Freud corrected the protected view of motherhood when he noted that mothers also may sexually traumatize their children, but his rivalry, rage, and fantasized revenge were displaced from his mother to his father and others. Matricide, a term which does not appear in Freud's oeuvre, as well as parricide, is part of the expanded Oedipus complex.[38] On Freud's 50th birthday, May 6, 1906, his closest colleagues presented

[35] Freud, letter to Eduard Silberstein, September 4, 1872. In: Freud, *The Letters of Sigmund Freud to Eduard Silberstein, 1871–1881*, ed. Walter Boehlich (Cambridge: Harvard University Press, 1990), 17.

[36] See Freud, *The Interpretation of Dreams.*

[37] Freud, letter to Fliess, December 21, 1899. In: *Complete Letters*, 392.

[38] Freud, *Three Essays on the Theory of Sexuality* (1905), *SE* VII: 123–246, here 226; and Blum, "Matricide and the Oedipus Complex." In: Peter Hartocollis (Ed.), *Mankind's Oedipal Destiny* (New York: International Universities Press, 2000), 209–228; as well as

their master with a remarkable bronze medallion. Freud was depicted in profile on one side and Oedipus confronting the Sphinx on the other side. Sophocles's ancient Greek verse "who divined the famed riddle and was a man most mighty" was inscribed with the figures of Oedipus and the Sphinx. Jones observed that Freud became pale, agitated, and demanded to know who had originated the gift. After Paul Federn acknowledged himself, Freud disclosed that when he was at the University of Vienna, he admired the memorial busts of famed professors. He had fantasized seeing his own bust with the same ancient Greek inscription.[39] The figure of Oedipus became a psychoanalytic symbol, an icon of Freud's creativity and the power of psychoanalytic insight. Freud placed a copy of Ingres's "Oedipus and the Sphinx" (1808) near his analytic couch, readily seen by himself and his patients. Oedipus and the Sphinx were painted on one of the archeological artifacts in Freud's collection, and he also had a separate Greek terra cotta artifact of a Sphinx.[40] The Oedipus complex was described as the "nuclear complex of neuroses."[41]

In 1910, Freud had described the Oedipus complex in terms of ontogeny,[42] but turned to a phylogenetic hypothesis in *Totem and Taboo.*[43] No taboo was needed if there was not a powerful wish, he averred, to commit incest. Having already identified the boys' threat of castration by the rival Oedipal father, Freud proposed that an all-powerful jealous father threatened castration of the sons in the primeval horde, imagined by Darwin. This dominant alpha male demanded exclusive sexual possession of the women, in effect his own harem. Sexually deprived, jealous, and resentful, the brothers bonded together to murder the reciprocally jealous father. Oedipal parricide was then followed by the band of sons' guilt and remorse. The murdered father was then orally incorporated as the totem animal in a ritual totem repast. The totem meal had analogs in extant tribal rituals, Christian belief in original sin, and the rite of holy communion.

James L. Fosshage, "Implicit and Explicit Dimensions of Oedipal Phenomenology: A Reassessment, *Psychoanalytic Inquiry*, 30 (2010): 520–534.

[39] Jones, *The Life and Work of Sigmund Freud*, ed. and abridged by Lionel Trilling and Steven Marcus (New York: Basic Books, 1961), 243–244.

[40] See Burke, *The Sphinx on the Table.*

[41] Freud "On the Sexual Theories of Children" (1908), *SE* IX: 205–226, here 214.

[42] Freud, "Fourth Lecture," *Five Lectures on Psycho-Analysis* (1910 [1909]), *SE* XIII: 3–58; here 47.

[43] Freud, *Totem and Taboo* (1913), *SE* XIII 1–161; see also Freud, "The Claims of Psycho-Analysis to Scientific Interest" (1913), *SE* XIII: 163–190.

Marriage was required to be exogamous and avoided the forbidden original incestuous objects; "motherfucker" became an ubiquitous curse. What was inherent and essentially new was not so much Freud's hypothetical excursion into historical anthropology, but his conclusion that the Oedipus complex was the foundation of morality, religion, society, and art. *Totem and Taboo* prefigured "Mourning and Melancholia" (1916) regarding the internalization of parental ideals and injunctions, the precepts of the later Freudian superego.[44] For Freud, the child's moral standards and values were primarily determined by father figures. The mother's role in conveying ideals, injunctions, standards, and values was elaborated in the evolution of psychoanalytic theory.

These ideas influenced the very development of institutional psychoanalysis. Freud's ambivalent reactions to what he regarded as irrational divergence or opposition led to the formation of a protective/punitive psychoanalytic group superego. Jones recommended a secret committee of Freud's closest colleagues to safeguard the fledgling psychoanalytic movement from dilution and distortion, modeled on the paladins of Charlemagne. Fortifying their genuine admiration and idealizing transference to him, Freud gave each a ring inscribed with Jupiter. His loyal sons then arranged a totem feast, celebrated on Freud's return from Rome to Vienna in June 1913. His former patient, Jones's wife Katherine, presented Freud with an Egyptian artifact for his ever-expanding collection. For Freud, the Oedipus complex had become a shibboleth, a password that "distinguishes the adherents of psychoanalysis from its opponents."[45] The political and narcissistic elements in the psychoanalytic movement (or "cause") fostered an unfortunate initial tendency toward orthodoxy and dogma, actually contrary to the ideals of psychoanalysis.

The Oedipus complex was subsequently expanded by Freud beyond the core complex of rivalry with the father for incestuous possession of the mother. Bisexuality and homosexuality were included in the "negative Oedipus complex" in which the son identified with his mother in rivalry for father's love.[46] The daughter identified with her father and his masculine role, a rival for mother's love in the negative Oedipus complex. Typically, however, the heterosexual positive Oedipus complex was

[44] Freud, "Mourning and Melancholia" (1916), *SE* XIV: 243–258; and Freud, *The Ego and the Id* (1923), *SE* XIX: 144–207.

[45] Freud, *Three Essays on the Theory of Sexuality*, *SE* VII: 226 (footnote 1920).

[46] Freud, *The Ego and the Id* (1923), *SE*: XIX: 3–16.

predominant, with greater defense against the negative Oedipus complex. Moreover, there may be individual permutations to the Oedipus complex. All parent-child relationships are by no means identical, nor are all families alike in structure. At least once Freud referred to the Oedipus complex as a family complex.[47] As we now appreciate, the Oedipus complex varies in form and content, based on culture, family structure, and individual experience. The Oedipus complex is not as fixed as first outlined and particularly undergoes revision during adolescence. For this reason, it is difficult to predict the adult character and personality from childhood.

The Oedipus complex of girls was far less developed in early Freudian theory. Freud's propositions regarding women were later subject to feminist criticism and psychoanalytic challenge to the initial emphasis on female penis envy, masochism, and narcissism.[48] Female development for Freud was obscure "a dark continent," possibly symbolic of the invisible female reproductive system. Realizing that his knowledge of femininity was limited, Freud left the psychoanalytic theory of female development to female analysts and the poets. His paper on femininity was published after the death of his mother in 1930. Freud's concept of a weak female superego has long been noted as obsolete, patriarchal, and culturally biased. The rearing of girls was very different in Freud's time and place, and women were deprived of male prerogatives and privileges. He never wrote a companion paper on masculinity or fatherhood. Analysts, feminists, neuroscientists, and sociologists all influenced the revision of psychoanalytic theories of femininity, which was never without controversy. For many theorists today, gender is regarded as more mosaic or fluid than had been considered previously. A non-linear model of the Oedipus complex integrating prior and later developmental phases would be more compatible with current analytic thought.

The Oedipus complex dominated psychoanalytic thought through the first generation of North American psychoanalysts following World War II. The Oedipal all-powerful father of *Totem and Taboo* may also be understood as incorporating pre-Oedipal infantile omnipotence and grandiosity infiltrating the Oedipal development.[49] Within psychoanalysis

[47] Freud, *On the History of the Psychoanalytic Movement* (1914), *SE* XIV: 7–66.

[48] Roy Schafer, "Problems in Freud's Psychology of Women," *JAPA* 67 (219): 503–526.

[49] Otto F. Kernberg, "Borderline Personality Disorder and Borderline Personality Organization: Psychopathology and Psychotherapy." In: Jeffrey J. Magnavita (Ed.), *Handbook of Personality Disorders: Theory and Practice* (New York: John Wiley & Sons, 2004), 92–119.

the Oedipus complex was no longer considered a procrustean bed in which all forms of psychopathology were fitted to size. Severe psychopathology was not simply reducible to unresolved regression from Oedipal conflict.[50] Attachment, separation-individuation, self-psychology, ego deficits, and neuroscience revised and influenced the centrality of the Oedipus complex in theory and practice.[51] Since Freud's death psychoanalytic focus on the Oedipus complex has waxed and waned.[52] Still the nuclear complex of the neuroses, Oedipal conflict is no longer regarded as the major pathogenic determinant of psychotic, narcissistic, and borderline personality disorder. Freud actually introduced the modified nuclear complex:

> Since this phase allows room for all the fixations and repressions from which we trace of the origin of the neuroses, it would seem as though we must retract the universality of the thesis that the Oedipus complex is the nucleus of the neuroses. But if anyone feels reluctant about making this correction, there is no need for him to do so. ... Our insight into this early, pre-Oedipus, phase in girls comes to us as a surprise, like the discovery, in another field, of the Minoan-Mycenean civilization behind the civilization of Greece.[53]

No long the heir to the Oedipus complex, superego development begins with the mother's indications of approval or disapproval, and continues through adolescence and adulthood with new identifications. Any individual may have highly specific Oedipal conflict, and any individual may have highly atypical Oedipal development or arrest.

The Oedipus complex undergoes modification in subsequent developmental phases rather than dissolution as Freud had originally proposed. Resolution or regressive revival of Oedipal conflict is important in later life, for example, upon becoming a parent. The Oedipus complex may now be conceptualized as an enduring yet malleable psychic constellation alive in all humanity. Oedipal antecedents of parental approval and disapproval, standards and limits, will have influenced later autonomous

[50] Kernberg, *Borderline Conditions and Pathological Narcissism*. New York: Jason Aronson, 1975; and Heinz Kohut, *The Restoration of the Self*, New York: International Universities Press, 1977.

[51] Rosemary M. Balsam, "Where has Oedipus gone? A Turn of the Century Contemplation," *Psychoanalytic Inquiry* 30 (2010): 511–519.

[52] Hans Loewald, "On the Therapeutic Action of Psychoanalysis," *International Journal of Psycho-Analysis* 41 (1960):16–33.

[53] Freud, "Female Sexuality" (1931), *SE* XXII: 221–246, here 226.

regulation of affect and impulse.[54] In fostering progressive developmental achievements the Oedipus complex leads to consolidation of our internalized values, ideals, and injunctions (the Super Ego).

Consoled by his discoveries in the pained twilight of his life, Freud asseverated: "If psychoanalysis could boast of no other achievement than the discovery of the repressed Oedipus complex, that alone would give it a claim to be included among the precious new acquisitions of mankind."[55]

[54] Elsa J. Blum and Blum, "The Development of Autonomy and Superego Precursors," *International Journal of Psycho-Analysis* 71 (1990): 585–595.

[55] Freud, *An Outline of Psychoanalysis* (1939), *SE* XXIII: 193–4.

PART II

The Oedipus Complex After Freud

CHAPTER 4

Freud's Oedipal Myth and Lacan's Critique

Jean-Michel Rabaté

Jacques Lacan's entire career can be inscribed under the banner of a "return to Freud," a motto launched against what he saw as the distortions operated by the second generation of Jewish psychoanalysts in exile, most of whom had gone to the United States and seemed eager to make money, thus readily compromised with American values and institutions. When he began his seminar, he would take a few canonical texts by Sigmund Freud, and comment on them at length. Over the years, he began taking more distance with Freud's texts, as we see in *Séminaire XVIII*, a later seminar from the last decade of his life, in which he begins to question the Oedipal foundation of Freud's system.

It is at the end of this seminar, when Lacan was examining Freud's 1913 *Totem and Taboo,* that he stated the need to remain critical even when facing what appears as Freud's main tenets. On the other hand, Lacan refused to psychoanalyze Freud himself, even if he noted that the Oedipal myth was his personal myth, and therefore his most durable invention. As he claims, Freud's texts should be reread with an attention to detail and the wish to keep a cutting edge. Freud's texts are not to be accepted or rejected blindly, but should be organized logically to be the

J.-M. Rabaté (✉)
University of Pennsylvania, Philadelphia, PA, USA
e-mail: jmrabate@sas.upenn.edu

L. Weissberg (ed.), *Psychoanalysis, Fatherhood, and the Modern Family*, https://doi.org/10.1007/978-3-030-82124-1_4

object of a Kantian "Critique" assessing the conditions of possibility of the main concept. This is what Lacan suggests when he says that we must "criticize" Freud's writings.[1] Here, it is indeed a critique of *Totem and Taboo* that Lacan is mounting. He begins by denouncing a widespread confusion in psychoanalytic literature that conflates the murder of the Father of the primitive horde with the Oedipus complex. One often reads that Freud's main idea is that the murder of the father that is posited as the root of civilization reenacts the Oedipus myth or presents an earlier version of it. On the contrary, according to Lacan, there is a "split" (*une schize*), a gap, a true epistemological break that separates the Oedipus myth from the founding legend of *Totem and Taboo* (S XVIII, 158).

Indeed, these two myths obey different logics. In the primordial myth of *Totem and Taboo*, Freud presents a domineering Father, a tyrant who enjoyed all the women of the horde; then the rebellious sons would have united against him and slayed him. Such a primal murder would have taken place after the sons had agreed that no one should succeed to the primal Father in his "gluttony for enjoyment" (S XVIII, 159). Then the sons devour the dead father, each eating a part of him, which creates a "first" communion, after which the dead Father returns because he has been idealized or deified after this murder by the sons. For Freud, this would provide the starting point for any subsequent social contract; in this unwritten contract, no male will touch not just the mother, but all the father's wives.

This myth cannot be aligned with the law that Freud presents as underpinning the Oedipus legend; in the Greek drama, we find a law that prevents incest with the mother, and as we know, such a law provides a foundation for psychoanalysis. In the Oedipus myth, the law of prohibition comes first; it is primordial in that it punishes anyone who contravenes it, even when the guilty party has done the deed innocently. In the Oedipus myth, the murder happens without the knowledge of the murderer who does not recognize that he is attacking the father. What the myth suggests is that the place occupied by the generating father, Oedipus's father in fact, is problematic. In the myth of *Totem and Taboo*, it is the reverse logic: Enjoyment comes first and is followed by the law that is

[1] Jacques Lacan, Jacques Lacan, *Le Séminaire, livre XVIII: D'un Discours qui ne serait pas du semblant,* ed. Jacques-Alain Miller (Paris, Édition de Seuil, 2007), 161. I will provide the translation and abbreviate this text S XVIII; further references will appear with page numbers in the text.

imposed to limit or prohibit it. A sacred cannibalism accompanies the fact that all women are prohibited, in principle. They are untouchable for the community of the males, a community that transcends itself in a ritual communion. Lacan then concludes:

> *Totem and Taboo* is a neurotic product, which is absolutely indisputable, without for all that my questioning the truth of the construction. That is even how it bears witness to the truth. One does not psychoanalyze an oeuvre, and that of Freud less than any other, is that not so? One criticizes it, and far from a neurosis making its solidity suspect, it is the very thing that solders it in this case.//It is to the testimony that the obsessional contributes about his structure, testifying that sexual relationship proves to be impossible to formulate in discourse, that we owe the myth of Freud. (S XVIII, 160)

If Freud's fascination with the murder of the father, from Oedipus to Moses, can make Freud appear as a neurotic, he was able to transform his neurosis into a productive agency. What does Lacan mean by "critique" or "criticizing" in this context? Soon after, in the last session of *Séminaire* XVIII, Lacan finally put his cards on the table and named Karl Marx as the true inventor of the notion of symptom (S XVIII, 164). This famous statement, often quoted by Slavoj Žižek, cannot but evoke Karl Marx's famous eleventh thesis on Feuerbach: "The philosophers have only interpreted the world, in various ways; the point is to change it."[2]

In the aftermath of May 1968, Lacan had elaborated his version of Freudo-Marxism by formalizing the social bonds as made up of four "discourses" in which the "discourse of the master" could be understood as the "discourse of the capitalist." Lacan was combining Louis Althusser's influential readings of *Capital* as having launched "symptomatic readings" of society and Foucault's critical historicism, also known as "genealogy."[3] Lacan needed only to insert what he called "surplus jouissance" (*plus de jouir*), a synthesis of Freud's *Lust* and Marx's *Mehrwert* (surplus value).

[2] Karl Marx, *Selected Writings*, tr. Lawrence H. Simon, ed. David McLellan (Oxford: Oxford University Press, 1977), 158.

[3] Michel Foucault, *The Archeology of Knowledge*, tr. Alan Sheridan, New York: Harper and Row, 1972; and Louis Althusser, Etienne Balibar, Jacques Rancière, Roger Establet and Pierre Macherey, *Reading Capital*, tr. Ben Brewster and David Fernbach, London: Verso, 2015.

I will give two examples of Lacan's symptomatic readings to show how they realize such a "critique." We will see that a great degree of criticism can be allied with a true fidelity to Freud's insights.

Hamlet

Freud's theory of desire was established in the *Interpretation of Dreams.* A section on "typical dreams" devoted to dreams of dead parents develops the implications for psychic life provided by *Oedipus Rex.* Then a long footnote develops the comparison between Sophocles and Shakespeare:

> Another great creation of tragic poetry is rooted in the same soil as *Oedipus the King*: Shakespeare's *Hamlet*. But the change in treatment of the same material reveals the difference in the inner life of these two cultural periods so remote from each other: the advance of repression over the centuries in mankind's emotional life. In *Oedipus* the child's wishful fantasy on which it is based is out in the open and realized—as it is in dreams; in *Hamlet* it remains repressed, and we learn of its existence—as we learn of a neurosis—only through the inhibiting effect it produces.[4]

For Freud, Shakespeare's play is a universal masterpiece not just because it offers an interesting riddle about murder and revenge, but because it teaches something fundamental about human sexuality, desire, and the evolution of culture. If we understand *Hamlet,* we can be aware of a deep change or progression in morality and ethics. The Greeks, on that view, would be less submitted to repression than us "moderns," like Hamlet. What was accomplished thoughtlessly by Oedipus has become quite impossible for Hamlet, hence for us. This is why the most obvious feature of the plot, its apparently meandering tale of hesitation, procrastination, and sadistic games cut by sudden outbursts of violence, can touch a nerve in us all. Freud continues his analysis:

> Hamlet can do anything—except take revenge on the man who removed his father and took the latter's place beside his mother, the man who shows him his own repressed infant wishes realized. The revulsion that should urge him to revenge is thus replaced by self-recrimination, by the scruples of conscience which accuse him of being, quite literally, no better than the sinner

[4] Sigmund Freud, *The Interpretation of Dreams: The Original Text,* tr. Joyce Crick (Oxford: Oxford University Press, 1999), 204. Further reference in the text.

> he has to punish. I have translated into conscious terms what is bound to remain unconscious in the hero's psyche; if anyone wants to call Hamlet a hysteric, I can only acknowledge that it is an inference my interpretation admits. The sexual revulsion which Hamlet expressed in the dialogue with Ophelia is congruent with it. (204)

Freud has called Hamlet a male hysteric because of the hero's well-known revulsion facing sexuality. If moral conscience conceals the unconscious knowledge of his incestuous desire for his mother, he will be defeated by his morality: he is no better than his uncle, who, at least, has had the courage to act and achieve the same desire. His sexual coldness facing Ophelia, whom he takes pleasure in torturing, his rejection of paternity and begetting, and finally his displacement of aggression from his father/uncle to the feminine pole embodied by Ophelia are, for Freud, typical signs of the hysteric's structure.

In the end, Hamlet brings down the punishment on himself, dying in the same way as his father, poisoned by the Oedipal rival, which confirms the identification to the father. Hamlet, both the character and the play, stands for modernity in so far as the treatment of repressed desire is concerned; *Hamlet* finds its most intimate root in the Oedipus complex, but it comes from a later period when repression has progressed:

> But the change in treatment of the same material reveals the difference in the inner life of these two cultural periods so remote from one another: the advance of repression over the centuries in mankind's emotional life. In *Oedipus* the child's wishful phantasy on which it is based is out in the open and realized—as it is in dreams; in *Hamlet* it remains repressed, and we learn of its existence—as we learn of a neurosis—only through the inhibiting effects it produces. (204)

This remained Freud's thesis about *Hamlet* throughout, even after he changed his mind as to who Shakespeare was.

Lacan's seminar VI, *Le Désir et son Interprétation*, displaces the Freudian reading of Hamle*t* as an Oedipus at one remove.[5] I will retrace its progression; Lacan did not realize at first that his reading would contradict the classical Freudian orthodoxy. In a first reading, he highlights the fact

[5] Jacques Lacan, *Le Séminaire,* livre VI: *Le Désir et son Interprétation,* ed. Jacques-Alain Miller, Paris: Editions de la Martinière, 2013. I refer to the French text by S VI and page number in the text; translations are mine.

that the ghost might be the Father who did not know that he was dead, a question leading the son to pursue the investigation. There is a first dig at Freud's theory when Lacan asks: "Why should the Moderns be more neurotic than the Ancients?" (S VI, 288). He decides to remain closer to the text.

Lacan distinguishes the ghost in *Hamlet,* who finally must know that he is dead, from Oedipus who "did not know," and whose tragedy derived from his relentless desire to know the truth. Lacan examines the core of Freud's argument: it is, as we have seen, the idea that Hamlet could not kill Claudius because Claudius is a successful rival, a rival who has dared to do what he did not dare to accomplish. The core of the play becomes then less the issue of knowing why Hamlet cannot act, that is murder his uncle, than fathoming what happens to his desire. There is something wrong with his desire, and the whole play, according to Lacan, could be condensed in Hamlet's request: "Give me my desire back!" (S VI, 401–419).

According to Lacan, Ophelia is one of the most fascinating characters in literature because her role is to throw light on the rationale of Hamlet's thwarted and impossible desire. This is not however because Ophelia might be called the object of Hamlet's desire. In fact, she triggers in Hamlet a paroxysm of "horror of femininity" (S VI, 292). Then Polonius intervenes as a "wild psychoanalyst" who jumps to hasty conclusions, as we know, when he believes that Hamlet's melancholia is the result of a forbidden love for Ophelia.

Lacan's main critique leads him to revisit Freud's central contention that Hamlet would be a modern-day version of an un-inhibited Oedipus. A close reading of *Hamlet,* the text written by Shakespeare, not the character's psychology, allows him to hit upon a snag in the usual Freudian reading. Lacan calls in question Freud's reliance upon an unexamined and questionable psychology. Indeed, Freud's Oedipal reading seems predicated upon a psychological reasoning that can be totally reversed. Here is what Lacan says about the Freudian *doxa* concerning *Hamlet*:

> What does the psychoanalytic tradition tell us? That everything hinges around the desire for the mother, that this desire is repressed, and that this is the cause for which the hero could not approach the act that is requested of him, namely the revenge against a man who is the current possessor, how illegitimate because a criminal, of the maternal object. If he cannot strike the person who has been pointed out for his vindication, it is because he himself has already committed the crime to be avenged. In as much as there is in the

> background the memory of an infantile desire for the mother, of the Oedipal desire to murder the father, Hamlet would in a sense become an accomplice of the current owner, *beatus possidens*, in his eyes. He could not attack this owner without attacking himself. Is this what they mean?—or he could not attack this possessor without reawakening in himself the old desire, felt as a guilty desire, in a mechanism that one feels everywhere in the play. (S VI, 330)

Lacan questions the pseudo-evidence hidden in what he calls a "non-dialectical scheme," for indeed, in this pattern, the main relations of power and desire could be reversed:

> However, should we remain fascinated by the aura of such a non-dialectical scheme? Couldn't we say as well that everything can be reversed? If Hamlet was to jump immediately on his father-in-law, could one not say that he finds in this an opportunity to quench his guilt finding a culprit outside of himself? (S VI, 330)

Lacan punches a hole in Freud's central contention that ushers in his Oedipal reading of the play. Freud thinks that Hamlet could not kill his uncle as a revenge for his father's murder just because Claudius has enacted his own repressed incestuous wishes. This reading, for Lacan, is "non-dialectical" because it rests on a psychology of imitation that might lead to different outcomes. Freud's psychologization of the main characters in a "French triangle," as James Joyce would say in *Ulysses*,[6] was founded on a common-sense view, and yet could easily turn into its opposite. It is not a stretch of imagination to suppose that Hamlet would want to punish a successful rival precisely because he has achieved what he was prevented from accomplishing himself.

Here, Lacan's shift from a subjective genitive (in which the "mother's desire" means "desire for the mother") to an objective genitive (for which the "mother's desire" is read as "her desire for another man") operates a dialectical reversal by refuting a psychology of mimetic desire that assumes that one could not punish someone who has acted out one's deepest longings. In this reversal, Hamlet's inhibition will be seen to stem from an archaic desire for his mother but not as an object: it is the mother as the source of alterity and desire that will concern Lacan. Hamlet's paralysis

[6] James Joyce, *Ulysses*, ed. Hans Walter Gabler (New York: Random House, 1986), 175.

will then derive from his bafflement facing the riddle of his mother's desire for another man, whether he is the uncle or indeed the father.

In order to avoid relying an intuitive psychology, Lacan argues that one needs to read the text itself (in the original language) more carefully and pay attention to a few recurrent signifiers. One of these is rather obvious for a psychoanalyst: it is the echo between Ophelia and phallus; this turns into a verbal point of connection. It is when Hamlet can wonder about the source of an Other desire in his own mother that the solution will be brought to him. Hamlet's progression will make him pass beyond the earliest object of desire, which was his mother in order to confront the complex reversals of the phallic object of heterosexual love. Then and only then will he reach an awareness of the place of the Other as determining desire. "Notice that what Hamlet is affronted to, and all the time, who he struggles with, is a desire. This desire has to be considered where it is in the play. This desire is quite far from his own. It is not his desire for his mother, it is his mother's desire" (S VI, 332). The key resides in a decentering of the hero's plight. *Hamlet* as a play not only articulates how desire and fantasy work together but above all shows human desire as determined by the mother's desire. Desire is not to be reduced to fantasy, since fantasy aims at the phallus concealed in the missing, shifting, and elusive *objet petit a*. Here is how Lacan sums up his thesis on April 22, 1959:

> Our first step ... was to express the extent to which the play is dominated by the Mother as Other, i.e., the primordial subject of the demand. The omnipotence of which we are always speaking in psychoanalysis is first of all the omnipotence of the subject of the first demand, and this omnipotence must be related back to the Mother. (S VI, 374)[7]

One just needs to reread the scene of moral torture in which Hamlet tries to make Gertrude renounce Claudius, and notice that it is only when Hamlet seems to have won, forcing his mother to confess: "Oh Hamlet, thou hast clef my heart in twain" (III 4, 157), when he has admonished her "go not to my uncle's bed" (III 4, 160), and when she sounds ready

[7] I am quoting from the partial English translation of Lacan's *Le Séminaire, livre* VI, published under the title of "Desire and the Interpretation of Desire in Hamlet" in: Shoshana Felman (Ed.), *Literature and Psychoanalysis. The Question of Reading: Otherwise* (Baltimore: Johns Hopkins University Press, 1982), 12. Hereafter abbreviated as LP and page number in the text. This has been the only available English version of Lacan's Hamlet seminar for a long time.

to follow his advice ("What shall I do?" III 4, 181)—that he suddenly and violently sends her back to the lover he despises. Hamlet is overwhelmed by his mother's *jouissance*, an excessive enjoyment of genital love-making that he cannot fathom or move her from.

Hamlet retrieves his desire only when he comes back from his sea-trip and sees Laertes in Ophelia's open tomb. He cannot stand that a rival should express mourning better than him. He shouts the passionate cry: "It is I, Hamlet the Dane" in the first scerne of Act 5. The phallus finally appears as a way of stopping the hole in the real that has opened for Hamlet when he jumped into Ophelia's tomb. The hole created by death is seen identical with the hole of the letter of literature. They both allow for the projection of a missing signifier without which desire cannot find its place. By a neat structural homology, what is revealed by literature has consequences for any subject's individual desire.

Lacan ends up reconciling his interpretation with the main tenets of Freudian theory. If *Hamlet* is both the "tragedy of desire" (S VI, 401) and if it is shown to fail because of an insufficient mourning, a key lies in the link between mourning and the phallus. Lacan argues that the only way for the subject to accept castration and "resolve" the Oedipus complex is to "mourn the phallus": "the Oedipus complex goes into its decline insofar as the subject must mourn the phallus." (LP, 46) Freud sees the phallus as determined by narcissism, a narcissism that the subject is ready (or not) to abandon; in Lacan's terminology, it is less an imaginary object than a "veiled" object that appears in brief flashes, in "epiphanies" or just "*phanies*" (LP, 48):

> And doesn't it seem that this is the point around which Hamlet's action turns and lingers? His astounded spirit, so to speak, trembles before something that is utterly unexpected: the phallus is located here in a position that is entirely out of place in terms of its position in the Oedipus complex. Here, the phallus to be struck at is real indeed. And Hamlet always stops. The very source of what makes Hamlet's arm waver at every moment is the narcissistic connection that Freud tells us about in his text on the decline of the Oedipus complex: one cannot strike the phallus, because the phallus, even the real phallus, is a *ghost*. (LP, 50)

One cannot kill the phallus because, like Hamlet's king, it is a "thing of nothing."[8] In other words, it does not exist. Hamlet will desire and kill his rivals after he has relinquished his narcissistic attachments. When he is mortally wounded and knows that he is going to die, he and Laertes exchange mutual blessings. They want to prevent other deaths—unlike the situation of Oedipus, in which the tragic *ate* is perpetuated and passed on to the next generation. By positing a Hamlet who is caught up in his mother's desire until he traverses death and the phallus—thanks to Ophelia and her sad fate—Lacan presents an original reading of the play. His approach remains attentive to the key-signifiers of the text while avoiding the usual interpretation of the play as a modern restaging of the Oedipus complex.

Schreber

Confronted with a perfect case of paranoia in Daniel Paul Schreber, Freud's thesis is simple: everything derives from a homosexual investment linking Schreber to his doctor, Paul Emil Flechsig, and then to his father, the formidable Daniel Gottlob Moritz Schreber, an educator and social reformer well known in Germany. The enjoying and abusive father of his fantasies provides a clear parody of these dominating fathers. The only way Schreber had to make his passive position and homosexual fantasies acceptable was to imagine a God that forced him to be transformed into a woman. Thus, he had to create an entire mythology, with Manichean structures recalling Ormuz and Ahriman, in order to justify his deep longing, which is why Freud can evoke Friedrich Nietzsche's *Zarathustra* when he reconstructs an interpretation of the case, which consists of a reading of the *Memoirs* published by Schreber.[9] For Freud, the elaboration of the delusion not only had a meaning but also a curative value. The delusion allowed Schreber to replay traumas inflicted by his father, a father who supplied many of his traits to this unwholesome God.

Schreber succeeded not only in liberating himself from his asylum, but even more in convincing Freud of the soundness of his allegations. Freud elaborated his theory of the libido and of God seen as a paternal projection with the Schreber case in mind. Even before completing his study, he had

[8] As Hamlet famously states: "The king is a thing—[…] Of Nothing." In: William Shakespeare, *Hamlet,* IV, 2, l. 2702.

[9] Sigmund Freud, *The Schreber Case,* tr. Andrew Weber (London: Penguin, 2002), 42–43.

announced, in a letter to Sandor Ferenczi: "I succeeded where the paranoid fails."[10] He recognized the proximity between paranoids as builders of delirious systems and his activity as a theoretician of libido. The essay devoted to Schreber is Freud's first psychoanalysis from a distance, that is to say, it is a text analyzing another text; it is a "discourse on method" about paranoia, which is revealed by an allusion to Kant. Freud writes:

> The two principal elements of Schreber's delusions, the transformation into a woman and the privileged relation to God, are linked up in his system by the feminine disposition towards God. An inevitable task for us will be to prove an essential, *genetic* relationship between these two elements; otherwise our elucidations of Schreber's delusions would lead to play the role described by Kant in the famous image from the *Critique of Pure Reason* as that of the man who holds the sieve under a billy-goat while another milks it.[11]

Here, Freud alludes to one of the rare humorous moments in the first *Critique* (he had also cited Kant's theory of laughter in his book on jokes), a passage from "Transcendental logic" introducing the division between analytical and dialectical logic. In this section, Kant challenges the idea that one can simply ask "What is the truth?" without grasping that this question always presupposes categories that will be used to answer.[12] The question is going to either embarrass the listener or impel him to give ridiculous answers—one will find oneself in the absurd position that Demonax, a cynical philosopher from the second century A.D., enjoyably depicted by an apologue describing two interlocutors, one who was asking stupid questions and the other who was responding in turn.[13] If they evoke a man who milks a goat while the other tries to collect what comes out in a sieve, we find the double impossibility of numerous *Witze*, contempt for sex being redoubled by the usage of a faulty tool.

[10] Freud, letter to Sandor Ferenczi, October 6, 1910. In: *The Correspondence of Sigmund Freud and Sandor Ferenczi*, ed. Eva Brabant, Ernst Falzeder, and Patrizia Giampieri-Deutsch; tr. Peter T. Hoffer (Cambridge, Harvard University Press, 1993), 43. Quoted by Colin MacCabe in his Introduction to: Freud, *The Schreber Case*, xii.

[11] Freud, *The Schreber Case*, 23.

[12] Immanuel Kant, *Critique of Pure Reason*, tr. Paul Guyer and Allen W. Wood (Cambridge: Cambridge University Press, 1998), 197.

[13] For the identification of this Athenian *Witz* from the Hellenistic era, reported by Lucian, see Kant, *Critique of Pure Reason*, 723–724.

The Freudian reference to Kant, so often suspected of being an impenitent moralist complicit in the formation of the superego, takes on a symptomatic value in the sense that what is at play is the interpretation of paranoia, that is of "reasoning delirium" or the "delirium of interpretation," a delirium the preserves all the appearances of rationality—and the observation has been made that the very term "paranoia," if it is not found in the classification of deliriums and mental illnesses in the *Anthropology*, is attributable to Johann Christian August Heinroth, a Kantian physician-philosopher.[14] Indeed, is there such a significant difference between Schreber's *Memoirs* and the treatises of certain mystics or founders of religious movements? Moreover, this was the reasoning used by Schreber to get himself released from the asylum—he surely had curious beliefs, in reality similar enough to those of a number of compatriots, but he could prove that they were not dangerous for others and only concerned himself. Even if he persisted in the belief that God had elected him to be a transsexual in order to regenerate the human race, that in no way would necessarily disturb public order; he was thus freed and can be lauded today as the first hero of anti-psychiatry.

Where Freud found libido and the father, Lacan discovers the Other and the *jouissance* of an obscene God. While Freud sees a transformation of repressed homosexuality into a delirium of redemption, Lacan insists on Schreber's perverse and transsexual dimension. Lacan does not hesitate to mark his disagreement with Freud's resolution of the Schreber case. He rejects Freud's idea that the key is to be found in a repressed homosexuality that would need to entirely rebuild the universe in order to "milk the goat" of the truth.

In "On a Question Prior to Any Possible Treatment of Psychosis," Lacan comments on Ida Macalpine's idea that "homosexuality, which is supposedly the determining factor in paranoiac psychosis, is actually a symptom articulated in the psychotic process."[15] Against the biographical and reductive reading of Freud, Lacan prefers to evoke a "transsexualist practice" related to perversion (474); this transsexualism would usher an

[14] In his *Anthropology*, Kant had distinguished *amentia* (simple mental confusion), *vesania* (perturbation of thought), and *dementia* (a type of methodical madness). See Pierre Fédida, "La paranoïa comme théorie de la communication." In Fédida, *Le Temps de la réflexion* V (Paris, Gallimard, 1984), 111–124.

[15] Jacques Lacan, "On a Question Prior to Any Possible Treatment of Psychosis," *Écrits*, Lacan, "On a Question Preliminary to any Possible Treatment of Psychosis," *Écrits: The First Complete Edition in English*, tr. Bruce Fink in collaboration with Héloïse Fink and Russell Grigg (New York: W.W. Norton, 2006), 445–488, here 455. Further references in the text.

Other, unnamable and excessive *jouissance*. For Lacan, nevertheless, the determining factor is the function of the Name-of-the-Father. The key for him is that it is a Name that Schreber had not been able to symbolize. Schreber is saved from a reductive reading not only because he was convinced by him that the truth of his system resembles his system of concepts, as Freud was, but more fundamentally because Schreber presented himself as a rebel against the authority of the Father. Schreber's Father was less a "symbolic father" or "dead father" than a father defined by his lies, his perversion, and his general imposture. Lacan's diatribe when glossing Schreber's opposition to social lies is worth quoting in full. The lies instigated the only true insanity that Schreber was obliged to survive, for since his early childhood, his body and his soul had been fashioned by the dictatorial orthopedics of an educator father. Schreber's father had had a mission, to make children stand up "straight":

> Further still, the father's relation to this law must be considered in its own right, for one will find in it the reason for the paradox whereby devastating effects of the paternal figure are found with particular frequency in cases where the father really functions as a legislator or boasts that he does—whether he is, in fact, one of the people who makes the laws or presents himself as a pillar of faith, as a paragon of integrity or devotion, as virtuous or a virtuoso, as serving a charitable cause whatever the object or lack thereof that is at stake, as serving the nation or birth rate, safety or salubrity, legacy or law, the pure, the lowest of the low, or the empire. These are all ideals that provide him with all too many opportunities to seem to be at fault, to fall short, and even to be fraudulent—in short, to exclude the Name-of-the-Father from its position in the signifier.
>
> The result can be obtained with still less, and no one who practices child analysis will deny that children see right through hypocritical behavior, so much so that it can be devastating to them. But who articulates that the lie thus perceived implies a reference to the constitutive function of speech? (482–483)

The answer to this rhetorical question can only be: Lacan! Otherwise, it would have been Schreber, whose proper name can be transcribed as *Schreiber*, the "writer" willing to expose the father's lies. Such is the function of writing in general, as Derrida has pointed out. The excess of meaning that he had to produce nevertheless allows for the function of truth to appear. Schreber flirted with the paradigm of the "beautiful soul"—his principal reason for allowing himself to be drawn into transsexual fantasies was that he felt it would truly "be *beautiful* to be a woman submitting during to the act of copulation" (455). He goes insane, but succeeds by traversing his insanity; he gets lost in genders and sexes, no longer knows if he loves a man in order to become a woman, or loves a woman, his wife, who seems to prefer the doctor who cured her husband to her husband. He is a writer and a poet, not a madman.

Lacan's Preface to the English translation of *Séminaire* XI, *The Four Fundamental Concepts of Psychoanalysis,* develops the idea that no certificate can provide credentials for psychoanalysts: They authorize themselves to practice, their legitimacy will only come from them. A different principle obtains if one looks at a birth certificate: "A certificate tells me that I was born. I repudiate this certificate: I am not a poet, but a poem. A poem that is being written, even if it looks like a subject."[16] Thus, if agency is required of psychoanalysts who should not rely on official papers given by schools, institutes, or any institution, the reverse is true for human subjects when they are born: their very births, inscribed in archives by a birth certificate, will confirm that symbolic markers like family names and first names, along with all other administrative details, are all set down before any agency is possible. Hence, I am always a being that is being written. My Unconscious functions as a living text, even if it remains undecipherable—I cannot claim to be the author of my fate.

This Preface is dated from May 17, 1976. One year later, Lacan returned to the same idea in a different key, applying the formula to himself. In the last session of *Séminaire* XXIV, Lacan explained that poetry is necessary because it replenishes language with new meaning. Poetry helps a psychoanalyst in the interpretation of the slips of the tongue and other unconscious productions presented by patients: "Only poetry … makes interpretation possible, and this is why in my clinical practice, I am not able to make it cohere any longer. I am not enough of a 'poet.'"[17] Lacan's regret that he had not been "enough of a poet" is an uncharacteristic admission of humility that contrasts with his usual bombast.[18]

[16] Jacques Lacan, *The Four Fundamental Concepts of Psychoanalysis,* tr. Alan Sheridan (New York, Norton, 1978), viii. Compare with Lacan, *Autres Écrits* (Paris: Édition du Seuil, 2001), 572.

[17] See Lacan, *Le Séminaire* XXIV, unpublished, session of May 17, 1977; gaogoa.free.fr/Seminaire.htm (access March 2021).

[18] Dany Nobus has given a wonderful analysis of this moment in "Once They Were Poets: The Function and Field of Sonority and Meaning in Psychoanalysis," paper presented at the APW Study Weekend on Lacan's *Le Séminaire* XXIV at Duquesne University, Pittsburgh, October 9, 2011.

Lacan's own Oedipal myth is a myth of paternity that ends up stating that we are born not only in language but also thanks to language. Such a birth does not constitute a final event, for it continues throughout our lives. This birth progresses thanks to the hieroglyphics, the coats of arms, and the runes that are being written in our psyches, those unknown and obscure signs inscribed in us, made flesh and blood after harsh contacts with the Reality principle. A psychoanalyst will know how to read these signs, hence must be conversant with literature and myth, which does not mean that every psychoanalyst is a poet. Poetry, however, will be indispensable for the practice of active interpretation, more pointedly for the Lacanian practice of hermeneutic equivocation, an actively dialogic game-playing with the signifiers presented by analysands, but this does not mean that all psychoanalysts must become poets.

CHAPTER 5

Deleuze-Guattari and the End of Oedipus

Dorothea Olkowski

Sigmund Freud introduces the theory of the Oedipus dream in the context of his work on the interpretation of dreams. He recounts the story of King Oedipus as written by the Greek poet, Sophocles, as a tragedy of fate, as the murder of a father, and as the guilt of the son. But as dream material, it is the story of a son who desires to marry the mother, a story of wish-fulfillment and sexual impulses directed to the mother, as well as hatred and violence directed to the father. For adherents of Gilles Deleuze's philosophy, Deleuze and Félix Guattari's approach to Freud's propagation of the ancient myth of Oedipus strikes at its heart, which is, the triangle of daddy-mommy-me, the dogma of the nuclear family, and the intervention and manipulation of the psychoanalytic priest, the psychoanalyst him or herself. Deleuze and Guattari's undoing of Freud's Oedipus Complex is situated largely within the pages of *Anti-Oedipus: Capitalism and Schizophrenia*.[1] But Deleuze also approaches Oedipus

[1] Gilles Deleuze and Félix Guattari, *Anti-Oedipus*, tr. Robert Hurley, Mark Seem, and Helen R. Lane, Minneapolis: University of Minnesota Press, 1987. Originally published in French as L'*anti-Oedipe*, Paris: Les Editions de Minuit, 1972.

D. Olkowski (✉)
University of Colorado at Colorado Springs, Colorado Springs, CO, USA
e-mail: dolkowsk@uccs.edu

L. Weissberg (ed.), *Psychoanalysis, Fatherhood, and the Modern Family*, https://doi.org/10.1007/978-3-030-82124-1_5

from the point of view of a second triangle, one that resonates with the first.

Deleuze's initial attack on psychoanalytic theory is also deeply implicated in pages of *The Logic of Sense*,[2] and perhaps originally appears in *Difference and Repetition,* where it is formulated—not in terms of the nuclear family—but as a function of another triple, that of the Id, Ego, and Super-Ego.[3] It is there that Deleuze first introduces the three syntheses of time, which form the structure for his account of Desiring-Production, the Body without Organs, and the Subject in *Anti-Oedipus,* leading to the analysis of capitalism and its limit, that is, to schizophrenia. If it's the case that Id, Ego, and Super-ego are the frame upon which Freud hangs his Oedipal theory, then the first, second, and third syntheses of time are Deleuze's radical reframing.

Deleuze begins his account of the first synthesis of time with David Hume's theory of sensation and ideas according to which repetition of a sensation changes something in the *mind,* that is, when "A" arrives, we *expect* "B." How do "A" and "B" become associated? They are associated in time. For Deleuze, imagination *contracts*, it synthesizes the two instants in the present. Past and future designate the dimensions of the present that contracts them. Thus, "time is subjective, but it has the subjectivity of a passive subject"; it happens to the mind, it forms the mind.[4] If the process stopped there, it would not in itself be enough to alter our idea of subjective mental states. Perceptual syntheses occur because they refer back to organic syntheses, the contraction of water, earth, light, and air that form living things (73). There is an original organic force that precedes and conditions perception.

This is why, in *Anti-Oedipus*, we find first, that processes of production are everywhere, because second, there is no distinction between humans and nature as processes of production, and third, production as a process (now called desiring-production) is everywhere, and of course, desiring-machines (natural or human) operate or *associate* in time as "'and …' 'and

[2] Deleuze, *Difference and Repetition,* tr. Paul Patton, New York: Columbia University Press, 1994. Originally published in French as *Différence et Répétition*, Paris: Presses Universitaires de France, 1968.

[3] Deleuze, *Logic of Sense,* tr. Mark Lester with Charles Stivale, ed. Constantin V. Boundas, New York: Columbia University Press, 1990. Originally published as *Logique du sens*, Paris: Les Editions de Minuit, 1969.

[4] Deleuze, *Difference and Repetition,* 70, 71. Further page reference in the text.

then ...'"[5] In other words, one so-called machine (in French *machiner*, to put together) connects to another, coupling continuous flows as well as fragments. No longer is there an instinctual Id, but in its place a machine that connects and flows. We discover it in Georg Büchner's *Lenz*, out for a schizophrenic stroll in the mountains "with other gods or without any gods at all, without a family, without a father or a mother, *with nature*."[6] Definitely he is with nature as a process of production, but he is also with the socius as industry extracts its materials from nature and returns its used-up garbage and pollution back to nature, so that production, distribution, and consumption all take place within the processes of production (3, 4).

The first synthesis also brings to light, not the problem of instinct but in its place, the "problem of habit," as habits unlike instincts are acquired through contemplation (73). As Hume sets this out, the process starts with an impression of sensation that is the contraction of signs from nature. What follows for Hume, is the idea, produced by contemplating the initial impression. Then the constant association of impression and idea forms habits, or better *habitudes*, not just the psychological sensory-motor habits of embodiment, but just as powerfully, the thousands of passive syntheses of which everything is organically composed, which are physical, and which *repeat* themselves as difference, that is, between two repetitions, there is always a difference.[7] This kind of habit—which is a habit of difference—is like the schizophrenic description of a table in that, "'Once noticed, it continued to occupy one's mind. ... It was not intended for any specific purpose. ... A table which lends itself to no function.'"[8] Furthermore, this first or passive synthesis is pleasure—the pleasure principle—meaning, it is the *emotion* of a contemplation-contraction, drawing from some impression or element to find an image of ourselves in the multitude of contractions.[9] This pleasure is a far cry from the Oedipal pleasure principle whose goal is to sublimate reality.

Clearly, however, the first synthesis calls for something more. Simply stated, the first synthesis of time—contraction or association or desiring-production or pleasure—is a present that passes, so there must be another

[5] Deleuze and Guattari, *Anti-Oedipus,* 5.

[6] Deleuze and Guattari, *Anti-Oedipus,* 2. Emphasis added. Further page references in the text.

[7] Deleuze, *Difference and Repetition,* 75, 76.

[8] Deleuze and Guattari, *Anti-Oedipus,* 6. Deleuze and Guattari cite Henri Michaux.

[9] Deleuze, *Difference and Repetition,* 74–75. Further page references in the text.

time in which the presents of the first synthesis pass, without which each would be eternal (79). It is the synthesis of memory that causes the present to pass, "the past in general is the element in which each former present is focused upon … as the particular," and the particular may then be represented as a former present in the current present which also represents or reflects itself (80). We find this at work in Marcel Proust's reminiscence of Combray that does not appear as it was but as a past that has never yet been present. This makes impossible the Oedipal return to so-called mother fostered infantile desires (85). The present *reflects* itself to form the memory of the former present. In this reflection, the past is contemporaneous with the present *it was*, and each present is also the entire past in its most contracted state. This is the past as the *active synthesis* of all time for which the past insists along with the former present and consists with the new present; it is, according to Deleuze, the a priori past (81, 82).

Yet the arrival of the pure past, the past of Reminiscence or Mnemosyne, is also erotic. The entire past contracted into each present constitutes a receptive being who does not initiate the activity of thought but who experiences it for the most part in terms of its effects. This being is subjected by the flow of presents, but in taking up memory as memory, a passive rather than an active synthesis of memory, memory emerges as the past that has never been present, the in-itself of memory (85). What has never been lived, what is purely past, is beyond Oedipal object choice, beyond the mother even while it coexists with them where they are. The pure past is Eros accompanying Mnemosyne, Eros or pleasure (passive synthesis and sexual drives) arising out of Mnemosyne (memory) and given to us to live with (85).

The role of reflection is related to Hume's argument that ideas are always derived from impressions—which produce either pleasure or pain—and when the original impressions fade, what is left is an idea that "returns upon the soul" to produce "impressions of reflection." Impressions of reflection are then repeated so that passions as well as understanding are, for Hume, an effect of reflection or contemplation. For Deleuze and Guattari, reflection does not reestablish the authority of a stable Ego but undoes it. It resists the desiring-machines, the organs, the connections, the processes of production in the second synthesis of time.

Given the role of Mnemosyne (memory), each present past is not a unity, but consists of a multiplicity of layers of "non-localizable connections, actions at a distance, systems of replay, resonance and echoes, objective chances, signs, signals and roles" transcending location and temporal succession and playing out the "same story, but at different levels."[10] Yet, this does not construct an Ego because each life plays out different lives as well connecting each life to everything else that is only apparently outside of it "as if the philosopher and the pig, the criminal and the saint, played out the past at different levels" (83). This *Whole* plays out difference between its multiplicity of coexisting levels.

This is why Deleuze and Guattari suggest that it would be much better if nothing works—although it does. The "full" body without organs would be unproductive, unconsumable, and unable to be extorted and absorbed. There would be no formed organs; desire can also desire death, the Death Instinct, the breakdown.[11] Judge Schreber, who so fascinated Freud, lived but also died, lacking or losing a stomach, intestines, lungs, esophagus, bladder, ribs, lacking actually, an image of the body as a unified whole. But the desiring-machines also desire life, and the Life Instinct is the working machine (8). Apart from his delusions, Schreber "showed lively interest, knowledgeable insights, a good memory, perceptive judgment ... he behaved in a nice and friendly manner."[12]

Yet Schreber suffers from the conflict between death and life, the body without organs and the desiring-machines, and his suffering produces the paranoic-machine, in this case the delusion of sexual persecution, his body transformed into that of a female that is subject to sexual abuse. For Deleuze and Guattari there is or must be some parallel between what Schreber suffers and the socius, that is, between desiring-machines and social-machines.

When the first synthesis of time is organized by the second, the desiring-machines encounter the body without organs (the schizophrenic table, the second synthesis), which repulses them, repulses their habituations, their productive organization. But something else happens as well. Freud often points to the oppressive effects of civilization that demands sexual repression and sublimation. This full body, the organized body of the socius also appears in *Anti-Oedipus,* not as sublimation but as Marx spelled it out, as the body of the earth, the tyrant, or capital. It is the social surface upon

[10] Deleuze, *Difference and Repetition,* 83. This structure is expressed most clearly by Henri Bergson's memory cone.

[11] Deleuze and Guattari, *Anti-Oedipus,* 8. Further page reference in the text.

[12] Sigmund Freud, *The Schreber Case,* tr. Andrew Webber (New York: Penguin Modern Classics, 2003), 8.

which all production is recorded and distributed for consumption, yet eventually also captured as surplus value, the effect of extorting surplus labor, that is, falling back upon all productive processes, appropriating and absorbing them as if they were its own productions. This is the means by which labor's social and productive forces appear as if they were produced by capital and not by labor.[13]

This is society's delirium, its delusion. If capitalists were once aware of the distinction between capital and labor, using capital to extort surplus labor, their delusion is that they forget this. Capital, in and of itself fluid but sterile, that is, non-productive, puts forth shoots and branches out, falling back upon production and appropriating it as its own. This "miraculating" process, this miracle, now coexists with the paranoic-machine—the body without organs—itself unproductive and unconsumable, which becomes the captured surface that records this discord, this contradiction. Poor Schreber attracts God and simultaneously, paranoically resists, but to what end?[14] Schreber comes to see his transformation into a woman fertilized by God's divine rays as serving the purpose of creating a new human being, a judge whose behavior toward those he judges undergoes an empathetic change.[15]

What can *Anti-Oedipus* do with this? Production has passed from desiring-machines to the body without organs, from production to recording, from labor to capital. The third synthesis will situate the "libido," the Life Instinct of the desiring-machines in the divine regime of the schizo's disjunctive syllogism "from which all secondary realities are derived by a process of division."[16]

In *Difference and Repetition,* Deleuze utilizes the philosophy of Henri Bergson to make sense of attributing repression or sublimation to the active motor habits of the body which Deleuze describes as, "the practical and useful consciousness of the present moment, that is to say, ... the sensory-motor equilibrium of a nervous system connecting perception with action," that binds us to the fascinating present.[17] This is not refuted

[13] Deleuze and Guattari, *Anti-Oedipus,* 10, 11.

[14] Deleuze and Guattari, *Anti-Oedipus,* 11. Schreber comes to believe that it is God who initiates or at least has knowledge of the assault on Schreber's body. Freud, *The Schreber Case,* 11.

[15] Freud, *The Schreber Case,* 12–13.

[16] Deleuze Guattari, *Anti-Oedipus,* 13.

[17] Bergson, *Matter and Memory,* tr. N. M. Paul and W. S. Palmer (New York: Zone Books, 1988), 95

in *Anti-Oedipus,* but the fascinating present has been expanded to take into account the role of the socius. Just as the socius records all production, the body without organs, unproductive and unconsumable, records all processes of production as if desiring-machines emanate from it, as if the first synthesis of habit emanated from the second synthesis, the pure past of time, a quasi-cause, which records or represents what was first produced.[18]

Confined by recording-representing, the schizo risks becoming trapped in an endless repetition in which each new situation forgoes its novelty, its difference, and is merely repeated on the model of a previous habit. In place of novelty, representations would be produced. Under such conditions, without reflection on difference, we discover nothing but resemblances. The question is, how to keep habit from inhabiting all productive connections, from taking over the "and then"? Desiring-machines attach themselves disjunctively to the slippery surface of the body without organs: disjunction being "either or." But the attachments must not form decisively either this or that organ, rather they take up the either or of differences sliding about on the body. "As in the case of Beckett's mouth that speaks and feet that walk: … 'Either he had finally nothing to say, or while having something to say he finally decided not to say it'" (12).

Deleuze and Guattari assert that the distribution of desire is a divine task carried out through disjunctive syntheses and object to the fact that Freud subjects the free-flowing syntheses of desiring-machines to the representation of Oedipus. Parodying Immanuel Kant, who identifies inclusive and exclusive disjunction with the transcendental idea of God, they characterize disjunction as the act of an imminent divine power that generates its objects by splitting apart every primitive machinic connection. The energy of the body without organs is for this reason divine, and secondary realities are derived from it by the process of division, that is, disjunction. And as was noted, Schreber calls the divine rays that penetrate him God, only to later divide them disjunctively into frontal and rear, lower and upper divisions even while remaining firmly skeptical in religious matters.[19]

What then is the relation of distributed desire to Oedipus? For Deleuze and Guattari, Oedipus is trivially a consequence of social reproduction, the existing social code of one's name, then that of father and mother, while

[18] Deleuze and Guattari, *Anti-Oedipus,* 11, 12. Further page reference in the text.
[19] Freud, *The Schreber Case*, 14, 15.

Oedipus completely bypasses the relationship with nature.[20] But the "subject" organized through the disjunctive syntheses has his or her own recording code, the fluid code of desire, no matter which organ-machines attempt to attach themselves to the body without organs. The "subject" scrambles codes, never records the same events in the same ways, and stuffs whatever she is forced into with disjunctions and more and more disjunctions (15).

In the temporal syntheses, the passive synthesis of contraction, the organic self, the "I am" arises first. Yet, the second synthesis of reflection, the "I think" is the determination that implies a previous yet undetermined existence, the "I am." Thus, the Cartesian "I think therefore, I am" is really the reverse of the order of the temporal process.[21] To this is added a third form, the form that orders the other two and in which the undetermined may be determined. It is in this sense a transcendental form, because *it makes possible* the first and second temporal syntheses as well as the difference between the determination and the undetermined, the "I think" and the "I am" (86). It is the condition of their syntheses. This occurs in time; the passive, receptive subject (I am) appears within time, but the "I think," we have already seen, appears only as the affection of and reflection on this passive self that experiences its own thought acting in and on itself; it is both passive and active. The "I is an Other," reflecting and acting, both affected and effecting within the form of time, producing the fractured self (86).

To be clear, the self, this "I" consists of two parts. There is the passive receptive ego (*moi*) that is in time and constantly changing, and the I (*je*) that is an act that carries out the active reflective synthesis of time. The "I," as the site of internal difference, emerges in the present and divides all time into past and future at each instant, so that ego and I are split, differentiated always in every act of thought by the form of time (86). Thus "I is an Other" and the subject "lives it like an Other within itself" (86). For Deleuze, time as the inner difference between ego and I means that ego and I, passive and active "self," can never be integrated; to do so would be to stop the flow of time.

As Deleuze points out, it is René Descartes who stops the flow of time. The Cartesian "I think" relies only on the instant and cedes time as continuity over to God. But for this reason, the pure and empty form of time,

[20] Deleuze and Guattari, *Anti-Oedipus,* 13, 14. Additional page reference in the text.

[21] Deleuze, *Difference and Repetition,* 86. Further page references in the text.

the third temporal synthesis, signifies the death of God, whose demise indicates a caesura, a before (God as continuity) and an after (the empty form of time) (86, 87). Yes, the schizo Schreber believes that God is emasculating him, but only as "master of the disjunctive syllogism," as the a priori principle, the pure form of time, which is to say, as an Idea.[22] The schizo's recording code is incommensurate with that of the socius to the extent that any use of the latter is pure parody.

Similarly, Freud understands disjunction as decomposition and characterizes it as characteristic of paranoia, but subverts it once again to Oedipal genealogy in the form of Oedipal triangulation—daddy, mommy, baby. Yet, as the effect of the three temporal syntheses, something along the lines of a subject begins to wander over the body without organs. It begins by situating itself disjunctively without a fixed identity and so, consuming what it finds and finding itself everywhere it experiences only residual pleasure.

We noted that the second synthesis brings about both an opposition and an attraction between the primary desiring-machines and the body without organs, and for the schizo, a parody of the God that guarantees continuity or of the Oedipus that triangulates. This new "conjunctive synthesis"—this and that—is identified by Kant as the transcendental idea of the World. In Deleuze's parody, conjunction produces "intensive quantities," states of pure naked intensity grounded in a profound *feeling*, a primary emotion arising from the conflict between repulsion and attraction. The movement from "I am" to "I think" to "I feel" has been presaged by Hume. Recall that, for Hume, perceptions of sensation result in either impressions (sensations, passions, emotions) or ideas, the fainter image of impressions in thinking or reasoning.[23] Original impressions of sensation leave ideas behind but they also directly affect the body as pleasure or pain, which we may also reflect on (11). These secondary impressions of reflection result in passions and passions may be calm or violent (276).

So it is the opposition and attraction between our original impressions and our reflection on the pleasure or pain they produce that leaves us with the "open series of intensive elements … that are never an expression of the final equilibrium of a system but consist instead of an unlimited

[22] Deleuze and Guattari, *Anti-Oedipus,* 13.

[23] David Hume, *A Treatise of Human Nature* (Oxford: Clarendon Press, 1968), 1. Further page references in the text.

number of stationary, metastable states through which the subject passes."[24] However, Hume stipulates that when we feel a passion, we act on it, unless it is founded on false suppositions or the means are insufficient to accomplish the desired ends. When it is founded on false suppositions or unable to achieve its ends, passion will be countered by reason's equilibrium.[25] This is not the case for the schizo.

Life, appearing first as desiring-production, then as recording or reflection, now appears as consumption and consummation—pleasure again—but extremely truncated. This so-called celibate machine, correlates with Schreber's experience of having been transformed into a woman by God's rays at least to the extent of having absorbed the nerves of "female voluptuousness," a sensation of voluptuousness he attributes to that felt by women, and for which he needs no sexual partner.[26] This strange subject exists alongside Schreber even after his recovery, and this voluptuousness, this intensive quantity grounded in pure feeling, is the "really primary emotion" arising from the two previous syntheses, their repulsion and attraction.[27]

There is no equilibrium for Schreber, not ever again. He passes through various "intense nervous states," exerting gentle pressure on his torso and attains the sensation of voluptuousness and the impression of female breasts and genitals.[28] These bands of intensities, say Deleuze and Guattari, bring the schizo as closely as possible to matter insofar as the schizo lives his intensity, consuming and consummating it and does not consume mommy-daddy. The schizo has from the beginning been a residuum alongside the three processes, the three syntheses, passing from one to the next without a fixed identity.

This "materialist psychiatry" is nevertheless not physicalist. Deleuze and Guattari mention Louis-Nicolas Clerambault's claim that certain symptoms of delirium are the effect of infections or intoxications, as well as automatism, that is, involuntary and unconscious acts due to neurological mechanisms. It is materialist in the sense that delirium occurs as the recording of processes of production of desiring-machines, processes strongly affected by syntheses and break-downs. Equally problematic are

[24] Deleuze and Guattari, *Anti-Oedipus,* 19.
[25] Hume, *A Treatise*, 416.
[26] Deleuze and Guattari, *Anti-Oedipus,* 17. Freud, *The Schreber Case*, 21.
[27] Deleuze and Guattari, *Anti-Oedipus,* 18–19.
[28] Freud, *The Schreber Case*, 21.

the idealist theories, all of which relate schizophrenia to the ego and the body-image, the "final avatar of the soul," a concept they take to be no less coercive than Oedipus.[29] At best, the idealists believe that desire produces a fantasy of psychic reality that lacks a real object (25).

But if desire is real, if desire is productive, it does not merely produce fantasies, and it lacks nothing; there are no objects missing from the world. Beginning with the first and passive synthesis, the contraction of nature, desire produces the real, the machine, and never stops producing, connecting one object to another. Thus, as has been noted above, social production and desiring-production are one and the same, the former being merely a determination of the latter (29).

This leads to the question of how it is possible for things to have gone so badly? Neurophysiologically, new work in genetics seems to point to a specific gene "C4," that may trigger too much pruning in the brains of some teenagers. Normally pruning eliminates excess connectivity in the brain for optimal functioning. Too much pruning is thought to impair mental development and has been correlated with schizophrenia.[30] But even if the neurophysiology is accounted for, this tells us little about the ways in which schizophrenia manifests in relation to its social production. Why do people without this disorder tolerate humiliation and enslavement both for others and for themselves even as people who presumably have this disorder refuse to accept even the notion of a stable "I"? If desiring-production is one with social production, then the answer seems to be that we do this to ourselves in a very specific manner.

The desiring-production of *homo natura* under certain determinate conditions, produces social production—*homo historia*—but since desiring-production is first of all social, *homo historia* comes first and determines *homo natura*. The structure of those determinate conditions is the topic of much of the rest of *Anti-Oedipus*.[31] Deleuze and Guattari add that desiring-production frees itself only at the end, but in their account, it

[29] Deleuze and Guattari, *Anti-Oedipus*, 22, 23. Further page references in the text.

[30] "Schizophrenia's Strongest Genetic Risk Deconstructed," National Institutes of Mental Health Press Release, January 27, 2016; http://www.nimh.nih.gov/news/science-news/2016/schizophrenias-strongest-known-genetic-risk-deconstructed.shtml (access March 2021).

[31] My essay, "Is Capitalism Determined? Deleuze and Guattari Between Capitalism and Calculus," appears in the *British Journal of Phenomenology* 45, 2 (2014): 91–106. It is an analysis of the determinate conditions under which capitalism developed and organizes desiring-production.

seems that this would happen only under the conditions imposed by schizophrenia. Perhaps the lack of synaptic connections due to excessive pruning gives the schizophrenic some deliverance from *homo historia* that the majority of human beings do not have.

In any case the body without organs does not project itself onto the social machine but is the residuum of the deterritorialized socius, even as the socius codifies, inscribes, and records desire so as to dam it up, channel, and regulate it. Of the three social-machines—the territorial, the despotic, and the capitalist—that Deleuze and Guattari designate according to Marx's analysis, only the last perpetuates itself "in all its violence, with all the powers at its command."[32] Capitalism takes its place in the wake of two kinds of decoding: one, decoded flows of production, freed from guilds and merchant associations; and two, decoded flows of labor, workers freed from servitude to a despotic ruler or from the system of journeymen. However, instead of generating a code that can be applied to the entire social field as the previous two social machines had done, capital, with no codes of its own, substitutes money, the "axiomatic of abstract quantities" which further deterritorializes the socius (33).

Why destroy it? Why make it a body without organs and why unleash flows of desire, the very mechanism of schizophrenia? Why not? Why not produce discord and disharmony at every level of society so as to reterritorialize in as violent and artificial manner as possible? As noted above, deterritorialization appropriates productive processes if they were its own productions, as if labor's social and productive forces were produced by capital and not by labor.

Let us recall that the third synthesis, that of the World, is the production of feeling. Conjunction produces "intensive quantities," those states of pure naked intensity grounded in profound *feeling*, the primary emotion arising from the conflict between repulsion and attraction in the body without organs. Profound feeling, the pure naked intensity of flows of social production arising due to the conflict between the violently unleased schizophrenic energy of social production—surplus value—and the violent and artificial reterritorialization by means of artificial, imaginary, and symbolic territories (34, 35).

Where are we now situated with respect to this? We appear to be situated in the conflict between nakedly intensive *deterritorialized* and profoundly felt calls for "freedom," "taking back," "change," or "revolution,"

[32] Deleuze and Guattari, *Anti-Oedipus*, 33. Further page references in the text.

and the *reterritorialized* artificial State, nation, family, community, culture, religion, technology, gender, ethnicity, political party, non-profit, all built with the surplus profits of labor and none of it real. If the real continues to flow, it is only in relation to the schizo who wanders and migrates, seeking the limits of capitalism. No wonder that Deleuze and Guattari conclude by saying that having introduced production into desire, psychiatry "cannot avoid posing in *eschatological* terms the problem of the ultimate relationship between the analytic machine, the revolutionary machine, and desiring machines."[33] If so, if they are correct, it is our eschatology too.

[33] Deleuze and Guattari, *Anti-Oedipus*, 35. Emphasis added.

CHAPTER 6

The Nuclear Family and Its Discontents: Freud, Jung, and Szondi and the Persistence of the Dynasty

Adrian Daub

Two Prehistories

Her name was Ida Bauer, but the world would come to know her as Dora. She was brought to the office of Sigmund Freud by her father, suffering from intermittent loss of voice and a nervous cough. In Freud's write-up of her case ("a Case of Hysteria"; 1905 [1901]),[1] we learn that she had a

Portions of "The Nuclear Family and its Discontents: Freud, Jung and Szondi and the Persistence of the Dynasty" first appeared in *The Dynastic Imagination: Family and Modernity in Nineteenth-Century Germany* by Adrian Daub.

[1] Sigmund Freud, "Fragment of an Analysis of a Case of Hysteria" (1905 [1901]). In: In: Freud, *The Standard Edition of the Complete Psychological Works*, tr. James Strachey, ed. Anna Freud et al., 24 vols. (London: The Hogarth Press, 1953–1974), VII: 3–124(edition will be abbreviated *SE*).

A. Daub (✉)
Stanford University, Stanford, CA, USA
e-mail: daub@stanford.edu

L. Weissberg (ed.), *Psychoanalysis, Fatherhood, and the Modern Family*, https://doi.org/10.1007/978-3-030-82124-1_6

brother, we hear that she has an aunt. Her mother remains a spectral presence throughout Freud's analysis. "I never made her mother's acquaintance," he notes, but adds that "from the accounts given me by the girl and her father I was led to imagine her as an uncultivated woman, and above all a foolish one" (20). We are introduced to a couple friendly with her parents, Herr and Frau K, who will become important in her analysis. Of her extended family we learn nothing. Freud seems determined to restrict his cast of characters, even when he gets to her mother his interest dwindles.

This pattern holds in Freud's other case studies. Sergei Pankejeff, immortalized by Freud as the "Wolf Man" (1918), had a wide variety of symptoms which Freud was able to trace to a moment of excessive closeness between an infant Pankejeff and his parents: sleeping in their bedroom he had witnessed his father take his mother from behind; this was the "primal scene" behind his infantile neurosis. In the case of "Little Hans" (1909), the patient who furnished Freud with much of his evidence for the Oedipus complex, Freud even deputized the young boy's father to act as his surrogate analyst.

In all of these cases, the nuclear family is the cause of, and the solution to, all of life's problems. "They fuck you up, your mum and dad," Philipp Larkin wrote,[2] and in Freud's estimation fucking you up appeared to be their exclusive job and prerogative. No one else got to do it. The unhappy families Freud met through his analytic work are self-contained affairs. Grandparents rarely figure into the story, and the kind of *lésion héréditaire* that dominates Émile Zola's fictional families are entirely absent. Later in life, Sergei Pankejeff pointed out how unlikely it was that he, child of Russian aristocrats, should have slept in his parents' bedroom at all—the kind of intimacy and self-containment presupposed by something like a "primal scene" simply hadn't existed in his household. There was something fantastical, almost phantasmatic about the closeness Freud imputed to his families. Even his own familial arrangement didn't adhere to the kind of structure he imputed to those of his analysands.

The families that appear in Freud's writings, be that in the theoretical texts or in the case studies, tend to be nuclear, even if their nucleus is frequently in tatters. They are certainly less complex than the family in which Freud himself grew up, in which his half-brother was his mother's

[2] See Philipp Larkin, "This be the Verse," included in Larkin, *Collected Poems*, New York: Farrar Straus and Giroux, 2001.

age, and seemingly a better match for her too. Whether through an act of repression, of canny marketing, or of methodological foreshortening, Freud usually presents families with parents and children and little more.

Persons beyond the nucleus factor into its dynamics, but usually as triggers and disturbances. In describing Dora's case, Freud settles on a series of culprits for Dora's symptoms—an aunt she adores, a friendly couple she tussles with, a governess, a cousin—all of which hail from outside the nuclear family. But in the end his gaze seems magnetically drawn to Frau K, and above all Herr K. Compared to the literary texts of Romanticism on which Freud so frequently drew for inspiration, the power of family members outside of the nucleus seems considerably weakened.

In later editions of the Dora case, Freud included a footnote about the role of heredity as the main etiological factor in hysteria. Here he emphasized that he did not want to create the impression that heredity "can be dispensed with."[3] But just as soon as he makes this admission, he circumscribes what sort of heredity he's most interested in—heredity that emerges directly from the parents' actions. For he allows that Dora's mother may well have inherited her hysteria and passed it on to her daughter, but insists that "there is another factor which is of more significance in the girl's hereditary or, properly speaking, constitutional predisposition" (4). That factor is the syphilis Dora's father had contracted either prior to marrying Dora's mother, or while married to her. Freud seems to regard the transmission of neuroses as proceeding according to a Lamarckian model of evolution, by which acquired traits can be passed down to future generations—but these traits hailed from one's immediate, rather than distant, ancestry.[4]

It was somehow for Freud more comfortable to blame a two-timing father than a contaminated heredity—and his predisposition agreed with that of many of his contemporaries. Viennese bourgeois of Freud's era tended to think of their politics, their society, their art as profoundly nuclear, in terms that Freud would eventually term Oedipal—a rebellion of sons against fathers.[5] The people who stepped through Freud's door were mostly scions of the self-made men that rose to prominence in the

[3] Freud, "Fragment of an Analysis," 20n.

[4] Sander L. Gilman, *Freud, Race and Gender* (Princeton: Princeton University Press, 1993), 90.

[5] Carl E. Schorske, *Fin de siècle Vienna: Politics and Culture* (New York: Vintage, 1981), xxvi.

mid-nineteenth century, and who had moved to Vienna only recently. They lived mostly in the ninth district, in grand new constructions not unlike Freud's own building at Berggasse 19—their Vienna was no longer that of the medieval ramparts, but the institutions clustered around the Ringstrasse that had replaced those ramparts. For them dynasties were other people; and their own lineage was frequently a bit of an embarrassment—whether they were small tradesmen who'd risen to the top of the heap through lucky investments or Eastern Jews shedding the dust and the pogroms of the Bukovina in favor of a *palais* in fourth district. The Freuds, of course, who hailed from rural Moravia and had moved to Vienna via Leipzig when Sigmund was three, were among them.

More generally, psychoanalysis proceeds from a central assumption that is anti-dynastic in character, although it may not appear that way at first. There is a simple reason why the people who matter to Freud's picture of sexual development are father, mother, and siblings: sexual development happens in early childhood. This may seem like a trivial point, but Freud's intuition that the etiology of neuroses was to be located inside the nuclear family was a minority opinion among those dedicated to puzzling out the origins of hysteria in the closing decades of the nineteenth century. Jean-Martin Charcot and Josef Breuer both insisted that hysteria was hereditary—that is to say, they located its origins in the past of the family, rather than the past of the individual.[6] Freud entertained this possibility early in his career, but starting with the so-called seduction hypothesis, he increasingly insisted that there has to be a non-hereditary element to the etiology of hysterical symptoms, and that it is to be sought in that part of the family history the individual was actually present for, even if they did not consciously register it.

Freud understood this as his original and revolutionary contribution to the theory of hysteria—and he would later make it a cornerstone of his picture of the mind. The text in which he did so, the *Three Essays on Sexuality* (1905), makes explicit that its theory of infantile sexuality is meant to replace theories that seek the origins of sexuality in a structure that might be called dynastic—that is to say in the prehistory of the family. Instead, Freud seeks to locate it in the immanence of the nuclear family—in the prehistory of the individual:

[6] Gilman, *Freud, Race and Gender*, 87.

> It is remarkable that writers who concern themselves with explaining the characteristics and reactions of the adult have devoted much more attention to that prehistory which is given to us by the lifespan of our ancestors, in other words have allotted such outsize importance to heredity, than the other prehistory, which already falls into the individual existence of the person, namely childhood.[7]
>
> *Es ist bemerkenswert, dass die Autoren, welche sich mit der Erklärung der Eigenschaften und Reaktionen des erwachsenen Individuums beschäftigen, jener Vorzeit, welche durch die Lebensdauer der Ahnen gegeben ist, soviel mehr Aufmerksamkeit geschenkt, also der Erblichkeit so viel mehr Einfluß zugesprochen haben, als der anderen Vorzeit, welche bereits in die individuelle Existenz der Person fällt, der Kindheit nämlich.*[8]

The concept of infantile sexuality, in other words, is intended as something of a replacement of dynastic modes of explanation. The individual subject is as ignorant about one as it is about the other, but on one picture the energies that threaten the nuclear family are (inherited) factors that transcend that nuclear family, in the other they are native to it.

We may well ask why Freud finds this fact "remarkable"—the nineteenth century had been, as we saw, obsessed with subsuming individual ends and drives into the dynastic force of the group, the family, the nation. It was commonplace to locate the mysteries of human psychology in the distant past, if anything it was Freud's claim that their explanation was far closer to hand that stood out. So why "remarkable"? Does Freud think his suggestion better because it locates the etiology of individual psychology closer in time to the adult individual? Is it supposed to be more commonsensical in some way?

Most likely, Freud understood his emphasis on the nuclear family to constitute a kind of residual humanism. Against the anthropologists, the biologists, the craniometers and physiognomists, against Zola and his experimental novel and Arthur Schopenhauer and the Will of the Species, he insisted that at long last the key to the mysteries of human experience were to be found --in human experience.[9] Of course, the unconscious is

[7] Freud, "Three Essays on the Theory of Sexuality" (1905), *SE* VII: 125–248, here 173 [translation modified for emphasis and accuracy].

[8] Freud, "Drei Abhandlungen zur Sexualtheorie." In: Freud, *Gesammelte Werke*, ed. Anna Freud et al. 17 vols, in 16 (London: Imago Publishing Co., 1940–1952), V: 27–146; here 73.

[9] Andrew Zimmerman, *Anthropology and Antihumanism in Imperial Germany* (Chicago: University of Chicago Press, 2001), 52.

no more recoverable, knowable, or domesticated on Freud's picture than it was, say, for advocates of evolutionary theory. But at least it came from us as individuals, from our lifetime, from decisions and misapprehensions that we in some way made, albeit before we became properly us. It also made Freud a late scion of Enlightenment thought: a believer in the anthropogenic character of our lifeworld and a believer in our ability to master that lifeworld by understanding our shaping of it more fully.

The paper in which Freud most decisively broke with Charcot, "Heredity and the Etiology of the Neuroses" (1896), makes clear that Freud also wanted to forestall ethnic or even racial categorization of neuroses—specifically the widespread idea of neurosis and neurasthenia as "Jewish" diseases. Against Charcot, he marshaled the fact that people of similar extraction can show very different symptoms, and that people of very different extraction can show strikingly similar ones. The break with dynastic pre-determination went along with an emphasis on the universality of hysterical symptoms and the universality of their psychoanalytic remedy.

With the discovery of infantile sexuality Freud became the Freud we now know. But in abandoning the hereditary theories of Charcot and Breuer he had initially entertained a different counter-proposal, and maintained it for quite some time. It was this picture of the etiology of neurosis, the so-called seduction hypothesis, that he abandoned in his now-classic treatments of hysteria. The seduction hypothesis proposed that hysteria originated from *actual* experiences during infancy—something happened to us and our infant mind was unable to assimilate the experience. Most frequently those actual experiences would be some sort of child sexual abuse. In the *Three Essays* he decided that hysteria emerged rather from the fantasy life of the infant, from erotic attentions the infant desired, not from ones it actually experienced.

This move could be seen (and was in fact seen by later feminist critics) as a colossal failure of nerve: Isn't it at least possible that Freud had stumbled on a pattern of victimization of girls by a patriarchal power structure, and had then decided that it was all in the girls' heads? Did Freud declare infants and children perverse in order to not have to accuse his own age of unconscionable perversity? Freud was not usually afraid of upsetting his contemporaries; in fact, he often delighted in doing so. Perhaps, then, the more likely explanation for Freud's rather jarring abandonment of the seduction hypothesis is to be sought in his theoretical premises. The step away from the seduction hypothesis emancipated the individual unconscious from the last vestiges of dynasticity: everything that roiled the unconscious now originated from the possessor of said unconscious (or, perhaps better, the one possessed *by* said unconscious). What mother and father *did* mattered no longer; what mattered instead was what the child's desire projected onto mother and father.

Psychoanalysis and the Dynastic Imagination

The decisiveness of these early bracketing gestures did not effectively banish the troubling possibilities presented by a dynastic unconscious. Sometime in 1904 Sigmund Freud stood upon the ruins of the acropolis in Athens, and in early 1936—"a generation" later,[10] as he puts it—he wrote about it. The open letter to Romain Rolland outlining "A Disturbance of Memory on the Acropolis" is a stealthy reflection on the psychoanalysis of inheritance, and of the heredity of psychoanalysis. The "disturbance" he identified was rather straightforward, but its explanation would preoccupy him for decades. He had, with his brother, decided to travel to Athens, after initially resisting. Once there he stood upon the acropolis gripped by a powerful feeling of derealization: he simply could not believe he was here. The origin of that feeling—perhaps unsurprisingly—turned out to be the Oedipus Complex, but in a peculiar variation: Freud is thinking about his own father and about his own daughter. About besting the earlier generation and about being outlived and bested by the next. About breaks with heredity and being outdone by one's followers. This Oedipus was, in other words, thinking dynastically.

Kept largely at bay in the classic case studies and in the work on infantile sexuality, the dynastic trajectory re-entered Freud's oeuvre before long. It remained largely absent from Freud's analytic work with patients, but of course Freud started publishing in fields that were only distantly tethered to the lavishly draped couch in Berggasse 19. In the years leading up to World War I he started training his analytic acumen on culture at large—the neuroses he sought to investigate in his writings now held entire populations, or even all of humanity, in their grip. He began, as he wrote to Rolland, "attempting [analysis] upon myself and then went on to apply it to other people and finally, by a bold extension, to the human race as a whole" (239). The concept of a phylogenetic memory that pitted human

[10] Freud, "A Disturbance of Memory on the Acropolis" (1936), *SE* XXII: 239–250, here 239.

beings against one another began looming larger in his thinking. At the same time, the dynasty began to infiltrate his personal life.

For Freud started to gain followers. And while most of the designations for the group he gathered around himself were intended to highlight the psychoanalytic movement's horizontal organization (it was a "society" with elected presidents, for instance), in his letters Freud instead cast the movement in emphatically familial terms. Freud called his younger followers, the first apostate Alfred Adler, the new heir apparent Carl Gustav Jung, and the loyalist Ludwig Binswanger, each "dear son," and wrote to the latter that Jung should "inherit the lot."[11] His younger colleagues followed his lead. Jung could write to Freud calling him "father," apologizing for "my pranks."[12] And, of course, Jung's unofficial designation as "Freud's crown prince" heightened the dynastic dimensions of the psychoanalytic community in its early years.

As Freud's ambitions grew, and as he began cultivating heirs to carry on his legacy, Freud began rethinking his opposition to the heredity of neuroses. A late text like *Moses and Monotheism* (1934–1938) relies quite heavily on the idea that a repressed memory might travel by way of heredity through the eons, all the way from the murdered Egyptian Moses to modern-day Jewry. Likewise, his insistence that the *Urhorde*'s murder of the Father was an actual historical event rather than a symbolic process seems intent on going back into the earliest prehistory at the expense of looking for the origins of human aggression in, say, early childhood development.

While the Freud of the *Three Essays* was content to linger within the immanence of the bourgeois nuclear family, the later works often labor under a mania for transcending it, for traveling up and down the dynastic chain. Starting in the 1910s, the term "archaic heritage" begins to creep into Freud's writings; by the 1930s it was ubiquitous. In his 1937 essay that can count as something of a sigh of resignation, entitled "Analysis Terminable and Interminable," Freud allowed for precisely such an "archaic heritage." And in *Moses and Monotheism*, Freud points out that

[11] Freud, letter to Ludwig Binswanger, May 14, 1911. In: *The Sigmund Freud-Ludwig Binswanger Correspondence 1908–1938*, ed. Gerhard Fichtner, tr. Arnold J. Pomerans, with Tom Roberts (New York: The Other Press, 2003), 64–65.

[12] Jung, letter to Freud, March 9, 1910. In: *The Freud/Jung Letters: The Correspondence Between Sigmund Freud and C.G. Jung, ed. McGuire*, tr. Ralph Manheim and Hull (Princeton: Princeton University Press, 1974), 302; see also Lionel Trilling, "The Freud/Jung Letters," *New York Times* (April 21, 1974), 489.

"the behavior of neurotic children towards their parents in the Oedipus and castration complex abounds in such reactions, which seem unjustified in the individual case and only become intelligible phylogenetically—by their connection with the experience of earlier generations."[13]

A famous passage in *Beyond the Pleasure Principle* (1920) suggests that the two—the heredity of neurosis and the dynastic project of psychoanalysis itself—were in fact linked in Freud's mind. When introducing the challenge posed to traditional libidinal theory by the compulsion to repeat, Freud mostly framed his analysis in terms of traumatic neuroses—stark, dramatic pathologies that afflicted shell-shocked soldiers and victims of violence. But then he points out that, in far less noticeable, far less obtrusive, and far less debilitating ways, the compulsion to repeat asserts itself in the life of "healthy" individuals as well. As so often in such instances, Freud demonstrates the prevalence of neurotic symptoms even among those who would see no need to seek out a psychoanalyst to alleviate them in their own person. For the portrait he offers, of a man for "whom every human relationship ends in the same way," is in fact a sly bit of autobiography:

> Thus one knows people with whom every human relationship ends in the same way: benefactors whose protégés, however different they may otherwise have been, invariably after a time desert them in ill-will, so that they are apparently condemned to drain to the dregs all the bitterness of ingratitude; men with whom every friendship ends in the friend's treachery; others who indefinitely often in their lives invest some other person with authority either in their own eyes or generally, and themselves overthrow such authority after a given time, only to replace it by a new one; lovers whose tender relationships with women each and all run through the same phases and come to the same end, and so on.[14]

The introduction of the death drive, and the repetition compulsion that constitutes its most pervasive symptom, thus coincides with a return of the dynastic family into the etiology of neurosis. Not only does Freud here tell a story of a man frustrated in his dynastic designs; the very experience that occasions his frustrations is no longer to be sought in the prehistory of childhood, but rather in the prehistory of the species. By a supreme bit of irony what frustrates this man's dynastic ambitions is something inherited.

[13] Freud, *Moses and Monotheism* (1939 [1934–1938]), *SE* XXIII: 3–140; here 99.
[14] Freud, "*Beyond the Pleasure Principle*" (1920), *SE*: XVIII: 3–66; here 22.

He does not act out some kind of Oedipal trauma with these men who are his friends until they disappoint him; he acts out a drive as old as the species, a ghost from the infancy of mankind, not of the individual.

This was the period in which Freud became obsessed with temporal origins, origins lying neither in the individual biography nor in the constitution of the organism. Events that happened once and transmitted themselves in culture. It would be easy to dissolve the doctrine of original sin into a simple operation of the human super-ego—Freud had done it before and continued to do it. But in *Totem and Taboo*, Freud found an actual event that had precipitated the idea—an actual guilt, an actual murder, an actual moment of fall. The fourth chapter of this 1913 exercise in speculative anthropology draws on Darwin's suggestion that early human communities may have been centered on a single alpha male from which male offspring were cast. As those outcast rebelled and slew the father, they gave rise in one moment to the Oedipus complex and to the guilt that, Freud believed, lay at the heart of religious feeling. The central structuring motor of the nuclear family, the Oedipus complex, was itself a dynastic inheritance of the oldest provenance, a *lésion héréditaire* on the entire species. *Totem and Taboo* opens the era of the primal horde or *Urhorde* of Abraham, of Moses.

This reverses the idea that opens Freud's essay on "Infantile Sexuality." Now the etiology of the individual's neuroses is, at least in one important respect, to be found in the history of the family rather than the history of the individual. The feeling of guilt that pervades the family is but a distant reverberation of a millennia-old guilt that has suffused the culture as religious doctrine. In *Moses and Monotheism*, his last published work, Freud famously proposes that Moses was not in fact a Hebrew, but rather an Egyptian named Tutmoses, who brought the monotheistic cult of Aton to the slave tribes of Israel, only to be murdered by them. It was a troubling argument, troubling no less to Freud himself who acknowledged in his preface that 1938 might be a uniquely inappropriate to make public a wild theory about the murderous roots of Jewish identity. The thought seems to have forced itself on Freud and *Moses and Monotheism* is a story about passing on ideas. Like genetic material certain suppositions are transmitted unconsciously from generation to generation in families, in tribes, in entire peoples. But *Moses* knows two such ways: Freud's historic Moses is one of the last adherents of a religion on the brink of eradication; to save the ideas of Akhenaten's Aton-cult, he imparts them to the enslaved Israelites, entrusts it to them for safekeeping. The very unlikeliness of this development for Freud vouches for its truth content; for this unlikeliness was preserved in memory. The God of Abraham who chooses "his" people, a small desert tribe out of all of the nations, is, Freud thinks, a distant echo of the incomprehensible decision that leads Tutmoses to entrust his defamed religion to his slaves.

But once Tutmoses is killed, his memory, now as Moses the Hebrew rather than Moses the Egyptian, passes along far less elective lines. As though to atone for the incomprehension with which they repaid the incomprehensibility of his grace, his followers transmit from generation to generation a *lésion héréditaire*—a memory of guilt. Or rather, a memory and a guilt, separately and distinct like motifs in a dream: The hereditary guilt that passes down from Adam, and the story of their forebear Moses.

Jung, the Crown Prince

In his seminal 1912 essay on transference, Freud raises once again the question of "the amount of etiological effectiveness to be attributed to" constitution and chance, and arrives at a middle-of-the-road answer, namely that this distribution "can only be arrived at in every individual case separately."[15] Some neuroses may have an etiology that exceeds the confines of the nuclear family, in other words, but those origins cannot be generalized. But that more distant etiology lingers over Freud's argument as a threat—and, quite characteristically, he banished it into a footnote. He closes the footnote by pointing out: "Incidentally, one might venture to regard constitution itself as a precipitate from the accidental effects produced on the endlessly long chain of our ancestors" (99n.).

Freud leaves it there, the note ends, the overwhelming question raised but not answered. "One might"—would one be right to do so? A good psychoanalyst, confronted with such a conspicuous loose end, would probably follow up. It is no accident that Freud couldn't, or wouldn't answer, at the time. For to answer would have led Freud into psychoanalysis's own unconscious. And to answer in the affirmative would have brought Freud into alignment with ideas held by his former favorite son, who was, by late 1912 fast in the process of becoming an implacable opponent. For Jung had ventured to regard our physiology as determinative of an inherited unconscious. He was a declared enemy of nuclearity, both in his view on the etiology of the neuroses and in his view on transference.

[15] Freud, "The Dynamics of Transference" (1912), *SE* XII: 7–108; here 99n.

Where Freud had assumed that in psychoanalyzing Dora, her resistance meant that she had integrated him into her family romance, turning him into a stand-in for her father (since they "both smoked," as he helpfully observed), Jung suggested that in transference analysands turned their analyst into something far less quaint and far more ancient. As Jung would explain in "On the Psychology of the Unconscious" (1917; an earlier version appeared 1912 as "Neue Bahnen der Psychologie") transference consists not simply in "making the doctor his father, mother, uncle, guardian and teacher, and all the rest of the parental authorities." Rather "still other fantasies appear, which represent the doctor as a savior or godlike being."[16]

It was, ironically enough, a moment of Oedipal resistance against a father figure cast as a rebellion against the concept of Oedipal resistance against father figures. In 1906, Freud turned 50. It was also the year Carl Gustav Jung, then 30, sent Freud a copy of his first book, *On the Psychology of Dementia Praecox* (*Über die Psychologie der Dementia Praecox: Ein Versuch*), which had just been published. Their ages matter: A young man looking for a mentor figure found a man at the threshold of old age looking for younger men to carry on his legacy. This was to both make and unmake their friendship.

It is no surprise that Jung's short book on schizophrenia kindled Freud's dynastic hopes. The preface is an unapologetic love letter to the "ingenious conceptions of Freud."[17] What led Jung to Freud, he claims there, was the empirical evidence: to come to terms with Freudian claims one has to put in one's time analyzing "daily life, hysteria and dreams" from Freud's standpoint—if one doesn't one "act like one of those lauded scientists who refused to look through Galileo's telescope" (iv). At the same time, Jung's list ("daily life, hysteria, and dreams") conspicuously downplays the area in which Freud and Jung most centrally disagreed: "When I recognize the mechanism of the complexes of dream and hysteria, for instance, that does not mean that I allot exclusive significance to the sexual traumas of youth, as Freud appears to" (iv).

This, as almost all historical accounts of their ill-fated friendship point out, was to be the sticking point throughout their friendship: Jung was on

[16] Carl Gustav Jung, "On the Psychology of the Unconscious" (1917). In: Jung, *The Collected Works of C.G. Jung*. ed. William McGuire et al., tr. R.F.C. Hull et al. 20 vols. (ser.) Bollington (Princeton: Princeton University Press, 1953–1979), VII: 9–88, here 64 (edition will be abbreviated *CW*).

[17] Jung, *Über die Psychologie der Dementia Praecox* (Halle: Marhold, 1907), iii.

board with the hysteria, the dreams, but he had serious misgivings with the libidinal engine of infantile sexuality that Freud had postulated in the *Three Essays*. The very fact that even in his rapturous dedication Jung seemingly neglects the fact that "daily life, hysteria and dreams" in Freud's reading are shot through with the residue of infantile sexuality, and moreover speaks of "traumas of youth" (when in fact Freud had moved away from a theory of trauma, and was thinking of *infantile* sexuality, not of the sexuality of youth) suggests not so much two thinkers destined to drift apart over time, but rather two thinkers destined to realize they fundamentally disagreed.

But for the moment both Freud and Jung remained almost purposefully blind to those disagreements. Freud was, as Reuben Fine points out, re-enacting an earlier homosocial relationship—just as a young Freud had latched onto Wilhelm Fliess as a kind of father figure, he now seemed to groom Jung as a kind of son and heir.[18] What exactly inspired him to do so is not clear: Jung's work at the time was capable, but not visionary; the works and ideas that would make him famous lay still in the future. But it was futurity that Jung had in spades, and perhaps that was primarily what Freud wanted. Jung was just the kind of heir Freud wanted for himself: a practicing psychiatrist, an empirical researcher, a Protestant, a gentile, and, most importantly, would young, one of those men who, as Freud wrote to Binswanger, would one day "continue my own life."[19] Jung must have appeared to him as the Moses who would lead psychoanalysis from the various theoretical and cultural ghettos in which he felt it was still confined.

But Jung would reject this role rather dramatically. While most biographers agree that the break between the two men had been some time coming, it seems both fitting and a bit ironic that Freud's dynastic bid was frustrated by the dynasty. The problem in 1913 was not that Freud and Jung differed on the transmissibility of unconscious content from generation, as they would have differed in 1905 when the *Three Essays* were published. It was that Freud's move toward the psychology of religion in *Totem and Taboo* (positing in its subtitle "Resemblances between the Mental Lives of Savages and Neurotics") expanded psychoanalysis into an anthropological realm that Jung seemed to consider his province.

In a letter to Freud, Jung complained that it would be "very oppressive to me, if you too become involved in this area. You are a dangerous

[18] Reuben Fine, *A History of Psychoanalysis* (New York: Columbia University Press), 83.
[19] Cited in: Peter Gay, *Freud – A Life for Our Time* (New York: Norton, 2006), 229.

competitor, if one wants to speak of competition."[20] The phrase was utterly revealing: Jung both *did* want to speak of competition, and disavow it, at least for now. The discoverer of the Oedipus complex apparently didn't notice that he seemed to inspire a distinctly Oedipal energy in his favorite son. Or perhaps he did notice, but thought that Jung would and should work through and master his aggressive impulses. Jung himself seemed to think of them that way—his sense of being crowded by Freud, he thought, was part of his own pathology.[21]

The issue that emerged as central in this disagreement was the role of collectivity, and in that collectivity the question of a family larger than the nuclear one emerged with renewed force. It did so in two ways: for one, if, as Jung claimed, there was a collective (or "interpersonal") unconscious preceding and conditioning the individual unconscious, then infantile psychology and the immediate family that shaped it ceded pride of place to something that came from the more distant past.[22] For another, it meant that unconscious content was transmissible in ways that differed markedly from the mechanisms that Freud had established, at least in his classical formulations.

Those mechanisms, above all the Oedipus complex, had drawn only on the fix points of the nuclear family, whereas Jung in his 1929 article on "Constitution and Heredity in Psychology" ("Die Bedeutung von Konstitution und Vererbung für die Psychologie") suggested that the two prehistories of the individual subject, the infantile and the familial combined to constitute the individual psyche.[23] This constituted a significant shift: The Oedipal family in a sense reconstitutes itself in each successive generation; Jung's family reached deep into the human past. "The psychic process does not start out of nothing with the individual consciousness, but is rather a repetition of functions which have been ages in the making and which are inherited with the brain structure" (110).

Jung remained ambivalent about how closely the process he supposed behind the collective unconscious resembled biological inheritance. His 1929 article linked it rather insistently to physiology. Rather than unconscious contents traveling from generation to generation directly, it was

[20] Cited in Gay, *Freud*, 223.

[21] Gay, *Freud*, 235.

[22] Jung, "The Structure of the Unconscious" (1916), *CW* VII: 263–292.

[23] Jung, "The Significance of Constitution and Heredity in Psychology" (1929), *CW* VIII: 87–91.

physiological traits that made the trip—and the physiological resemblance of each generation to the previous permits for the structural resemblance of certain ideas, associations, and images. Nevertheless, these physiological traits could be acquired and passed along much further down the dynastic chain than an Oedipal infatuation with a mother figure. What is more, Jung often talked as though this continuity went well beyond a function of physiology. In the same essay he claims that "psychic processes antedate, accompany, and outlive consciousness. Consciousness is an interval in a continuous psychic process" (110). This was precisely the picture of human inheritance Freud's essay on infantile sexuality had been intended to rebuke: the Schopenhauerian view, whereby the individual is just a blip in the relentless unfolding of the psychic process of the species.

In his final years Jung arrived at the palatably universalist conviction that mythemes, ideas, and associations had redounded from some common ancestor to all humans. But in decades prior he had not always been so sure. In his 1929 essay he casts the constituency of the collective unconscious as a family collective, remarking on the "astounding cases of mental similarity [that] can be found in family" (111). Jung wavered between the picture of a familial and racial collective unconscious and a universalist heredity shared by all mankind. His vacillation, often trafficking in rather noxious anti-Semitic tropes, became particularly acute in the years between his break with Freud and the Nazis' rise to power.

In his 1918 article "On the Unconscious," Jung made a distinction between distinctly Jewish and distinctly German forms of the collective unconscious. Jung's vocabulary in the essay is troublingly redolent of later Nazi-jargon (he speaks of the Germans as a "host people," implying that Jews are parasites; his Germans are the "blonde beasts" of Nietzsche's later aphorisms; he assumes a thoroughgoing distinction between Jews and Germans; and he gives the old canard of Jewish double loyalty a psychoanalytic sheen). But behind this objectionable rhetoric lurks a deeper point: Jung seems intent on dealing with the notion that psychoanalysis is a Jewish discourse addressing specifically Jewish problems, and is ill-suited to the German psyche. And while his erstwhile friend and mentor turned to the death drive and the Mosaic legacy to comprehend the rise of fascism, Jung located its origins in the German psyche.

In March of 1936, Jung published an article entitled "Wotan" in the *Neue Schweizer Rundschau*. It is in this essay that Jung describes a specifically German collective unconscious and spells out what it means for his own age, the age of the "rebirth of Wotan."[24] Jung proposes a dynastic unconscious that can go dormant for centuries, only to then re-emerge and take hold of Germans in a moment of *Ergriffenheit*, "a state of being seized or possessed" (184). But he also claims a different extraction for his own analytic project: he cites the German Youth Movement, he cites Richard Wagner, Friedrich Nietzsche, Stefan George, Ludwig Klages, and Alfred Schuler, but he also cites Nazi rallies. They understood, like Jung, that Wotan helps illuminate a phenomenon "so strange to anybody not a German, that it remains incomprehensible even after the deepest reflection" (184). The "anybody" who was not a German and whose "deepest reflections" had to miss Wotan, was most likely Freud.

To be sure, Jung in this article evinces no triumph over having understood what Freud could not—if anything, he is quite worried. Wotan "is a fundamental attribute of the German psyche, an irrational psychic factor which acts on the high pressure of civilization like a cyclone and blows it away." But at the same time, he allows that "the Wotan-worshippers seem to have judged things more correctly than the worshippers of reason" (186). There lingers in a text like "Wotan" a persistent whiff of self-satisfaction of having been vindicated in his analytic instincts—Jung's fear of having his worries about the German unconscious borne out were largely trumped by his satisfaction at having been right.

More troublingly, all his obvious misgivings about the rise of Nazism notwithstanding, Jung's texts about the Wotanic extraction of Nazism reverberate with an off-putting awe at the reason-shattering power of the German soul. And the terms in which Jung frames Freud's incomprehension before the rise of Nazism itself has troubling racial implications. For on the one hand, it seems Jung wants to argue that German gentiles, rather than Jews, have more urgent need for psychoanalytic intervention. They are half-domesticated, he writes, while half of them roils with "the remainders of prehistory [*Vorzeit*], with the collective unconscious." The Jew, by contrast, "has his ancient culture, and additionally has acquired the culture of his host people. He has two cultures."[25] This can make it sound as though Jung assigned psychoanalysis the role of civilizing the uncivilized Germans. On the other hand, in light of other writings of the

[24] Jung, "Wotan" (1936), *CW* X: 179–193; here 180.

[25] Jung, "Über das Unbewußte"(1918).In: Jung, *Zivilisation im Übergang*, *Gesammelte Werke*, 20 vols., ed. Lilly Jung-Merker and Elisabeth Rüf (Olten: Walter Verlag, 1958–), X: 15–42; here 25 (edition will be abbreviate *GW*).

time (above all "Zur gegenwärtigen Lage der Psychotherapie," 1934), it becomes clear that Jung means to distinguish between two *forms* of analysis: the rationalist, reductive, erotomanic analysis of the Freudian type can only understand Jews, and cannot understand true Germans—it stirs in "the garbage bin [*Kehrichtkübel*] of unfulfillable childhood wishes and unresolved family resentments," and misses the "hidden depths of the Germanic soul."[26]

By contrast, Jungian techniques, aiming as they do at the collective unconscious, only work when applied to a people that still retains a strong collective unconscious. Jung is not subtle in suggesting that Freud, for racial reasons, was constitutionally unable to see this collective unconscious. Freud's problem, in other words, was his focus on the nuclear family, on infantile sexuality, and more generally Freud's "fanatical one-sidedness" in focusing on "sexuality, on desire" (184); and his concomitant inability to understand collective (and ancestral) forces at work in the etiology of the neuroses. Rather than fetishizing the childhood of the individual, Jungian analysis harnesses a spirit "not yet fully alienated from youthfulness" (191).

Hitler's rise to power did not serve to nuance this juxtaposition, but Jung began to sound increasingly worried about the semi-domesticated state of the German soul. His affirmation of Germanic depth and the cradling certitudes of Wotanic archetypes gave way to an anguished insistence that Germans begin to psychoanalyze the undomesticated depths of their soul.[27] Hitler himself emerged as a direct protuberance of the collective unconscious—in the so-called Knickerbocker-interview Jung gave in 1939, he is portrayed as its pure carrier as much as its hapless victim.[28]

After the war, after the end of Nazism, or, as Jung's one essay reflecting on events put it, "after the catastrophe," Jung largely abandoned the idea that the collective unconscious was different from one racial group to the other, or that some groups had more of it than others. Instead, he retreated to what may have been his initial instinct anyway, namely that the family that was relevant for the collective unconscious was the human family, not some tribal subset of it. He had entertained this universalist opinion

[26] Jung, "Zur gegenwärtigen Lage der Psychotherapie" (1934). In: Jung, *Zivilisation im Übergang*, *GW* X: 181–200; here 191.

[27] Barbara Hannah: *C. G. Jung. Sein Leben und Wirken* (Küsnacht: Stiftung für Jung'sche Psychologie, Küsnacht 2006), 273.

[28] Robert Ellwood, *The Politics of Myth: A Study of C. G. Jung, Mircea Eliade, and Joseph Campbell* (New York: SUNY Press, 1999), 37.

throughout. Even in a 1929 essay, four years before "Wotan," five years before his essay on the "Present Situation of Psychotherapy," he merely claims to have entertained the idea "that such things could only happen to people belonging to the same race," but to have been convinced otherwise. And in his essay "On the Psychology of the Unconscious," for instance, he claims that these ideas have "been stamped on the human brain for aeons. That is why it lies ready to hand in the unconscious of every man."[29] After the war, this became his exclusive view.

But psychoanalysis after the World War II, of course, was "after" several overlapping events. It is likely that Jung was reacting mostly to what Dan Diner called the "break in civilization" (*Zivilisationsbruch*)—the holocaust and associated German barbarities.[30] But the late 1930s and most of the 1940s were for the international psychoanalytic community a moment of disarray, which, while of course not of the same order of magnitude as the convulsions of war and genocide, nevertheless had a profound impact of how the practice located and conceived itself within the broader project of Western modernity.

For one thing, psychoanalysis post 1938 meant psychoanalysis in the diaspora. The practitioners of psychoanalysis, once mostly concentrated in central Europe, were now scattered across the globe, and had to adjust their practice to a variety of countries, and in each of them which adjust it to a peculiar, and peculiarly agitated, political situation. Often regarded with suspicion, sometimes interned or unable to find employment, they had to find intersections with a local infrastructure that forced them to adjust and distend their practice, and that would shape their theorizing going forward. Questions of lineage raised themselves differently for these scattered, frequently fractious groups.

For another, psychoanalysis post 1939 meant psychoanalysis post Freud. It was the dynastic moment par excellence—the death of the sovereign, a moment where a distinction between psychoanalysis's two bodies had to ensure both continuity and the possibility for adaptation. During this interregnum, two eminent psychoanalysts came to wrestle with a related question: the controversy between Melanie Klein and Anna Freud dealt less (or less obviously) with what gets transmitted between the generations, for how long and how far down the family tree. At least on the

[29] Jung, "On the Psychology of the Unconscious," 69.

[30] See Dan Diner (Ed.), *Zivilisationsbruch: Denken nach Auschwitz*. Frankfurt: Fischer Verlag, 1988.

surface it instead focused on the role of psychoanalysis in accompanying this process. But the dynastic, the phylogenetic lurked behind this question as well.

Anna Freud, the Athena

Freud's analysis of his experience on the Acropolis in Athens is curious in a way typical of Freud's texts. It is deeply perceptive about certain questions and details and seems downright oblivious in treating others. It is both most perceptive and most oblivious in thinking about Athens. The Freud brothers, he tells us, had initially intended to go to Corfu, but had been pushed toward Athens instead, a decision that felt at once inevitable and contrary to their inclination. He is quick to locate the reason for their resistance, and the root of his feeling of derealization ("so all this really *does* exist, just as we learned at school!" 241) once he actually arrives at his destination, in his childhood and above all in his relationship to his father.

Freud quickly surmised that his feeling that the Acropolis cannot be real stems from a sense that it *must* not be real—that it was "a materialization of our conscience, of the severe super-ego within us, itself a residue of the punitive agency of our childhoods" (243). Growing up impoverished in Vienna, wishing to get away from his family and his roots, "I could really not have imagined it possible that I should ever be granted the sight of Athens with my own eyes" (243). Specifically, he points to the limitations of his father—a self-made businessman with comparatively little education—and his own sense of guilt over having exceeded his father's accomplishments—"as though to excel one's father was still something forbidden" (247). He does not mention that the limitations faced by his father, the "limitations and poverty of our condition" (247), were strongly connected to his Jewishness, and that the opportunities that had opened up for him had everything to do with having born a Jewish boy in 1856 and not in 1815. His guilt is the guilt of a young man who has outdone his father.

But while it may not have contributed to Freud going to Athens, the text strongly suggests there is a reason Freud held onto the memory of his derealization experience in Athens. And it comes through in his analytic categories: experiences like derealization, Freud explains, are defense mechanisms, "they aim at keeping something away from the ego, at disowning it" (245). These defense mechanisms were being studied—and would indeed that same year be made famous by—"my daughter, the child analyst."[31] The slightly dismissive reference to Anna as a "child analyst" (or is it a child who is also an analyst?) is striking by itself, but even more striking that Anna would not be on Freud's mind when considering how his trip to Athens has lingered in his memory. Anna is about to continue her father's work, and here is Sigmund reflecting in depth on how he outdid his own father. In this regard, it seems worth noting that Sigmund Freud is using his daughter's elaborations of his own theories while reflecting on a place dedicated to a goddess who was born parthenogenetically from her own father's forehead—what Faye Carey has called "the parthenogenesis on the Parthenon."[32] Fantasies of parthenogenesis are surely about virgin birth, but they are also about transmission of heredity without interference from a mate. They are fantasies of eternal life. "A Disturbance of Memory on the Acropolis" can be read as a dying man contemplating his legacy, but being unable to countenance that this legacy might be too distinct from him.

Freud doesn't seem to have discussed his "disturbance of memory" with Anna either at the time or when he wrote his letter to Romain Rolland. But Anna was a spectral presence in the text. By 1936, Freud had vacillated for decades between pride in how closely daughter followed in his footsteps, and a slight unease at the lack of an oedipal break between the generations. In a letter to Lou Andreas-Salomé, Freud proudly claimed his daughter's *An Introduction to the Technique of Child Analysis* (*Einführung in die Technik der Kinderanalyse*, 1927) that had just appeared was independent of his: "you will not believe how little I contributed to her book," he wrote, calling it "completely independent work." (All he had done, he claimed, was the political work of "curtailing her polemic against Melanie Klein."[33]) At the same time, he clearly worried about her dynastic potential—he confided to Andreas-Salomé that he worried his daughter had "no sexual life," and lamented that Anna "clings to women friends, one taking the place of the other" (541). He could not have failed to notice the resonances with his own homosocial experiences with father and son figures, the repetition of which he had thematized in *Beyond the Pleasure Principle* (1920). There he had illustrated the concept

[31] Freud, "A Disturbance of Memory on the Acropolis," 245.

[32] Faye Carey, "'Derealization': In the Shadow of the Son," in Jonathan Burke (Ed.), *Psychoanalytic Perspectives on the Shadow of the Parent: Mythology, History, Politics, and Art* (London: Routledge, 2018): 75–92; here 75.

[33] Freud letter to Lou Andreas-Salomé; see the discussion in Gay, *Freud*, 541.

of a compulsion to repeat by pointing to "people with whom every human relationship ends in the same way," clearly thinking about himself; now Anna's own repetition compulsion worried him, not just in itself, but as a repetition of his repetition. If the Oedipus complex is about managing repetition and difference, Freud's relationship to Anna seemed to worry him on both counts.

The woman who manages to be at the center of the text's fantasy, and remain unacknowledged as that center, is herself noteworthy for appearing to refuse the meanings her father seems intent on imposing on "the child analyst" in his open letter. Similarly, her great antagonist in the immediate aftermath of the patriarch's death, Melanie Klein, in her essay on the *Oresteia* positions Athena as a figure beyond the Oedipal, precisely because she has "appropriated the father."[34] Compared to the expansionary, oedipal energy of the crown prince Jung, Anna Freud's version of ego psychology and Kleinian psychoanalysis seemed to go the opposite route. Gone were invocations of collective, or hereditary unconscious, gone were the laborious investigations into the far reaches of the family tree. Rather than extend the family further outward, it seemed to further tighten the nucleus that Freud had relied on in his classic studies: by centering actual children in their practice, and by decentering the discursive aspect of psychoanalysis, both Klein and Anna Freud restricted the etiology of psychic disturbance to a limited set of interactions around (and almost exclusively with) the infant. There was no massive family tree or parental prehistory to consider. Klein was most radical in this regard: the family mattered only insofar as it was present or absent for the infant *in infancy*. For her, the only entity that truly mattered was a toddler playing with plasticine. Julia Kristeva in her biography of Klein claims that, compared to others, Klein "did not focus on the political aspects of the madness that tainted the twentieth century."[35] The politics of Kleinianism consisted precisely in not having an (overt) politics.

Neither Klein nor Anna Freud ever cast this restriction in these terms, but their justifications of focusing on early childhood occurred during a moment of disordered paternity. Both Klein and Freud had come to England as immigrants, Freud in fact as part of what she explicitly

[34] Melanie Klein, "Some Reflections on *The Oresteia*" (1963). In: Klein, *Envy and Gratitude and Other Works, 1946–1963* (New York: Macmillan, 2002), 275–299; here 285.

[35] Julia Kristeva, *Melanie Klein*, tr. Ross Guberman (New York: Columbia University Press, 2001), 15.

understood as a new diaspora. Sigmund Freud died shortly after his arrival in the UK, and questions of the extraction and portability of psychoanalytic technique were front of mind not just for the two women, but for most of their colleagues as well. At their most general, the "Controversial Discussions" of 1942–1946, and the broader schism within the British psychoanalytic community that culminated in them, were about what Freudian orthodoxy and Freudian apostasy would look like going forward. Klein's interventions—gleaned, unlike Anna Freud's insights, in working with children directly—proposed that Freud had erred in his timeline of the Oedipus complex and thus in pinpointing the creation of the super-ego. Both were present almost at birth, and almost certainly predated the ego defenses Anna Freud would make the lynchpin of her psychoanalytic theory.

Both Klein and Anna Freud claimed to be extending rather than upending Sigmund Freud's insights. And, serious though their disagreements were to prove for the methods and politics of psychoanalytic theory, when it came to their picture of unconscious content inherited through the family the two actually moved in tandem, and moved beyond the famous father figure. For in this respect, Anna was less-than-Freudian. She if anything further reduced the inherited component of the psyche, but a lot of what was not inherited might as well have been. What is acquired so early in childhood does not accommodate itself easily to analytic intervention—and is thus close to innate. "Much that used to be considered innate," Anna Freud would later explain in "Difficulties in the Path of Psychoanalysis" (1968), "can now be shown to have been acquired during the first year of life and to have been added to the inherited constitution." At the same time, she added, "The new technical proposals aimed at the beginning of life imply the assumption that whatever is acquired is reversible. This is by no means proved. It may well be that the very basis on which personality formation rests is, in fact, bedrock."[36] This would seem to repeat Freud's injunction at the beginning of the first of the *Three Essays* that our theories of the mind should focus on "that other inheritance" at the expense of the faraway reaches of family extraction. But at the same time, Anna Freud denies the distinction her father has made: if they are made early enough, certain personality traits *might as well* be a family

[36] Anna Freud, *Difficulties in the Path of Psychoanalysis; A Confrontation of Past with Present Viewpoints* (ser.) Freud Anniversary Lectures. New York: International Universities Press, [1969].

inheritance. Collapsing this distinction—even though it was essentially forced upon them by their empirical research on infants—meant that the hereditary would continue to haunt both Melanie Klein's and Anna Freud's work, even as they seemed to move decisively beyond it.

The two women differed from their male colleagues by their focus on early childhood, which raised one of the knottiest questions in psychoanalysis: what exactly could be hoped for in treatment. Sigmund Freud himself had vacillated on this score, with some of his early works (such as the *Three Essays*) seemingly imputing to the psychoanalytic project a potentially progressive function, and with especially the later works of anthropology being far more pessimistic—a work like *Beyond the Pleasure Principle* might be able to explain, but it could do little to change the course of human affairs. In Jung's reaction to the Nazi ascendancy in Germany, meanwhile, one could see where this kind of thinking could lead: Jung saw Germans so caught in the strictures of their own collective unconscious that his diagnostic work bordered on quietism. All analysis could do is show just how powerless human reason was before the Wotan-principle.

The figure of the infant permits no such quietism. Whatever is hoped for when intervening in infants or young children is hoped for by others—by parents, by society. The question of what analysis can accomplish is thus both unavoidable and perhaps more obviously tied to a political project than it was in, say, the case of the Wolf Man or Dora. Behind it lies the question that would divide Klein and Anna Freud: the question of education. Was the analyst an educator or not? Or, put differently: Was the analyst an analyst *of* the hereditary process by which neurosis traveled from one generation to the next, or was it somehow part of that hereditary process? Anna Freud's research focused on the nexus between nursery schools and the psychoanalytic profession, she offered seminars for nursery school teachers and worked in educational institutions throughout her life. Melanie Klein by contrast worried that "if the analyst, even only temporarily, becomes the representative of the educative agencies, if he assumes the role of the super-ego, at that point he ... becomes a representative of the repressive facilities."[37] The heredity that Anna Freud and Melanie Klein came to disagree over no longer concerned the collective unconscious of Jung or the phylogenetic memory of Freud père—it was the question of the eternal transmissibility of the super-ego itself.

[37] Klein, *Contributions to Psycho-Analysis, 1925–45* (London: Hogarth Press, 1965), 182.

For Anna Freud recent experiences of Nazi barbarity likewise loomed large in her emphasis on the child as a site for reproduction of societal aggression. Much depended for her on the notion of the infant largely propelled by erotic drives, and she was bound to resist a theory like Klein's that seemed to suggest that some aggression was evident even in the youngest children. Both of them could claim portions of the Freudian corpus for their conclusions—Anna Freud on the analytic practice and the classic case studies, Klein more the later work. Even though Klein supposed no phylogenetic memory of any kind, her picture of the infant mind seemed to draw preferably those works of Freud's that had operated with this and similar notions. Freud and Klein in their own ways offered a response to what appeared to them an unprecedented breakdown in European civilization. Anna's emphasis on education, as Deborah Britzman has pointed out, went along with an emphasis on responsible, democratic citizenship.[38] Klein, by contrast, seemed to fear that psychoanalysis itself might be drafted into the mechanisms of state power.

In her theoretical works, Klein drew extensively on the later Freudian oeuvre, in particular the Eros/Thanatos distinction: these two instincts were mediated by the ego in a tug-of-war that ultimately determined how the infant's ego was constituted. And it was here that the *longue durée* of family history re-entered the picture: In 1908, shortly after having dismissed and then readmitted the familial unconscious in the *Three Essays*, Freud suggested (in an essay entitled "Character and Anal Eroticism") that a predisposition toward anal eroticism ran in families. In 1924, Karl Abraham similarly suggested "what is really constitutional and inherited is an over-accentuation of oral erotism in the same way that in certain families anal erotism seems to be a preponderant factor from the very beginning."[39] Drawing on both forebears, Klein theorized that there was a "connection between the preponderance of the one or other instinct and the strength or weakness of the ego."[40] It was this "very beginning" on which Klein focused in her own form of analysis. And it was a beginning that raised the question of transmission: how did a factor like this become

[38] Deborah P. Britzman. *After-Education: Anna Freud, Melanie Klein, and Psychoanalytic Histories of Learning*, Buffalo: SUNY Press, 2003.

[39] Karl Abraham, "A Short History of the Development of the Libido, Viewed in Light of Mental Disorders." In: Karl Abraham, *Selected Papers*, ed. Ernest Jones, tr. Douglas Bryan and Alix Strachey(London: Hogarth, 1948), 418–501.

[40] Klein, "Envy and Gratitude" (1957). In: *Envy and Gratitude and Other Works, 1946–1963* (New York: Macmillan, 2002), 176–235; here 229.

"preponderant"? Was it a biological fact? Was it transmitted by the way parents interacted with their infant? Or was it part of a familial unconscious after all?

The Dynastic Unconscious: Léopold Szondi's "Fate Analysis"

The fact that even Jung retreated from a dynastic conception of phylogenetic memory after the "catastrophe" makes it particularly remarkable that after the war the idea of a collective unconscious belonging to a family of descent rather than the species as a whole was fully embraced by a Jewish holocaust survivor from Hungary, and not too far from Jung's Küsnacht home. Léopold (Lipot) Szondi drew on the same sources as Jung—Schopenhauer, Neo-Nietzschean thought—but arrived at a very different picture of what he called "the familial unconscious." Jung's Wotan had been "on the one hand the God of rage and fury [*Wut und Raserei*], on the other a reader of runes and a speaker of destiny [*Schicksalskünder*]."[41] Jung was both frightened and excited by the former guise of Wotan; Szondi interrogated the latter valence of the collective unconscious.

Jung had flirted with the idea that families and races could have their own unconscious; the late Freud had seemed to suggest that something like it might well exist. Among the ranks of the rapidly scattering psychoanalytic community, ideas like this were largely greeted with bafflement—it smacked of racism and of nineteenth-century *Völkerpsychologie*, and it bode ill for the portability of psychoanalytic technique beyond its native soil, on which so much depended now for so many. Jung's own insistence on a racially specific familial unconscious in his "Wotan"-essay and others served to widely discredit him during and immediately after the war.[42] American ego psychology, for one, doubled down on the anti-dynastic thrust of Freud's early work; for them, Freud's main mistake had not been the elision of the extended family, but rather an overemphasis of the family in general, above all the Oedipus complex. Even Freud's own heir Anna admits to having "always more attracted to the latency period that the pre-Oedipal phases."[43] Her theory of ego defenses was less interested in the

[41] Jung, "*Wotan*," 213.

[42] Deirdre Bair, *Jung: A Biography* (Boston: Little, Brown and Company, 2003), 510.

[43] Cited in: Elizabeth Young-Bruehl, *Anna Freud: A Biography* (New York: Summit, 1988), 455.

pressures that bear upon the ego from without, but in the lengths to which the ego goes to do battle with them.

The Hungarian psychoanalyst Szondi, however, pursued the opposite instinct: that there existed a familial unconscious, transmitted by uncertain mechanisms well beyond the nucleus. On Szondi's picture, familial arrangements could influence descendants, even if they had never actually experienced those arrangements. Why do, he asked, individuals seem to seek out marital partners that mirror in their pathologies those of their ancestors, even if they are not aware of those pathologies, or perhaps even those ancestors? Why are people drawn to certain professions or life choice? This was what Szondi called "fate" (*Schicksal*), and its therapy, by means of what would later become known as the Szondi-test, was called "fate analysis" (*Schicksalsanalyse*). Szondi put entire families on the couch—just as Freud had felt quite confident in diagnosing Dora's mother as a neurotic housewife sight unseen, Szondi cast his analytic net far beyond the actual patient sitting before him.

In the bargain, Szondi also recast the familial extraction of psychoanalysis itself. For what he proposes to analyze as "fate" is really sexual choice—not the *type* of object a drive takes, but the specific person one ends up with. It is important to note that this is anything but a new question in the theory of sexuality—if anything, it is the oldest question there is. It was the question of Oedipus, whose problem was after all a very specific object choice. It was the question Aristophanes' famous story in the Plato's *Symposium* was supposed to answer: how come we experience a particular person as our soul mate, our better half? But for that reason, it was a question that Freud had given little thought to. It was a philosophical question, it seemed basically unanswerable scientifically, and Freud was intent on doing empirical science.

Philosophers were still trying to answer this question in the nineteenth century, up to Freud's own day. Schopenhauer thought that through sexual choice a child attempted to will itself into existence—and that it looked for one parent to complement the other parent's traits. Otto Weininger thought that each individual sought out a partner that had the exact converse distribution of male and female traits. Freud read both of them with some interest, but he was otherwise careful not to place himself in their company. Theirs were grand metaphysical speculations, neither intended to furnish medical insight, nor especially liable to do so. And both Schopenhauer and Weininger were basically cranks—not the kinds of patron saints you call on for an enterprise as precariously situated between science, art, and voodoo as psychoanalysis.

Szondi's gesture of readmitting this banished question back into psychoanalysis turns out to be characteristic of his approach more generally: he seems to have had no problem with uncomfortable ancestors. Freud might relegate Schopenhauer to the deepest footnotes, might confine his fascination with Weininger to letters; Szondi cheerfully adopted them, and their uncomfortable question, as forebears to the analytic project. Problematic ancestors, the prehistory provided by one's forebears rather than one's infancy, were central to Szondi's analytic undertaking. Where Freud eclipsed the ancestors in favor of that "other prehistory" of infantile sexuality, Szondi typically begins his case studies with an exhaustive rundown of the family tree that produced the person.

Why did he feel the need to be so specific? Unlike Jung's collective unconscious, which is simply passed along from generation to generation, the familial unconscious Szondi identified seemed to be able to skip generations, to become invisible only to reappear again. Why did analysands come to Szondi with symptoms only to discover that their great-grandmother suffered from the same? Why did a woman seek out his help for the same neurosis her mother-in-law once saw Szondi for? It was because psychological traits, like physical ones, could be dominant or recessive. Szondi is indeed the rare psychoanalyst to refer to Mendelian inheritance law as much as the works of Freud in discussing his cases. But where the determinists of the nineteenth century had traced how imbecility, moral defects, or addiction traveled directly from one generation to the next, Szondi believed that a family line could carry a certain defect (say, a neurosis or a mania) without ever showing any symptoms.

This idea would seem to invite Hegel's famous objection that one can have a murderer's brainpan, but unless one actually murders, one is not a murderer.[44] How can we insist someone is mentally ill, in spite of not showing any symptoms? How can one be a paranoiac without a fear of surveillance? Szondi's answer to this problem is rather ingenious: the carrier in whom such a defect is latent, may not show symptoms, but he or she will seek out sufferers of this very defect. The disease is indeed present in those individuals in whom it fails to assert itself, but it is unconscious, as Szondi puts it, a *repressed* trait. That repressed trait predisposes the indi-

[44] G.W.F. Hegel, *The Phenomenology of Spirit*, tr. Terry Pinkard (Cambridge: Cambridge University Press, 2018), 196.

vidual toward falling in love with someone in whom the same trait is expressed. The very neurosis that the individual fails to express in their own person, they express through their object choice. In our mates, we seek out our ancestral defects—this Szondi called "genotropism." Where Freud had insisted that object choice depended centrally on the perversions introduced by the family nucleus, Szondi proposed that "love develops between the healthy, defectless descendants of people suffering from some common hereditary disease."[45]

Szondi reverses the way heredity and disease were thought to relate among nineteenth-century determinists. Zola, for instance, had posited that certain compulsions are the result of hereditary processes—a *lésion* that is passed down from individual to individual. Fate Analysis proposes instead that rather than being the carrier of the unconscious, heredity is an effect of the unconscious. A disease seeks to perpetuate itself in a population and compels the individual to pass it on.

Szondi, like Jung, doesn't assign sexuality pride of place. Sexual choice may be the most significant decision to be swayed by the familial unconscious, but so are vocational choices, friendship choices and even the way in which individuals die. In examining the story of Moses, for instance, Szondi makes none of Freud's adventurous conjectures, but interprets Moses as a palimpsest of the familial relations around him—not only is this Moses not an Egyptian, he is all of his ancestral tree in compacted form.[46] And instead of Oedipus, Szondi insisted on a "Cain complex," which derives precisely from the friction between the ego on the one hand and a person's heredity and their cultural milieu on the other.[47]

This radical decentering of the subject (which is the result of perversion, rather than the site of it) came to ensure the afterlife of Szondi's rather fringe theories. For it shared important features with the post-structuralist account of subjecthood, post-structuralism's own dissatisfaction with the oedipally determined nuclear family. When Gilles Deleuze and Felix Guattari undertook to free psychoanalysis of myth (and thus rethink what it meant to *repeat* the ancestral past), when they sought to

[45] Léopold Szondi, "Contributions to Fate Analysis," *Acta Psychologica* III (1937): 1–80; here 26.

[46] Szondi, *Moses—Antwort auf Kain* (Bern: Huber, 1973), 105.

[47] Szondi, *Kain, Gestalten des Bösen* (Bern: Huber, 1969), 115.

"de-oedipalize" and "undo the daddy-mommy spider web,"[48] Szondi became one of their path beyond Freud.[49]

At the same time, Szondi retains far more of Freud's humanism than Deleuze and Guattari suppose. He insists that treating genetics as "fate" is not simply to reverse Freud's more humanistic focus on the individual. Szondi distinguishes between an old and a new anancology. The Greek root *ananke* has two senses—on the one hand necessity, force, limitation by outside forces, and on the other hand consanguinity. Traditional anancology, for instance in Schopenhauer, focused entirely on the first sense; Szondi proposes to found his anancology on the second sense. His dynasties are half fated, half chosen—we end up with the family (and the familial unconscious) we have without having a choice in the matter; but while there are certain compulsions that guide our choice in partner (and though our partner is "genverwandt," or genetically related), we do choose. It is for that reason that Jens de Vleminck has dubbed Szondi a "tragic humanist"[50]: his obsession with genetics does not preclude human action or evacuate our choices of their meaning.

In his book *Freiheit und Zwangim Schicksal des Einzelnen* (1968), Szondi spells out how this shift changes the questions we may pose about fate: Since our genetic material is heterogeneous and different traits and drives vie in us, we do not have *one* fate in the mold of Oedipus. We have a choice and a certain degree of agency in expressing the many, frequently contradictory, traits that seek to dominate our daily actions. The question for "fate analysis" then becomes how to identify, analyze, and ultimately strengthen that faculty in us that could take on a reflective position vis-à-vis our multiple "fates." The subject thus carves out a kind of freedom, not *from* the dynastic chain, but rather *within* it. It is not that everything is possible for us; but we can be led to recognize the range of possibilities that heredity has left open to us. "Fate," Szondi writes, "is the totality of all inherited and freely choosable modes of existence."[51]

Was this perhaps also a way of addressing the problem of the psychoanalytic project's own vexed heredity? Freud had posited an oedipal family

[48] Gilles Deleuze and Félix Guattari, *Anti-Oedipus,* tr. Robert Hurley, Mark Seem, and Helen R. Lane (Minneapolis: University of Minnesota Press, 1987), 123.

[49] See Deleuze and Guattari, *Anti-Oedipus,* 319.

[50] Jens de Vleminck, "Tragic Choices: Fate, Oedipus, and Beyond." In: Arthur N. Cools and Thomas K. M. Crombez (Eds.), *The Locus of Tragedy* (Boston: Brill, 2008), 197–214; here 198.

[51] Szondi, *Freiheit und Zwang im Schicksal des Einzelnen* (Bern: Huber, 1968), 21.

as something liberating, and had sensed in the encroachment of the dynastic a threat. From the compulsive neurotics that returned from the war, to the political exploiters of the Death Drive, humanity's familial unconscious seemed to represent those forces that endangered Freud's life and work. It was what made him a refugee, what threatened to "demote" psychoanalysis to a specifically Jewish cultural practice, a kind of self-analysis of Moses' murderers. Jung, meanwhile, abandoned himself to the reassuring undulations of the collective unconscious with troubling ease. That its stark anti-humanism threatened to eclipse psychoanalysis's mission seemed to matter little to him.

Szondi's way of holding up compulsory fate (*Zwangsschicksal*) against free fate (*Freiheitsschicksal*) offered a third way. *Schicksal* in German is the thing that is sent to you, the hand you are dealt. But Szondi was insistent that your double heredity always deals you more than one hand. Psychoanalysis, in its guise as fate analysis, creates the space in which you can take stock and choose which one to play. What could have been more attractive as the Nazis scattered the psychoanalytic community throughout the world, sent Szondi and his young children to Bergen Belsen, and exterminated his community? But what could have been more attractive to the older Szondi, living by then in safety in Switzerland, not too far from Jung, than the idea that the question of whether psychoanalysis is Jewish or not, is German or not, is bourgeois European or not, might be in each case a false one? To Szondi, psychoanalysis could have multiple heredities, the trick was to look at them honestly, and then to choose from among the options they left open. Wotan, Jung had thought, seizes you in a state of *Ergriffenheit* (being deeply moved; literally: being grabbed), the individual has no say with regard to the past's claim on him or her. Szondi's form of psychoanalysis was premised on the conviction that, understood correctly, you could choose what seized you from the past.

Szondi's very designation of his enterprise represented one such moment. "Schicksalsanalyse"—no one could hear it without the thudding associations of what Heidegger would call the *Geschick*, "the history of Being as the *Geschick* of being."[52] It would be the analysis of that which is sent to us without our input; but also the analysis of what opens up for us without any action of our own. This is precisely not what Szondi has in mind: what fate and family bring to us we can master. In introducing his

[52] Martin Heidegger, *The Principle of Reason*, tr. Reginald Lilly (Bloomington: Indiana University Press, 1996), 110.

method to his English-speaking audience, Szondi tips his hand and implies that in fact his term has itself a dual extraction. It stands, as all of us do, at the intersection of two family trees. Throughout the English-language article in which he sought to introduce Fate Analysis to a broader readership, Szondi describes hereditary diseases as "matchmakers." It may strike one as an odd metaphor to use, at least it is one that has fallen out of fashion in modern genetics—we no longer think of passing on genes in terms as archaic as an extended courtship.

But in using the metaphor Szondi connects "fate analysis" to a longer lineage, a lineage that psychoanalysis had frequently repressed. After all, the matchmaker (*shadchan*) was still a common figure in Jewish culture and literature in the early twentieth century. And the term for the magical work performed by the *shadchanim*, somewhere between accident and necessity, between destiny and convenience, was *bashert*—fate. Szondi is thus culling his term for the notion of a dynastic unconscious from specifically Jewish custom. And at the same time, he is suggesting a dynastic unconscious for psychoanalysis: for much of Freud's life, psychoanalysis had avoided the question of how Jewish a practice it was. Szondi was suggesting it was Jewish through and through—but this parentage was not binding or determinative. In fact, *beshert* has also something of the German *Bescherung*; it is a gift we receive without having asked for it. Its multiple parentages were not its liability, they were its past's great gift. It was up to psychoanalysis to make its heritage its own.

PART III

Private and Public Fathers

CHAPTER 7

Black Fathers, Oedipal Issues, and Modernity

C. Jama Adams

Thesis

The African American father carries his own cultural and subjectively informed models of being fathered and being a father. Given the systemic racism that informs his life choices he is often struggling with a series of conflicts that exacerbate the aggression and competitive issues that are a feature of the oedipal. Central to these conflicts is the oedipal-like struggle with the cultural white father, whose ethos he admires but is also a source of rage given the constraints it places on him. In this chapter I review the historical and contemporary perspective on the oedipal and supplement them with a perspective on the role of race. Case vignettes are used to illustrate some ways in which intrapsychic and interpsychic struggles around oedipal issues are played out on both a cultural and familial level.

Research on African American fathers has historically focused on a very dysfunctional subgroup and then generalized to all fathers. When combined with the marginalization of fathers it is difficult to understand

C. J. Adams (✉)
John Jay College of Criminal Justice, The City University of New York, New York, NY, USA
e-mail: cadams@jjay.cuny.edu

L. Weissberg (ed.), *Psychoanalysis, Fatherhood, and the Modern Family*, https://doi.org/10.1007/978-3-030-82124-1_7

the role and intrapsychic dynamics of this population.[1] As an extension to that assertion, contemporary psychoanalytic theorizing and clinical work reflects an indifference to Black cultural experiences and their effects on intrapsychic functioning. Such lack makes it challenging to speak with confidence about Black oedipal issues. From a classical psychoanalytic perspective, the male child is fated to engage in an intrapsychic struggle to displace and exile the father as the mother's primary love object. At the same time the boy fears that the father in retaliation may castrate him. This generates high levels of anxiety given that his sister was castrated for harboring similar wishes.

The tactic for relief from this potentially castrating and alienating competition is to identify with the father and renounce his wish for the mother. Such a reversal opens the risk of a defensive hyper-masculinity as the basis of male gender development.[2] This process is presented as an inherent feature of being male and its working through is necessary for the development of a healthy masculine identity.

Modifications of the Classic Oedipal Complex

Formulating a less primitive response Nancy Chodorow notes that masculinity is a psychosocial as against a biological challenge for a boy.[3] The challenge for the boy is being parented by a woman, his dependency on her, and ambivalent identification with her, given that is not a male. At the same time the wish to be like the father is in tension with the wish to get rid of the father. The temptation is to reject the dependency and to deny the identification. Jessica Benjamin notes that switching the identification to the father does not resolve the issue of intrapsychic feelings of omnipotence.[4] The sense of masculinity may thus be linked to

[1] See C. Jama Adams, "Poor African-American Fathers: Healthy Moves." In: Kirkland C. Vaughans & Warren Spielberg (Eds.), *The Psychology of Black Boys and Adolescents* II (Santa Barbara: Praeger, 2014), 469–486; and Adams, "Black fatherhood in a time of fluidity," *Psychoanalytic Perspectives* 16 (2019): 326–339.

[2] Chris Blazina and Anne Bartone, Anne, "Moving Beyond Essentialism in the Contemporary Psychodynamic Psychology of Men: Implications for Theory and Research." In: Y. Joel Wong and Stephen R. Wester (Eds.), *APA Handbook of Men and Masculinities* (Washington: American Psychological Association, 2016), 105–122.

[3] See Blazina and Bartone, "Moving Beyond Essentialism."

[4] Jessica Benjamin, "The Omnipotent Mother: A Psychoanalytic Study of Fantasy and Reality." In: Donna Bassin, Margaret Honey, and Meryle Mahrer Kaplan (Eds.), *Representations of Motherhood* (New Haven: Yale University Press, 1994), 128–146.

both a negative identification with the mother and a positive identification with the father. Such dis-identification is damaging and constitutes boyhood trauma resulting in a fragile masculine self that uses primitive defenses such as splitting.[5] Adrienne Harris notes that many fathers are socialized as sons to be separate, and therefore often lack the pleasurable experience of intimate relating.[6] The emphasis is on separation and autonomy, as a consequence of which many fathers carry a sense of melancholy due to this lack and are experienced as remote. Michael Diamond argues that reframing the oedipal as a triad instead of a dyad offers rich possibilities for a less contentious realignment of identifications.[7] He posits a gradual process of dis-identification that embraces the masculine over time and need not be damaging. Such an approach is not dichotomous but instead integrates aspects of both gender styles as manifested by his parents. This view echoes the spirit of Margaret Mahler's separation individuation perspective through which individuality emerges as a function of selective identification with both parents.[8] This model eschews brittle independence but instead promotes healthy interdependence. The father is a model for the healthy modulation of affect; he is a protector and also demonstrates good-enough qualities such as tenderness traditionally identified with the essentialized mother.

Diamond notes that contemporary models of fathering are grounded in actual observations and clinical findings; theory informed by experience: "This work led to a deeper understanding of the intrapsychic impact entailing bodily/sensory, emotional, and intellectual interaction and attachment in the dyadic relationship."[9] Diamond goes on to note that the father is understood to signify a complex interaction between his actual presence, symbolic functioning, and internal representation in the child's mind as well as the mother's. The father, co-existing with mother and child, is both a symbolic figure and a real person and is thus less likely to

[5] Blazina and Bartone, "Moving Beyond Essentialism."

[6] Adrienne Harris, "Melancholic Fathers; Dangerous Fathers." Paper presented at the American Psychological Association: Division of Psychoanalysis Conference. New Orleans, April 2018.

[7] Michael Diamond, "Recovering the Father in Mind and Flesh: History, Triadic Functioning and Developmental Implications," *Psychoanalytic Quarterly* 86 (2017): 297–334.

[8] Margaret Mahler, Fred Pine, and Annie Bergman, (1975) *The Psychological Birth of the Human Infant.* New York: Basic Books, 1975.

[9] Diamond, "Recovering the Father in Mind and Flesh," 307.

be eclipsed in Tabitha Freeman's terms "under the shadow of the omnipresent nurturing mother."[10] This advance directly establishes the impact of both maternal and paternal subjectivity (309). Diamond further notes "Fathering's most important characteristics are discussed in accordance with father's actual and symbolic functioning within triadic reality and the familial context-including the mother's vital role in establishing and maintaining the paternal function" (298). Crucial for healthy function is his penetration of the mother-child dyad. Among other uses this creates space for adult intimacy. The father is also what Diamond refers to as a separating agent and an attracting object. Therefore, there is no definitive way of doing masculinity but instead multiple healthy ways. This speaks to not only a range of masculinities within a culture but within the self.[11]

Robert Grossmark and others have argued that an important theme in the Oedipus myth that is evident in fathers is that of not knowing.[12] There is the expectation of the enactment of a role of assertiveness, if not aggression, buffering, and tenderness that lacks an experiential base. The reality is that of ignorance as to how to engage with their particular internalized father and with their expectant sons. Beginning at birth is the ever-evolving developmental tasks of individuation, identification, and the management of the accompanying affective and cognitive vicissitudes.[13] In that regard one fruitful approach to interpreting the oedipal phase is that of a tension between intrapsychic struggles around omnipotence and helplessness and an awareness of the subjective reality of significant others.[14] On the level of subject reality is an awareness of significant others as gendered, racialized beings with varying degrees of authority. On the intrapsychic levels is the managing of developmentally driven feelings around control and fears of abandonment. The challenge is not to privilege one set of tensions over the other but to develop good-enough ways of managing them. Recognizing the difference between the projection of a feeling into a significant other and recognizing the subjective reality of the

[10] Cited in Diamond, "Recovering the Father in Mind and Flesh," 309.

[11] See Blazina and Bartone, "Moving Beyond Essentialism."

[12] Robert Grossmark, "The Anguish of Fatherhood and the Crisis of Subjectivity." Paper presented at the American Psychological Association: Division of Psychoanalysis conference. New Orleans, April 2018.

[13] Karen Gilmore, "Psychoanalytic Developmental Theory: A Contemporary Reconsideration," *Journal of the American Psychoanalytic Association*, 53 (2008): 885–907.

[14] See Benjamin, "The Omnipotent Mother."

other as an individual separate from one's projection is crucial for managing feelings of omnipotence and helplessness.

The challenge for all caregivers is to productively hold and work the tension between their fantasies of omnipotence, including the lack thereof and the reality of their lived experience as influenced by race, gender, and class, and their intergenerational heritage. As Benjamin among others have noted, psychoanalytic theorizing has tended to focus on the intrapsychic aspects of parenting as embodied in the mother-child dyad and has marginalized the interpersonal and larger social reality as embodied by the father and the subjective realities within which the triad is embedded. This is especially relevant to Black fathers who, given the reality of their marginalization, struggle with the intrapsychic conflicts around omnipotence, dependency, and identification. Benjamin proposes a model that does not overly privilege intrapsychic fantasies or cultural and subjective realities. She argues that a crucial tension that informs oedipal issues is the tension between the intrapsychic fantasies of the mother and the subjective reality of her. The fantasies around the mother's omnipotence and the child's helplessness are modulated by his perceptions of the mother in reality. Oedipal issues in terms of having mother to the exclusion of father recedes in the son's growing awareness of his mother subjectivities and his inability to meet her needs.

As part of that reality is his realization of gender imbalances around authority that would lessen his sense of her as omnipotent. His continued dependency on her can fuel feelings of helplessness. His ability to hold these states in tension as he matures limits intrapsychic fears of being engulfed or wishing to destroy the mother. It strengthens his sense of being separate from her and having developmentally appropriate notions of self and autonomy. The mother's stance toward the father as observed by the son also contributes to his identity work. As a function of her own paternal history, she might well enact a dominant and unsatisfactory patriarchal model that rejects matriarchal inter-dependency and marginalizes the father. Alternatively, she may facilitate an inclusive fathering by coaching him on both tenderness and routine childcare. They may also renegotiate breadwinner roles where possible.

Managing these tensions is challenging for the father given that his own childhood experiences may have included a bias toward unattainable fantasies given the lack of a father and the elusiveness in reality of the mother. Then again, the reality of the limits of the mother's authority in the context of poverty or an overbearing father may have exacerbated a heightened sense of helplessness. The child's subjective perception of his father's omnipotence in relation to the mother, and in the context of his relationship to larger realities will also influence his own approach to his gender identity and sense of authority. The child will observe the pragmatic obstacles to achieving goals such as the low quality of education, bleak employment possibilities, and the stultifying costs of respectability.[15] They will also understand the illusion of meritocracy when one is not granted the resources to achieve outcomes held in high esteem.[16] This is alongside models of assertiveness by white men, and exceptional Black men doing healthy masculinities against the odds and those doing attractive but often costly enactments.

These positions on the oedipal have been critiqued. Neil Altman argues that the contemporary models reflect the dominant ethos of competition and aggression and resource insufficiency.[17] Love is a scarce commodity that one must compete for, but ultimately one ends up dissatisfied and feeling incomplete. In a similar vein Todd McGowan speaks to the tendency of capitalist systems to sculpt desire in pursuit of an ever-elusive sense of being assuaged.[18] Despite an apparent abundance of resources, the contemporary individual does not feel assuaged. Psychoanalysis focuses on the intrapsychic sense of lack with regarding to desire satisfaction but appears oblivious to the social reality of resource insecurity experienced by so many including Black fathers.[19] The illusion is that all desires can eventually be assuaged, which implies that resource desire is purely an intrapsychic lack, reflective of the neoliberal attempt to portray the good-enough society as an everyday reality.

Such a patriarchal position highlights the critique of the tension between the symbolic father and the father in reality. There is a paradox

[15] Adams, "Respect and Reputation: The Construction of Masculinity in Poor African American Men," *Journal of African American Studies* 11 (2007):157–172.

[16] Marianne Cooper, "*The False Promise of Meritocracy*," *The Atlantic* (2015); https://www.theatlantic.com/business/archive/2015/12/meritocracy/418074/ (access March 2021).

[17] Neil Altman, *The Analyst in the Inner City: Race, Class and Culture Through a Psychoanalytic Lens*, Hillsdale: The Analytic Press, 1995.

[18] Todd McGowan, *Capitalism and Desire: The Psychic Cost of Free Markets.* New York: Columbia University Press, 2016.

[19] John Creamer, *Inequalities persist despite decline in poverty for all major race and Hispanic origin groups.* United States Census Bureau, 2020 https://www.census.gov/library/stories/2020/09/poverty-rates-for-blacks-and-hispanics-reached-historic-lows-in-2019.html (access March 2021).

here as the father is symbolically all powerful even as he is marginalized within the triad. "Indeed, psychoanalytic theory recreates the fundamental paradoxes of patriarchy by giving central place to the father as a symbolic figure of authority while eclipsing men's relationships with their infants under the shadow of the omnipresent nurturing mother."[20] Diamond and others have argued that the symbolic father is remote, the enforcer of the law, and always potentially punitive. In this regard Harris notes that contemporary fathers "are burdened by the psychic labor of holding up and representing the symbolic, of being the practitioners of limit setting and lack while being starved of bereft of tenderness, the imaginary, the going on being as Winnicott imagines early relatedness."[21] This resonates with Diamond's points regarding the father's marginalized position in the triad, in tension with the social expectation of dominance. This is often exacerbated in Black fathers with an expectation of performance but a lack of experience and resources. Harris goes on to note that given their lack of the appropriate paternal competencies, some fathers will present a brittle hyper-masculinity and illusory omnipotence. Therefore, the risk is that the father will re-enact his own rage at the lack of insufficient nurturing and protection, that in turn can lead to attacks within the triad or flight.

There is a twist to the interpsychic and intrapsychic reality of the Black father that goes unaddressed in contemporary American psychoanalysis. He must struggle to make sense of the legacies of his biological father and that of the cultural white father, who invariable dominates, exploits, and constrains. This need for both intrapsychic and relational vigilance often sculpts a fathering stance that is aggressive and punitive in the service of protection.[22] Paternal nurturing is often expressed as constraining developmentally appropriate self-assertion by his child. The intent is to protect the child against the rage of the cultural white father. It is often manifested in a punitive manner, given the father's own lack of a model of paternal tenderness.

[20] Tabitha Freeman, "Psychoanalytic Concepts of Fatherhood: Patriarchal Paradoxes and the Presence of an Absent Authority," *Gender and Sexuality* 9 (2008): 113–139, here 115.

[21] Harris, "Melancholic Fathers; Dangerous Fathers," 1.

[22] Adams, "Social and Psychoanalytic Perspectives on the Use of Physical Punishment among Low-Income African Americans," *The Psychoanalytic Study of the Child,* 73 (2020): 73–90.

The Culturally "White Father"

Black fatherhood can be manifested in myriad ways all influenced by his family culture and also by the pervasive cultural white father. These competing narratives create conflicts that can be well managed and need not be enacted as negative oedipal struggles. The core paternal function is to tutor a son in a healthy model of masculinities in relation to body, and affective, cognitive, and relationship management.[23] The quality of fatherhood that is enacted is subject to the influence of intergenerational legacies, contemporary resources, and the facilitating or constraining role of the State. The values of a traditional white male elite masculinity profoundly influence the way Black fatherhood is enacted. Intergenerational legacies speak to both healthy and dysfunctional models of fatherhood passed on from one generation to the next. Central to "good-enough" fathering is the availability of opportunities necessary to acquire the capabilities to generate the requisite material and psychological resources.

By the State, I mean the political directorate, teachers, criminal justice officials, and the healthcare community with its swelling ranks of surveilling and therapeutic agents. Related actors such as the business community and the media have a long history of being complicit with the State, in both influencing and reinforcing its constraining and racist policies. Black fathers must therefore be vigilant of the actions of the State given its oppressive and at times murderous stance toward its Black citizens, especially Black males. So, the Black father struggles with a series of Oedipal conflicts arising from his intrapsychic relationship with two fathers; the patriarchal white father who seeks dominion overall, and his Black father who often presents as a petit patriarch.

I use the term "white father" as the embodiment of an ethos articulated and enforced by a form of white masculinity. The core theme is domination and control in the service of maintaining white masculine hegemony. This controlling ethos speaks to a deep fear of helplessness and the resulting vulnerability that comes from depending on the Other, such as the Black, the female, and those necessarily viewed as inferior. Acknowledging commonality and inter-dependency would mean relinquishing power and the sense of superiority and domination and that comes with that. For the

[23] Donald Moss, *Thirteen Ways of Looking at a Man: Psychoanalysis and Masculinity*. New York: Routledge, 2012.

white father the son qua Other is a risk in the sense of evoking feelings of dependency, envy, and love.

Forever vigilant and fearful, the cultural white father deploys racism and within-white wariness and competition. His ethos has its roots in divine rights, patriarchy and capitalism, and the subordination of the Other. It profoundly influences self-making and therefore the intrapsychic actions of all persons in the American space. As such it is internalized by whites and Blacks, men and women who often enact it in an unreflective way. This system of white patriarchal control is continuously evolving in its attempts to maintain its hegemony. What remains consistent is its adroit pursuit of traditional masculine forms of control and as such it is firmly embedded in the institutions of power. This facilitates it continuing to inform all race and gender-based assertions and constrains attempt at challenging its hegemony. At this point in its evolution, it is less crude, less visible but still effective in oppressing and co-opting. Especially effective is its capacity to co-opt and generate petit patriarchs through the granting of treasure and status, in exchange for obedience and silence.

Specific to fatherhood, the white father is the ultimate father who in classic oedipal style views his cultural offspring with ambivalence. He admires the Black male's strength and creativity, but also fears it might be deployed against him. Given the racist nature of American patriarchy, the Black father is therefore a subjugated being. He is subjected to high degrees of surveillance and control with limited access to resources, status, dignity, and parental autonomy. He must forego any firm assumptions of having his paternal agency consistently respected and supported.

Arising Conflicts

Such restraints create a series of conflicts for the Black father that are enacted in the arenas of work and relating. These conflicts are mediated through institutional practices and within the Black father's own family system. The Black father is often in conflict with the white father as he both identifies with him, given his own patriarchal fantasies, while also raging against his racist constraints. He has internalized the white patriarchal model and its ethos of dominance, envies the white father's authority, and therefore often strives to be like him. The refusal by the white father to validate his aspirations, by not granting him resources and respect, engenders feelings of anger and despair.

The second core conflict arises from attempting to guide his son's developmentally appropriate strivings in the assertion of self. The father must often constrain such strivings and thereby distort his son's development, given realistic fears of the racist predations against his child by state and private actors.[24] This conflict can result in punitive measures by the father that speak to both an attempt to protect the child and his own fears of the child's threat to his own patriarchal tendencies.[25] The model of his own father that he carries intrapsychically might very well be that of a petit patriarch mimicking the White father. However, given the constraints, the Black father's frustrations are displaced unto his son. This then becomes the adult's son legacy to his own son.

Given the entrenched and enduring nature of racism these conflicts can never be truly resolved; at best they are managed with varying degrees of efficacy. One costly approach is to challenge the white father, to take on the system, which inevitably results in harsh disciplining if not death. Black men experience high rates of homicide, suicide, and incarceration, and these adverse outcomes speak to often rage driven enactments against the white father or displacement unto peers and family. Despair and flight as a defense against feelings of being ineffectual are also quite common. Aware that he lacks the resources to attack the system he turns the rage against himself and withdraws from the role of father.

The adaptive management of a third conflict offers guarded hope. Here the father struggles to adopt "feminist" and healthy African American parenting strategies. This in turn requires him to relinquish racist and misogynistic interpellations that mimic the cultural white father but alienates the Black father from himself and from the triad. The hope in reorienting is the gratification derived from a grounded role in the triad that draws on healthy cultural practices and eschews fantasies of dominance and the attendant frustrations and displacements.

Social Aspects of the Oedipal

Psychoanalytic development theories are ideally informed by principles of development that provide a context for theorizing about the unfolding and effect of the oedipal, among other foundational issues. Karen Gilmore has written cogently on these framing principles. She broadens the

[24] Nancy Boyd-Franklin, *Black Families in Therapy*. New York: The Guilford Press, 1989.

[25] Adams, "Social and Psychoanalytic Perspectives."

emphasis on environment as a facilitating factor in the nature and quality of the development that is observed: "The theory should recognize the demands imposed by the larger near environment and the still larger remote environment, including the cognitive and social expectations of each developmental epoch as realized in a given culture, such as attitudes toward gender, morality, and the future. It would consider how these affect the individual child as a product of a particular culture in a particular time."[26]

Examining lived experience from a sociologically informed perspective can enrich psychoanalytic theorizing and treatment. This emphasis allows us to have some insight into the life of Mike Tyson, the former heavy boxing champion. Tyson's mother was mentally ill and there apparently was no father or well-functioning complimentary caregiver. Rather than nurture and protect him, she apparently oscillated between neglect and abuse.[27] Tyson's self-awareness began to coalesce around anger and flight. His speech impediment made him a target for peers, who one sensed had their own rage, lack of protection, and injurious projections. Tyson learned to fight to stay alive.

In the absence of any substantive surrogate ego, fate smiled on Tyson in the form of Gus D'Amato, a renowned boxing coach who tutored Tyson in the art of fighting. Equally important he lived with D'Amato and his wife in a home where there was structure, protection, and emotional nurturing. Tyson thrived as a person and as a boxer, but unfortunately his beloved coach died. He was left adrift in a world of grifters, violence, and disingenuous appeals to his primitiveness and fragile sense of self-control. Not surprisingly he was incarcerated for rape. His necessary internalization of toxic masculinities facilitated his survival on the street but the identifications he adopted did not contribute to competencies around aggression management, reflective functioning, or verbal dexterity. There was no sustained safe space to work on understanding his rage or to mourn the absence of a good-enough parents. Here the oedipal resolution is primitive with an over-identification with the powerful, rageful, and punitive father but also with the narcissistic and predatory mother.[28]

[26] Gilmore, "Psychoanalytic Developmental Theory," 898.

[27] Daphne Merkin, "*Mike Tyson moves to the suburbs*," *New York Times* (2011); https://www.nytimes.com/2011/03/20/magazine/mag-20Tyson-t.html (access March 2021).

[28] Harold Blum, "The Dawn of the Oedipus Complex: A Tale of Two Letters," Published in this volume.

Again, someone saw good and possibilities in him. He married a caring and grounded woman, Kiki, who like his adopted parents protected and loved him. She withdrew him from the gritty, overstimulating, and dangerous precincts of his youth and ensconced the family in a gated community in Arizona. Tyson is now a much calmer and thoughtful individual who can love and control his volcanic rage. Tyson's receptivity to work on his self-regulation skills speaks to caution around over-privileging culture or early experiences.[29] He worked with his coach, on harnessing his aggression, enabling him to stay safe while incarcerated. With his wife he demonstrated the crucial ability to be available to embrace introjects that strengthened his ego, his capacity for intimacy, and healthy defense deployment. Equally important he did not demonstrate the possibly fatal loss of freedom that can occur with the narrowing of options that can come with the maturation and solidification of, what in Tyson's case, would be a toxic ego style.[30]

Individuals in the multiplicity of roles that they play are embedded in cultures that frame and influence how they play those roles. Through the avenue of the social unconscious their imaginations are tutored as to the expectations of everyday behaviors.[31] These expectations invariably reflect the interests of dominant and mostly white male elites. Here we see the structuring of agency in ways that do not necessarily serve the best interest of the individual. The Black father must therefore struggle with ideological disingenuity in which he often internalizes the dominant models of masculinity but often is denied the cognitive, material, and rights resources to be a good-enough father. There is an ironic aspect of the cultural oedipal here as the identification with the cultural white father is encouraged only to a point. The long history of Black intergenerational truth-making cautions the Black father on the white cultural limitations on his attempts to be a good-enough father.[32] Many rage against these limitations making them ineffective in the triad, while others are vigilant

[29] See Benjamin, "The Omnipotent Mother"; and Gilmore, "Psychoanalytic Developmental Theory."

[30] See Gilmore, "Psychoanalytic Developmental Theory."

[31] Phia S. Salter and Glenn Adams, "Provisional Strategies for Decolonizing Consciousness." In: Felice Blake, Paula Ioanide, Alison Reed (Eds.), *Anti-Racism, Inc.: Why the Way We Talk About Racial Justice Matters* (New York: punctum books, 2019), 299–325.

[32] Tommy Curry, *The Man-Not: Race, Class, Genre and the Dilemmas of Black Manhood*. Philadelphia: Temple University Press, 2017.

in ways that project into the child a model of manhood overly attuned to caution and obedience.[33]

The normative family model has always been a nuclear one, ideally headed by the father and fairly independent of supporting kin. One takes as a given that many within the contemporary African American population have been socialized into this model. The model was supported by the patriarchal structure of the society enshrined in its laws and enforced through its economic structures. Azille Coetzee references the work of Judith Butler, in noting that kinship ties are often socially constructed as seemingly non-ideological, and therefore natural and unquestioned.[34] The privileging of the Western nuclear model and the provision of legal and material supporting structures was for the most part limited to white families. Given these constraints Africana persons have sought to maintain elements of their African-based family practices that have evolved over time in the American cultural space.[35] The ambivalence of the dominant culture to Africana kinship arrangements was costly not only to the Africana community but also to America in general. Coetzee's makes the general point about the distorting and pathological effects of patriarchy and capital on kinship ties.

By way of illustration, Black males were often valued for their role in the sexual aspect of reproductive success—ensuring biological enslavement—while being unconsciously socialized and structurally prevented from making substantive cognitive, emotional, and material contributions.[36] Here we see the use of an essentialist seeming formulation deployed for dehumanizing and commodifying desire. Elements of such oppression and the attendant poor outcomes are still evident in contemporary times, as reflected in terms referring to fathers as "sperm donor" and "Deadbeat Dad." This discriminatory treatment created a moral conflict for the white elites. Their religious mores spoke to the humanity and equality of all human beings, including enslaved persons. So, they could not be thought of as being non-human. This conflict was operationally but not dynamically resolved by acknowledging enslaved persons as humans, but of a lesser order. On a hierarchy of beings, they

[33] Adams, "Social and Psychoanalytic Perspectives."

[34] Azille Coetzee, "Antigone, Empire, and the Legacy of Oedipus: Thinking African Decolonization Through the Articulation of Kinship Rules," *Hypatia* 14 (2019): 464–484.

[35] Boyd-Franklin, *Black Families in Therapy*.

[36] Jay Wade, "African American Fathers and Sons: Social, Historical, and Psychological Considerations," *The Journal of Contemporary Social Services* 75 (1994): 561–570.

were inferior and lacked the higher intellectual qualities to ever be the equal of their white counterparts.[37] Not only were they intellectually inferior but were also less able to control their primitivity.[38]

This disingenuous intellectual sleight of hand solved four problems. It met the religious mandate to "care" for others. It sustained white domination of whites over Blacks which allowed for their continuing political subjugation and economic exploitation. Black gendered bodies, through their purported primitiveness, became a container for the projected and disavowed sexuality and aggression of the whites. The intellectual lie that Blacks were inferior was crucial for supporting the shaky edifice of white superiority and independence. As children of a politically harsh and withholding cultural white father, they were also excluded from the political sphere where, as free thinking and respected citizens, they could advocate for change. So, many Africana persons underperformed given their lack of the resources necessary to acquire formal capabilities.

Finally, from an intrapsychic perspective, these "reigning regimes of representation"[39] established the cultural white father as the unconsciously immoral father of all, thereby usurping the role of the Black father. The white father enacted his own oedipal rage by often symbolically, and sometimes literally killing off the Black father thereby stripping him off his parental authority, and his exclusive sexual right to his intimate partner. He would often sexually abuse and claim the Black mother as his own. One can think of the symbolic white father as the original abusive, unsupportive, and absent father. Equally important were these predations including the marginalization of healthy Black family structures, such as extensive kinship groups. These were routinely decimated, through the sale of kin, the lack of property rights, the theft of their surplus, all in the service of economic gain and political control.[40] Part of the pain was the reinforcing of the lack of authority of Black parents and a disregard for the psychological importance of the parent-child triad.

[37] Ogunnaike Oludamini, "From Heathen to Sub-Human: A Genealogy of the Influence of the Decline of Religion on the Rise of Modern Racism," *Open Theology* (2016): 785–803.

[38] Franz Fanon, *Black Skin, White Masks.* New York: Grove Press, 1967; and Stephen Frosh, "Psychoanalysis, Colonialism, Racism," *Journal of Theoretical and Philosophical Psychology* 33 (2013): 141–154.

[39] Judith Butler, referred to in Coetzee, "Antigone, Empire, and the Legacy of Oedipus," 468.

[40] Eric Williams, *Capitalism and Slavery.* Durham. NC. Duke University Press, 1994.

Given that a marker of a "good" father was that he was productive citizen, the structurally facilitated under-resourcing and limited opportunities, constrained the ability of many Black parents to meet the nurturance and protective needs of themselves and their children. It also fueled the age-old canard of them as having some fundamental lack. What is crucial here is that while the white nuclear model devalued the work of women, the racist model of Black family life devalued the work of both mothers and fathers.

With regard to kinship norms in contemporary culture, Coetzee cites Butler who notes that, "kinship has become fragile, porous and expansive."[41] She further cites Butler as attributing these changes as having occurred "because of global displacements of people, divorce and a proliferation in sexual orientations and sexual identities, among other things" (468). Butler asks, "what will be the legacy of Oedipus for those who are formed in these situations, where positions are hardly clear, where the place of the father is dispersed, where the place of the mother is multiply occupied or dispersed, where the symbolic in its stasis no longer holds" (468). Again, in the service of domination and exploitation, the privileged kinship rules informed how we—including psychoanalysis—assessed good-enough parenting. Marginalized kinship rules, such as Africana ways, had to be considered less than civilized. In this regard, Coetzee notes "different forms of familial and gender organization betray deviance and monstrosity, (associated with Blackness and proving necessary inferiority)" (469). One perspective on the history of whiteness is its within-whiteness porousness and its vigilance in excluding the remotest whiff of Blackness.[42] Africana kinship structures are therefore still not part of the "civilized" repertoire of good-enough parenting or rigorous theorizing about kinship. A troubling consequence is that Africana family epistemologies are not known. Given the normative frames of reference and projection needs, those kinship models become the site of that which we cannot afford to acknowledge about certain forms of white Western kinship. These would include the debilitating effects on predatory capitalist practices on family functioning.

[41] Butler, cited in Coetzee, "Antigone, Empire, and the Legacy of Oedipus," 468.

[42] Coetzee, "Antigone, Empire, and the Legacy of Oedipus."

Capitalism and the Issue of Resources

The dominant model for resource distribution is capitalism. Individual identity and family roles are tightly yoked to the capacity of the individual and family unit to generate the resources necessary to love and work. Success in this task is often linked to the acquisition and deployment of cognitive resources necessary to generate the treasure and material acquisitions by which success is measured. The capitalist is adroit at manipulating emotional states that result in unthoughtful consumption in the pursuit of fleeting pleasure or the temporary reduction of pain.

Capitalism is an amoral system of resource acquisition that when framed by ethics can facilitate exploration and innovation in the service of good-enough well-being. Outside of an ethical framework it lends itself to primitive enactments through the pursuit of immediate pleasure, and satisfaction at the cost of caring for others and for the environment. In this regard ethical forces as embodied by the state have retreated from their role of constraining unethical practices and protecting the commons.[43] In the spirit of a progressive ethical stance, the failure of the state to contain the primitive leaves unprotected the vulnerable and the disenfranchised.

Regarding the immoral ways in which capitalism can be deployed, it puts men who unthoughtfully enact traditional masculinities—including fathers—at risk for marginalizing affective awareness in the areas of controlling aggression and embracing tenderness. The emphasis on a market-oriented cognitivism and on consumption entrenches traditional and limiting gender roles. The father orients toward the market to fulfill his role as the provider of worldly knowledge and material goods, staying on the periphery of the emotional aspects of the triad.

Capitalism has also been deployed as the handmaiden of subjugation and has been central in enslavement, genocide, and environmental despoliation.[44] Its role in the marginalization of the despised Other, the unwilling recipient of projected rage and envy has had especially dire consequences for Black fathers. Again, the cultural enactment of the oedipal drama is instructive. The white construction of Blackness imagines the Black as child-like and inferior, a conception necessary to justify their subordinate and exploitive status. At the same time due to unremitting

[43] Dirk Philipsen, "Economics for the People" (2020); https://aeon.co/essays/the-challenge-of-reclaiming-the-commons-from-capitalism (access March 2021).

[44] Williams, *Capitalism and Slavery*.

resistance against dehumanization, Blacks affirm their capacity to be productive and caring. The intrapsychic challenge for the white elites is how to manage their desire to continue to exploit Blacks, while acknowledging their demand to be treated in a humane fashion. For the white elites there is a realistic need to subdue the Black, whom if acknowledged as an equal, might well psychologically kill him by challenging his intrapsychic illusion of superiority. The Black challenges the cultural white father who through oedipal-like enactments responds with muted rage, but more importantly resource and rights deprivation.[45]

In the hyper-individualistic iteration of late capitalism, the state is less inclined to facilitate equal opportunity to access the resources necessary to live a good-enough life. For low-income Blacks this often results in a scarcity of good-paying work, with much low paying work available and by necessity taken by low-income women and mothers. This systemic gender and racial discrimination results in the under-resourcing of Black family life thereby adding stress to the triad. To the degree that Black parents' privilege unattainable and archaic gender roles, they exacerbate oedipal tensions. The mother and father may both feel that he is failing to "man up" to be the head of the household and the provider of material resources. Such a failure may result in a mutually agreed upon withdrawal from the triad, expulsion by maternal fiat, or an adoption by the father of illegitimate approaches to acquiring resources. One might also observe regressive enactments in which the father becomes another son, overly dependent on the often-meager resource capabilities of the mother. In these scenarios there is an unconscious expectation of an unattainable level of family self-sufficiency, given the lack of systemic support.

Black Fathers and Oedipal Issues

Blackness comes unbidden to the individual and influences but does not define him. As with all other social constructions it constrains and facilitates self-development and is subject over time to the contingent acts of a reflective and agentic self. As such there are infinite ways to define and assert a sense of Blackness within and between racialized, gendered, and

[45] Valerie Wilson and Jhacova Williams, "Racial and Ethnic Income Gaps Persist Amid Uneven Growth in Household Incomes." Economic Policy Institute (2019); https://www.epi.org/blog/racial-and-ethnic-income-gaps-persist-amid-uneven-growth-in-household--incomes/ (access March 2021).

class-informed social arrangements. As a resistance to oppression a weak commonality across the infinitely individualized sense of the community of Black persons is a sense of struggle for human rights, dignity, and resources.[46] This is both an intrapsychic and interpsychic reality that influences self-definition, fantasy, affect regulation and relating. Specific to Black fathers, but not limited to them, are some core issues that will be discussed in detail: *managing dyadic and triadic demands; self-management with a focus on aggression and tenderness; re-imagining gendered parenting roles, the contributions of the (maternal) co-parenting to good-enough fathering, managing the non-(maternal) co-parent relationship*, and *managing inter and intra-generational introjects.*

Central to healthy fathering is the willingness and the capacity to be immersed in the triad with child and co-parent and in separate but related dyads with the child and with the co-parent. Such involvement is mutually beneficial and strengthens internalizations of distinct and loving minds. Real experiences that are well managed constrain the more toxic and feared aspects of the triad in mind. Given the lack of healthy parenting skills many fathers approach their task with some trepidation. This concern around having the capacities to be a good-enough father was evident in a case discussed in an earlier paper I was working with an inexperienced father who was feeling frustrated and incompetent in managing his toddler.[47] The toddler suddenly stopped whining and started laughing. The father's first thought was one of aggression given that he felt his son was aggravating him, but he was able to contain the impulse and realized that his son was "playing him," upon which they both laughed. He was not only able to see his son as a distinct person but was also able to see himself in his son. His openness to being engaged by his son, on the child's terms, facilitated the insight that shifted him from anger at the child, to one of jocular mutuality.

Managing negative oedipal urges means coming to terms with the psychological reality of the child rather than the fantasy of the desired child. Accepting the differentiation that comes about as the child

[46] Radley Balko, "There's Overwhelming Evidence that the Criminal Justice System is Racist. Here's the Proof," *The Washington Post* (2020); https://www.washingtonpost.com/graphics/2020/opinions/systemic-racism-police-evidence-criminal-justice-system/ (access March 2021); and Christine Benz, "75 Must-Know Statistics About Race, Income, and Wealth." *Morning Star* (2020); https://www.morningstar.com/articles/987356/75-must-know-statistics-about-race-income-and-wealth (access March 2021).

[47] See Adams, "Poor African-American Fathers."

individuates and celebrating his role in that process, compensates for the necessary mourning of the disappearance of the imagined child. For fathers with potent and often unacknowledged fantasies of creating the son that they never were, fathering often results in a relationship of coercion, resistance, and disappointment. We have all seen the sons who became reluctant physicians, and under-performing athletes as a result of a denied opportunity to individuate.

Given their less than adequate sense of themselves as emotionally competent fathers, some will defensively flee from the triad. They must cope with the shame of perceived paternal incompetency and the anger at the internalized competent father. This is especially pressing for Black fathers, some of whom are raised exclusively by female caregivers, themselves often single and with absent or peripheral male co-parents. My own experience is suggestive of a similar dynamic between Black males. As a college professor I regularly interact with the relatively few Black male college students. One student was hungry for my attention and sought to use me to work out his sense of being abandoned. Apparently, his father frequently read to him prior to withdrawing from his life. So, the student was drawn to me because I was knowledgeable but also angry at me because I was not as available to chat with him, nor would I explore in depth with him his father hunger. Avoiding the temptation to defensively double down on being didactic and remote, I was able to nurture him sufficiently for him to follow up on a therapy referral that I gave him.

A Case Vignette

Many years ago, I met Winston, a twenty-eight-year-old Black man, while I was walking down the street. A car with heavily tinted windows pulled up close to me and I noticed pedestrians quickly distancing from me. A passenger called out to me, *Doc, can I talk to you.* The driver and the three passengers were all hard-looking men. The entire scenario said that I was dealing with a feared drug dealer and his bodyguards. I didn't know this person and thought to myself: *This is different.* I went over to the window, stuck out my hand, and introduced myself. He paused, shook my hand, and said: *I know who you are.* I waited. He wasn't a current undergraduate student of mine, nor was he my therapy client at the nearby community clinic where I worked. I also could not recall him being present at the workshops I did with parents of preschoolers at two local schools.

"*Can we talk?*": I thought it prudent not to ask him for a topic in the presence of his henchmen. Working class Black men, cum drug dealers do not generally acknowledge having psychological problems, nor do they routinely seek therapeutic consultations. Even if they are interested in therapy, they are often reluctant to come into a clinic or therapy office. I suggested to him that we take a stroll through a nearby park, an approach that I have successfully used in the past.[48] He explained that the mother of his three-year-old son had attended a workshop I gave on how to raise healthy Black children. She had shared with him my point that children needed fathers and wanted him to be more involved in their son's life. He was not sure he wanted to be more involved and that even if he did, he wouldn't know what to do.

Winston exuded aggression in the combative way he walked, and through his definitive, don't-even-think-of-arguing-with-me style of speaking. At the same time, I sensed that he was eager to connect with me, that there was something that I could do for him, and that he was insightful enough to know that he could not coerce me into doing it. I wondered about what the child's mother had said to him, and how she had said it in a way that he could hear and act on it. I had to think quickly, as here was an appeal for help from a man who exuded aggression and was feared. I was intrigued by the idea of working with him, yet given his lifestyle, strolling through the park was perhaps not the safest way for me to do work with him. His reputation and his antipathy to therapy meant he would not come to the clinic. I asked him where he would be comfortable meeting and he suggested a local coffee shop. He was quick to tell me that he would pay me, whatever my rate was in cash, and did not need a receipt. We set up an appointment and I told him I would need to meet with him four to five times to get a sense of the issues and to have something useful to say to him.

As I wended my way home, I thought about the challenges of being a father given the risks in also being a manager or "Don" in a drug dealing enterprise. There was also the issue of my personal safety given the endemic violence that was a part of that business. I made some calls and confirmed who this individual was. Winston was a "senior" distributer who was feared but also admired for his philanthropy and his intolerance of violence, other than what he meted out. The middle-aged female receptionist at the

[48] Adams, "Poor African-American Fathers."

office said she liked him because he respected and protected women and children.

Winston would not agree to a consistent meeting time and sometimes weeks would pass before he would schedule his next appointment. We met on and off for over three years, although rarely did we have more than three sessions in a month. There were breaks of up to three months, but I noted an interest variation of emotional refueling. Winston knew my work location and schedule. With little predictability, during the long breaks, he would sometimes just happen to be driving past when I was entering or leaving the building. I would wait for him to wave and then wave back; he would then continue on his way. I never commented on my sense of the dynamic reasons why he needed to intermittently distance from me and yet maintain contact. I did stress my availability when he called, and I declined his offer to pay a handsome premium to be able to see me at short notice.

Winston was the only child for a father who spent long stretches incarcerated for crimes of violence resulting from distributing guns. Winston was proud that the police were never able to convict his father for gun possession. His mother, who worked in retail, would take him intermittently to visit his father in jail although both parents were ambivalent about exposing him to that environment. Winston was fascinated by the men he saw there and would interrogate his father as to the crimes they had committed. His father would not indulge these queries and would tell him to focus on his schoolwork and listening to his mother. Winston's father made a point that stuck with him. "He told me that everyone in jail had fucked up, that they had made mistakes and gotten caught. But it didn't stop there. He said that there were a lot of really smart guys there who like him, had made dumb choices. He pointed to one who he called a philosopher, and another who was the go-to expert on legal issues. I asked him what he made of all of that. He was silent for a while. I think he wanted better for me. He died in jail from tuberculosis when I was 13. I think it's too late for me, but I want better for my son."

Winston portrayed his mother as loving but "wounded." She had apparently tried to get his father to pursue legitimate paths to success, all to no avail. On numerous occasions she perjured herself to protect him and transported weapons and cash for him. She had managed to keep Winston on the straight and narrow with support from his father, but that ended when the father died. She was astute enough to know that he needed a male relationship but could not find a Black therapist and

Winston had no interest in sports or karate. Winston took to the street under the tutelage of older veterans of street life and drug dealing. Winston's intellectual prowess kept him out of jail, and his focused rage made him feared and appeared to keep him physically safe.

Winston respected the mother of his child but was at times wary of her: "She takes really good care of our son and she is not after my money, although I make sure they are well taken care of. She doesn't hassle me, but like my parents, she thinks I could do better than drug dealing. She doesn't preach about it, just a look, or a comment every now and then. I feel I am disappointing her in a funny kind of way. So, I think that makes me sometimes keep my distance." They were no longer intimate partners, although they would intermittently socialize as a triad. Like many men, he struggled in how to be emotionally available to his son. He tended to turn every engagement into a structured tutoring activity, re-producing the relationship and the shortcomings of his relationship with his father. He showered his son with gifts and took him to events but it was hard for him to just play with him. Spontaneity and relaxing were dangerous luxuries that required Winston to lower his guard. Not only was he afraid of external dangers but he was also afraid that these periods of tender reverie would surface disavowed self-states of tenderness and paternal hunger. He described an incident where he was on the floor with his son and the child fell asleep against him. "I could feel his heart beating. I can't describe how I felt, but it was like I was both happy and crying inside": Here, his concerns were not so much his aggression, but his hunger for love and his fears of being abandoned again. He noted that while he punished those who stole from him, he became especially enraged and violent in response to acts of betrayal. He was able to hear that it was difficult to love when potentially every adult could betray you.

Winston struggled to make sense of his intense but very carefully if costly managed aggression. He was able to make tentative links to his structured relations on one hand and at other times his unleashing violence on threatening persons. Winston felt he lacked the skill, and perhaps the desire, to find a middle way to be dominant, respected, and yet not be violent.[49] Cognitively smart and financially prudent, he had begun to invest in legitimate businesses as he was weary of the vigilance and violence of drug dealing. Here we see the influence of the father within, who exhorted him, to be smart, and not just aggressive.

[49] Adams, "Respect and Reputation."

Although the painful links to his father were evident, he felt a need to protect that memory of him as a good father. Of course, the reality of being abandoned kept resurfacing and that would trigger the withdrawals. He valued the relationship with his son but was afraid that somehow his son would continue the family pattern of male violence as a result of paternal failure around aggression management. We explored his thought that he should simply withdraw from his son's life so that he did not, according to him, "infect him with violence." I noted that his father had done that and wondered how he thought that had affected him. He spoke about still longing for him and being angry at him, and that he didn't want that for his son.

I felt that Winston was hungry to take in as much of me as possible as he was always curious about me. He commented on how smart I was, and that people liked me in the community. I thought to myself: I am you without the intense aggression. Initially, he attempted to both seduce me with offers of making me referrals or seeking to pay exorbitant fees. Perceiving me as rebuffing his well-meaning but austere offers of affection, he would show his sense of hurt and anger at me by describing acts of violence he had visited on his enemies. He was always careful to describe punishments that, by his moral code, were justifiable and proportionate to the rule infraction. I wondered if this was his way of managing the mutual affection. I never felt endangered but felt sad at times, as I knew he was at high risk for betrayal, resulting in incarceration, serious injury, or death. He both indulged in and defended against his fantasy of me being the good father he never had by literally fleeing at times, while being reassured by my steady availability and me not becoming enraged at him. At times in sessions, he would appeal to the professor in me and draw comfort by discussing abstract ideas. There would be a meeting of minds that was mutually gratifying and the intellectual nature of the discourse muting longing and the melancholy of loss. There were sporadic musings on going to college and him wondering if he could get credit for lived experience. While we were both bemused at the thought of him requesting credit for the unethical aspects of some of his experiences, we also explored his strengths around intellectual rigor and people management skills.

For most of the therapy the women in his life were shadowy and obliquely acknowledged objects. The good therapeutic work that Winston did was greatly facilitated by the ability and willingness of his mother and the child's mother to love him with little demand of overt reciprocation. At the same time neither his mother nor his co-parent could be seduced by his transparent substitution of material goods and advice for love. Yet, they created safe spaces where he could tentatively explore being with his child on the child's terms. These women both signaled their faith that he had the potential to reciprocate their love and that is a piece of work that both attracts and scares Winston. Ever so gradually his aggressive outbursts and his need to flee diminished. Winston spent more time with his son and could tolerate following the child's lead in play activities and sharing affection. The process of becoming a legitimate businessman quickened and Winston moved out of the neighborhood to a two-family home in an upscale neighborhood. He hints that he is re-engaging the mother of his son as an intimate partner, but he still walls off the feminine within. He periodically calls and we have the occasional lunch.

The oedipal machinations here are variations on the core oedipal theme of the healthy management of love and aggression. Winston's father abandoned the son as an act of love, viewing himself as toxic to the triad. Despite this, Winston's strong identification with his father's aggression and fear of intimacy had him immersing himself in violent enactments and contemplating abandoning his own son. With the absence of the father in the real there is an intrapsychic lack of the ability to resolve the desire for omnipotence that can lead to rageful enactments or whimpering helplessness. In this oedipal triad, Winston's mother managed to avoid neglecting him, while also not inappropriately embracing him as a substitute for the father. She did not offer the intrapsychically costly option that he would become the "man of the house." Many Black young men struggle to embrace a sense of tenderness that is in healthy tension with aggression when the co-parent bearing the aggression is absent. There is then fear of engulfment, given reality-based maternal fears of them being hurt by the state or peers. As a consequence, some mothers will harshly curb their son's developmentally typically assertions of aggression. In his rage against his father and his fear of his mother, Winston sought validation and tutoring from equally, primitively enacting male peers.

One could argue that a parallel Oedipal battle was taking place where both men had challenged the cultural white father—the vigilant, punitive, and un-nurturing state—with mixed results. Here the state is the father of all men, but especially of Black men, intensifying their aggression through its failure to nurture and protect them. That failure to provide equal opportunity enrages and dehumanizes while the failure to protect heightens aggressive enactments against self and all others. Families and cultures crumble when patriarchs neglect or murder their sons. Winston's father lost his battle with the state and sought to tutor his son not to initiate such conflict less he too loses. Winston was able to hold on to that loving gesture by his father and avoid a brutal and inevitably costly, if not fatal battle with the culturally white father.

The way in which the Oedipal is manifested is influenced by cultural practices both bequeathed and re-signified. African America culture has developed effective and live affirming ways of managing oedipal constructs. The presence of a close and extended kinship system and the practice of child shifting can buffer children from primitive parental enactments. While that may be interpsychically helpful, it often leaves unresolved how to manage the pain of the missing parent. Melancholy sits alongside desires that can never be assuaged. As some compensation African American kinship networks sought to sublimate the expression of male aggression by flight into the armed forces, entry into competitive sports, and creativity in the performing art. A harsh maternal parenting style and the attendant constraints is intended to be protective. It can however be counter-productive, given the absence of a buffering co-parent, especially a father. This can sow the seeds of rebellious enactments and misogyny.

With many boys there is a multitude of lacks that can be attributed to the father. Given systemic racism African American families struggle with inadequate resources and a lack of civil rights. These deficiencies reduce the space in which fathers can manage their aggression and tutor their sons. Resource deficiency makes a typical African American man question his manhood, as measured by his ability to meet the material needs of his family. Many by mutual agreement with the child's mother withdraw from the triad or are extruded. With Winston, there was no lack of material goods. What was not bequeathed to him by his father was how to be open to love and how to manage his aggression. Both men struggled to love themselves in a manner that was not dangerous to others. Again, we observe withdrawal as a defense against feelings of inadequacy and dangerousness.

Increasingly, gendered behaviors are not particular to biology and they can be thought of as ways of thinking about oneself on a spectrum as against a binary. Given then that intimacy or aggression are not limited to a particular sex, oedipal issues can play themselves out in the varied ways in which parents are sexed and in how they enact their sexualities. This presents an opportunity for males to identify with tenderness and demonstrate an enlightened masculinity that does not require them to renounce their maleness.[50] Initially Winston's marked wariness with regard to the social feminine and the feminine within immobilized him in his ability to love his son. Yet with the unconscious support of his mother and his female co-parent he was able to acknowledge and demonstrate tenderness without a crisis about his manhood. It seemed also that this shift moderated his aggression and his need to act out. Alongside this one might well observe some mourning over the retreat of the "traditional" masculinity and some melancholy over the lost father.

The good therapeutic work that Winston did was greatly facilitated by the ability and willingness of his mother and the child's mother to love him with little demand for overt reciprocation. They created safe spaces where he could tentatively explore being with his child on the child's terms. These women both signaled their faith that he could reciprocate their love and that is a piece of work that both attracts and scares Winston. This in turn also enabled Winston to re-engage his partner around non-parental intimacy. Winning the oedipal battle can be thought of as a skirmish for many men, in the larger struggle of managing the desire and risks of being truly emotionally inter-dependent.

Conclusion

The model of good-enough fathering requires a decoupling from the patriarchal model of dominance, inherent in an oedipally driven parenting dynamic. It requires a good-enough ability to contribute material, intellectual, and emotional resources to the triad. This can be especially daunting for Black fathers given systemic racism. It also speaks to the capacity to develop discipline to manage the internalized petit patriarch with the fatal oedipal wish to battle the white cultural patriarch. This requires both taking pleasure in a nurturing and protective role, managing the pain of the constraints on agency and mourning the loss of petit patriarchal fantasies.

[50] Diamond, "Recovering the Father in Mind and Flesh"; and Harris, *Melancholic Fathers*.

CHAPTER 8

Does a Father Need to be a Man?

Trans* Embodiments and Parenthood

Patricia Gherovici

What is a father? Who can be a father? What is the relationship between a man who impregnates a woman, a male parent, a founding patriot, the head of an organized crime family, and He, the one up there in the clouds who hears our prayers, the Heavenly Father? *Pater semper incertus est* (the father is always uncertain) while the mother is *certissima*, is a Roman-law principle meaning that the mother of the child is always known while there can be doubts on the identity of the father. This principle of maternal certainty that is dependent on a woman's childbearing capacities was used for many centuries until 1978 when the technique of in vitro fertilization was successfully used to fertilize an egg outside of a human body. These evolving methods of assisted reproduction problematize a simple notion of paternity and kinship more generally, with modern reproductive technology that is able to harvest and freeze sperm, eggs, and embryos, use embryos from donors, and in some cases, employ a gestational carrier. Current IVF methods allow a gestational surrogate to carry an embryo to birth without having any genetic ties to the baby. Thus, children

P. Gherovici (✉)
Philadelphia, PA, USA

L. Weissberg (ed.), *Psychoanalysis, Fatherhood, and the Modern Family*, https://doi.org/10.1007/978-3-030-82124-1_8

conceived and gestated with assisted reproduction may have three "mothers": a genetic one, a natural or birth mother, and a third one who will raise them. As for the father's identity, thanks to new DNA analysis technologies, biological paternity can be more clearly established. But is a father just a genitor?

In ancient Rome, being the father involved acting like one. The Roman father played a pivotal role in maintaining order, both publicly and privately, and as such was quite different from the Greek father who was absent from family life.[1] He had absolute power over his children throughout their lives: the right to arrange marriages or force divorce, to abandon a newborn child, to disown, sell, or even kill his children. The Roman father assumed his *patria potestas* (father's power) not because of biological kinship, but as the result of a formal social act. The father held his son in his arms and lifted him into the skies to indicate his desire to take on parental responsibility. All his progeny were not treated equally: for a daughter, he simply ordered that she be fed. In this sense, in ancient Rome, all "true" fatherhood was a ritualized adoption of legal obligation rather than a simple biological destiny. In the present, a time of assisted reproduction, sperm banks, and families with same-sex parents, why do we hold on to the notion of the "father"?

Sexual Determinants of Procreation

Sigmund Freud elevated Sophocles's *Oedipus Rex* tragedy to a universal model of psychic organization, giving the father a main but complex role not only in the family but most importantly in the family romance. He saw a son's love for his mother and jealousy of his father as "a universal event in early childhood." Freud generalized this milestone, positioning the father as the one against which the child experiences the "first murderous wishes."[2] The child loves his mommy too much, becomes envious of daddy, and wants to kill him—the Oedipus complex is a *father* complex! Well, what about the daughter? Freud's Oedipal complex may explain the

[1] See Luigi Zoja, *The Father: Historical, Psychological and Cultural Perspectives*, New York: Routledge, 2001.

[2] Sigmund Freud, *The Interpretation of Dreams* (1900). In: Freud, *The Standard Edition of the Complete Psychological Works*, ed. James Strachey in collaboration with Anna Freud, tr. James and Alix Strachey. 24 vols. (London: The Hogarth Press, 1953–74), III: 262. The Standard Edition is here abbreviated *SE*.

sexual development of the boy but leaves the question of why girls would love men and not their mothers unanswered.

What is common to both girls and boys in this model is that the father is someone who lays down a law, be it of sexual difference, the law of the prohibition of incest, or the laws of language. The father works as a diplomat, as an agent of a metaphor. The father is not an individual, but a principle of separation. It is a fourth term that breaks down what psychoanalysis describes as the mother-child-phallus triangle. A child of any gender has to renounce being the mother's phallus. The father is a function, someone or something intervenes as the representative of the law, the law to which they are subjected and of which they are an effect. Fathers will only be able to limit or "castrate" insofar as they are "castrated"—if they were not incomplete, they would not "need" to separate mother and child. But fathers need to be themselves castrated, that is, subject to the law and not identified with it; they will want to ensure the mother/woman recognizes them as a partner, so that the mother makes room in her desire for the father as well, abandoning the completeness the child may offer. Castration introduces a double dimension of privation and promise, of renunciation and substitution.

Fathers are simply agents, representatives of a position that transcends them and survives them, or as Freud puts it, they become "the mortal vehicle of a (possible) immortal substance."[3] Moreover, Jacques Lacan claims that it is only in relation to the experience of death that the true meaning of being a father can be grasped.[4] Psychoanalysis discovered that in the unconscious there is no awareness of our own mortality, a fact not unrelated to the often-conflicted desire to become a parent and the impossibility of fully performing that role. In this chapter, I ask whether a father needs to be a man. The perhaps obvious, negative answer to this question points to the specificity of the paternal function. The father is not a person or a gender but a position, an agent of separation (what psychoanalysis calls castration); the father is what separates the child from the mother (or main care-taker), the mother from the child, and what represents an order that also subjects them. The father is the knot that fastens drives and cultural conventions.

[3] Freud, "On Narcissm" (1914), *SE* XIV: 67–102, here 78.

[4] Jacques Lacan, *The Seminar of Jacques Lacan III: The Psychoses 1955–1956*, ed. Jacques-Alain Miller, tr. Russell Grigg (New York: W.W. Norton, 1993), 293.

The father is the space at the origin of subjectivity that disjoins the lethal imaginary trappings of any dual relationship. The role of the father is complex and perverse since Lacan plays on the homophony in French of *perversion*, that is, "père-version," or "the father's version." This "perversion" has to do with the fact that a father has to possess something that nobody can have or be: the phallus. The paternal function is structurally identified with the phallic function: the father has to appear as the one who has something that nobody can have. The paternal imposture refers to pretend to have the phallus (as a function and not an anatomical organ); the phallus as "stand in" for the object of the mother's desire that renders impossible the child's identification with the mother's object of desire.

According to Freud's interpretation in *Totem and Taboo* a good father is a dead father, a symbolic father whose foundation is the primal exceptional father, a father whose death inscribes the incest taboo, a father whose prohibition will be all the more necessary and severe once he is dead.[5] The primal father is called by Lacan the "at least one," that is, the exception to the law (there is at least one man not subjected to the law of castration). According to the myth elaborated by Freud, the sons get together and kill the all-enjoying father who kept all women; they eat him and feel guilty afterward. The sons identify with the father by incorporation (this cannibalistic identification is described by Freud in *Group Psychology* in a way I'll sum up as "We love you so. We'll eat you up. Daddy, are you mad at me?") The tyrant becomes a father post-mortem, and thus he becomes the exception supporting the universal law of castration: all are subjected to castration.

The Problem with Father

The question "Does a father need to be a man?" is especially relevant when examining families with parents with non-binary gender, biology, or whose sexual orientation resists easy classification. Though earlier I suggested that a father is no more than a figure, freeing this role from associations with sex assigned at birth, psychoanalysis' stance on the father could be read as hostile to transgender parents. Lacanian psychoanalysis' history of linking transgender expressions of sexuality with severe pathology dates back to 1955–1956 when Lacan reread Freud's text on President Daniel Paul Schreber and re-wrote Freud's theory of psychosis. There, he

[5] Freud, *Totem and Taboo* (1913), *SE* XIII: vii-162.

summarized Freud's Oedipus complex in his formula of what he called "the paternal metaphor" and later condensed as the "Name-of-the-Father." Freud's speculation was that Schreber's psychosis was the result of the repression of his passive homosexual position vis-à-vis his father. According to Freud, Schreber's rejected homosexual feelings toward to his father were reawakened by his relationship with his doctor, Professor Flechsig. Schreber developed a massive transference that led to his persecutory delusion centered on his eventual transformation into God's wife. Not only did Schreber derive progressive pleasure in the cultivation of the feminine, he speculated that once the transformation into a woman was fully completed, he would become God's companion. After an inevitable apocalypse, the fruit of Schreber's womb would repopulate the world.

Schreber's concerns are not really homosexual, and it would be more accurate to call them transsexual.[6] Deviating from Freud's interpretation, Lacan focused on what he called President Schreber's transsexual enjoyment. In his study of the famous President's memoir, Freud stated that Schreber's "idea of being transformed into a woman was the salient feature and the earliest germ of the delusional system. It also proved to be the one part of it that persisted after his cure, and the one part that was able to retain a place in his behavior in real life after he had recovered."[7] Developing Freud's observation, Lacan stressed the crucial function of Schreber's transformation into a woman and wondered whether this was a "properly psychotic mechanism, one that would be imaginary and that would extend from the first hint of identification with and capture by the feminine image, to the blossoming of a world system in which the subject is completely absorbed in his imagination by a feminine identification."[8] In his commentary of the Schreber, Lacan observed the mechanisms that he later systematized under the name of the "push-towards-Woman."[9]

Lacan's term *pousse-à-la-femme* (push-towards-Woman) could be rendered in English as "driving one to become a woman," if "drive" was

[6] Russell Grigg, "From the Mechanism of Psychosis to the Universal Condition of the Symptom: On Foreclosure." In: Dany Nobus (Ed.), *Key Concepts of Lacanian Psychoanalysis* (New York: Other Press, 1999), 48–74, here 55.

[7] Freud, "Psychoanalytic Notes on an Autobiographical Account of a Case of Paranoia (Dementia Paranoides): The Case of Schreber" (1911), *SE* XII: 1–82; here 20.

[8] Lacan, *The Seminar* III, 63.

[9] This section updates an earlier version of a discussion of Lacan's "push-toward-Woman" that appeared in my *Please Select Your Gender: From the Invention of Hysteria to the Democratizing of Transgenderism* (New York: Routledge, 2010), 173–181.

not already a technical concept translating Freud's *Trieb*.[10] The concept was accurately described by Renée Richards, the famous transgender tennis player, who created a media frenzy in 1976 when she went to court and won the right to play as a woman in the U.S. Open. She was asked at age seventy-two about the motivations for her gender transition more than thirty years before. Richards described her decision to change gender as resulting from an unyielding "pressure to change into a woman."[11] This could be an adequate translation of Lacan's expression *pousse-à-la-femme*. Richards also said that she wished she could have something that could have stopped that "pressure" and prevented the surgery: "What I said was if there were a drug, some voodoo, any kind of mind-altering magic remedy to keep the man intact, that would have been preferable, but there wasn't."[12] Richards seemed to express regrets about something that she had felt as inevitable: "Better to be an intact man functioning with 100 percent capacity for everything than to be a transsexual woman who is an imperfect woman."[13] However, the imperative to turn into a woman had been a way of warding off suicide: "The pressure to change into a woman was so strong that if I had not been able to do it, I might have been a suicide."[14] Schreber's description of his transformation into a woman also conveys this sense of an imposed force, of a drive pulling him into an inevitable sexual metamorphosis.

Freud's thesis has the merit of simplicity. For him, Schreber's transformation into a woman implied a feminine position toward the father. In this view, Schreber's evolution was made up of a rejection then an acceptance of his transformation into a woman. Finally, in his cure, the cultivation of a feminine persona was meant to have a stabilizing effect that gave him a sense of futurity. For Lacan, homosexuality played a secondary role in the interpretation of the case, as for femininity, "In no way has President Schreber ever introjected any type of feminine form."[15] What precipitates Schreber's psychosis would have been "an irruption in the real of

[10] Lacan, "L'etourdit," *Scilicet* 4 (1973): 5–52, here 22.

[11] Renée Richards, *No Way Renée: The Second Half of My Notorious Life*. New York: Simon & Schuster, 2007.

[12] Joyce Wadler, "At Home with Renée Richards: The Lady Regrets," *New York Times* (February 1, 2007); https://www.nytimes.com/2007/02/01/garden/01renee.html (access March 2021).

[13] Wadler, "At Home with Renée Richards."

[14] Wadler, "At Home with Renée Richards."

[15] Lacan, *The Seminar* III, 85.

something he has never known, the sudden emergence of a total strangeness that will progressively bring on a radical submersion of all his categories to the point of forcing him into a veritable reshaping of his world." (86) The missing meaning for Schreber "involves the feminine function in its essential symbolic meaning … at the level of procreation" (86). In the end, this drive had to transform Schreber into a woman, not just any woman but God's wife, the anointed person who would be the bearer of a new human race. The freedom of the psychotic resides precisely in this rejection that foregoes both the phallus and the Name-of-the-Father, and that ends up requiring an invention to anchor jouissance.[16]

"Push-towards-Woman," Effect of the Irruption of One-Father

Lacan uses the phrase "push-towards-Woman" in 1972 when he refers to Schreber's transformation into a woman, a transformation that he explains as the result of the sudden, violent entrance of a father.[17] But the coining of the phrase "push-towards-Woman" recalls Lacan's earlier text "On a Question Prior to Any Possible Treatment of Psychosis." In this essay, written in 1958, the "One-Father" is present at the dramatic conjuncture that marks the beginning of each case of psychosis. This One-father is not the subject's own father, but a representative, the "signifier" of paternity. The unique father is the agent for a metaphor, an agent represented by a signifier summoned by a contingency of life. This missing or foreclosed signifier "presents itself to a woman who has just given birth, in her husband's face, to a penitent confessing her sins in the person of her confessor, or to a girl in love in her encounter 'with the young man's father.'"[18] The One-Father, foreclosed in the symbolic, comes back as real jouissance, and it can be embodied in a female form.

[16] "Jouissance" is a term does not translate easily into English. Lacan himself suggested a combination of "enjoyment" and "lust." The word connotes a form of enjoyment not necessarily accompanied by pleasure or joy (as in "it hurts so good"). Indeed, jouissance conveys enjoyment not just with a gratifying surplus benefit but a violent, climactic bliss closer to loss, death, fragmentation, and the disruptive rapture experienced when transgressing limits.

[17] Lacan, *Le Séminaire XIX … ou pire. Le savoir du psychanalyste (1971–72)*, ed. Miller (ser.) Champ Freudien. Paris: Éditions du Seuil, 2011.

[18] Lacan, "On a Question Preliminary to any Possible Treatment of Psychosis," *Écrits: The First Complete Edition in English*, tr. Bruce Fink in collaboration with Héloïse Fink and Russell Grigg (New York: W.W. Norton, 2006), 445–488, here 481.

Before discussing clinical examples to further explore the father function as understood by Lacan, I will add that in the same way that we do not believe in death within the Freudian unconscious (as the negation of life by time) and behave as if we were immortal, there is no representation or symbol of the masculine-feminine opposition. Sexual identity for both males and females is always precarious because the human infant *becomes sexed* without ever fully symbolizing unconsciously a "normal," finished gender positioning. Assuming a gendered positioning is a process of becoming. Lacan introduces the notion of "sexuation," which is based not on anatomical borders but on modalities of enjoyment (*jouissance*). Lacan's sexuation formula is a matrix that proposes a set of mobile modes of sexual positioning. He proposes distinguishing the phallus, as an instrument, from the penis, as an organ, which clarifies the opposition between sexuality (he called it sexual difference or sexuation), anatomical sex, and symbolically constructed gender.

Keeping these elements in mind, I will explore the case of an analysand I will call Sergei, a young male musician who lived as a man until his early twenties when the identity that had comfortably sustained him in a male role suddenly failed.[19] His career as a soloist was faltering but he had recently auditioned for an important academic job teaching at a prestigious music conservatory and was waiting to hear back, expecting to get the position. If he was offered the job, he was going to relocate to another city. For him, the wait was unbearable. After several nights of insomnia, an idea came to him: He had the conviction that he was going to become a woman. Such a realization surprised him; the thought triggered on the one hand the most extreme anxiety, and on the other, it elicited a terse, humbling feeling—it was an inevitable destiny. Tormented but resigned to accept what he experienced as an inescapable fate, Sergei went to a bar, met a man, and had sex with him. He found the experience revolting; his anxiety increased. Sergei felt he had no choice; his feminization was "excruciating but inevitable."

Sergei had identified as a cis heterosexual male and never before did he question his gender or felt any attraction for men. The precise moment at which this idea of a sudden transformation into a woman appeared was revealing. Sergei's "imposed metamorphosis," as he called it, took place

[19] This section expands an earlier discussion of this case in my *Please Select Your Gender: From the Invention of Hysteria to the Democratizing of Transgenderism* (New York: Routledge, 2010), 186–9.

when this job opportunity meant that he was about to compete with his father professionally. Sergei's father enjoyed a brilliant international career and was also a reputed musician with an impressive academic standing. A dream in which Sergei came back home to his European childhood home "*to check whether there was mail (male) in the mail (male) box*" showed that he was dealing with what he unconsciously experienced as a passive position toward his father. By receiving his help, his support, and his endorsement, he was going to occupy a position that he unconsciously equated with femininity. The rejection of actual sex with a man expressed a masculine protest and implied a tentative at positioning himself as a male, rejecting the potential of an experience of receptivity, what he imagined as a forced feminization. Sergei's certainty of becoming a woman, which caused him intense psychic pain, was in fact a response, an attempt to deal with an excess that he could not symbolize. The shocking irruption of the transformation into a woman as he imagined it was Sergei's way of resolving an impossible situation: It compensated for the insufficiency of previous identifications that could no longer sustain his positioning as a man at a moment when he was to compete decisively with his father.

Sergei's family background was atypical. Not unlike Freud's patient "Little Hans," he had been called "little Sergei" (*malenkey/маленкей*) in his family. *Male*nkey, almost a male, but not quite. Whenever he compared himself to his father, he felt belittled. While an important figure in the world, his father had been placed in a degraded position by Sergei's mother. Through her, it was the whole position of being a *man* that was questioned. The answer to the question "Am I a man?" that was haunting Sergei was becoming more and more like an obscure riddle. He had been raised in a very homophobic town whose name in his native language, he noted with irony, is a transliteration of the slang word for a gay male. This small city, by the way, had been made famous as a result of the artistic achievements of Sergei's father. Sergei had left his native town at a very early age, with encouragements from family members who all insisted that he would do well because he was already a "man." Then Sergei had moved to a faraway city to pursue more intense studies with a leading figure in his field, at first, accompanied by his mother who left behind the rest of the family. Finding it hard to adapt to the new city, his mother became depressed. She missed her husband and two other children; at the time, the father was having extra-marital affairs. Sergei and his mother developed a semi-incestuous bond: the mother was totally devoted to her son's career; they shared a bed and she developed increasingly exhibitionist behavior, often going around the house naked. Eventually the father came to fetch his wife and bring her back home. The mother was torn between her prodigious son, her successful husband from whom she felt estranged, and her other children left at home. She chose to return home. Sergei stayed alone and continued studying and progressing. Eventually, he got a big career break when he was awarded a scholarship that gave him the opportunity to study in the United States.

And yet, for Sergei, the gifted son, choices in life appeared limited, overdetermined by a talent that could not be wasted. He had not yet reached adolescence, but in order to appease their separation, his mother claimed that "he was already a man," that he was mature well beyond his years, hence strong enough to be in New York without her. Sergei arrived alone in *Man*hattan where he studied in the prestigious conservatory *Man*nes College of Music. He later continued his studies in the *Man*hattan School of Music. All the rewards of his career accomplishments did not assuage the negative associations to the signifier "man" that referred to a degraded place, at least according to his mother. There was, however, an option left, which was to join the other side, namely the side of women. Sergei gradually devoted less time to practicing his instrument, his grades in school dropped, and he started drinking heavily and using drugs. He eventually left New York to move back to the town from which his father's family came, which was not where his father and family lived. There, he was mentored by a woman who shared a first name with his mother and, most importantly, with the woman who later became his wife. With the help of this woman, and in a short time, Sergei was able to gather the courage to "get clean" and recover the motivation to return to the United States to complete his music studies.

Between Man and Woman, Husband

Sergei did not express a wish to become a woman, for he felt his feminization as oppressive and anguishing, an imposed destiny. Early in the treatment, he told me that he had decided to get married in what initially looked like an impetuous decision primarily motivated by a visa about to expire and the need to have "permanent resident" status in the United States. This marriage, however, allowed him to assume himself not only as a "green card holder" (a card that he observed was in fact pink, a color that he was aware was a symbol for various LGBTQ identities) but also as something that exceeded the man/woman binary. Sergei forged a new identity in his role as "husband."

Let us backtrack a little. Paradoxically, while his father enjoyed continuous professional success, he was looked down upon by Sergei's mother, who eventually divorced him "for being a womanizer." "I believed everything my mother said and forgot my father," Sergei said. "I had to take sides and chose my mother's." His mother professed to despise men, especially Sergei's father who was, according to her, "a great artist, a bad husband, and a horrible man." On the other hand, she was totally devoted to her talented son. Thus, Sergei appeared caught in a double bind: his virility was sustained by his mother's adoration for his being a boy, which made him her favorite, and was contrasted with the negative regard his mother had for men. Not only was his father seen as a horrible man, but being a man was seen as a horrible fate. "Women are better than men," his mother proclaimed. His mother's view had deeply influenced him, and he worked hard trying to become "a great artist." The possibilities of becoming "a bad husband" or "a horrible man" were carefully avoided.

Sergei's belief that he was going to become a woman was assuaged by a gesture of nomination. He and his father had the same first and last name, which was not uncommon in his country. Sergei complained that he was often confused with his father, something that he experienced as a mixed blessing. When he decided to get married, in order to distinguish himself from his father and become "a good husband," he hyphenated his last name and added his wife's maiden name to his. Soon after, the certainty of an eventual transformation into a woman subsided: he was no longer sure that it would happen and the fantasy of emasculation appeared transformed. It went from being the certainty of an inescapable destiny to being the fear of a contingency. The space for uncertainty opened up.

The "artistic name" that Sergei created in order to be able to make a name for himself and end the confusion with his father acted as a supplement that provisionally made up for the deficiencies in what Lacan calls the Name-of-the-Father, made up for the failure in his father's function as a support for a symbolic function of separation and inscribed a first trait of difference in the genealogy. His given name contradicted the nominative function: he felt that it did not qualify him as unique and individualized. Sergei added hyphenated his last name with his wife's, which is also a male first name. This "middle name" that he "borrowed" from his wife was the first trait of difference between him and his father. This name, however, functioned in a more limited manner due to the role it played in his identity as a husband who takes his wife's name. It was not his own invention; the wife had the name that she had received from her father, another distinguished man who played an important role for the patient as an idealized yet "fallen" father; this devoted father had sacrificed his own life to promote his daughter's career (another musician). Sergei's solution was precarious but it allowed him to find an outcome facing the riddle of sexual difference. Sergei's sudden "push-towards-Woman" can be explained as a precarious and tentative precipitation of meaning. Both he and his father were exceptional figures, but the father's fame had transformed his last name into a name that, like a brand, became his trademark, a name that he could not transmit to his son. In other words, the Name-of-the-Father had not been operative.

Usually, in neurosis the place of exception is relegated to the phallic function corresponding to the father. For Sergei, however, the father was actually someone "exceptional"; unlike a father who is subjected to the law, he represents an "exception" to the rule. Sergei's father was placed in a position equivalent to the exception of the primal father presented by Freud in *Totem and Taboo* (1913). Sergei was supposed to follow the family's tradition and become like his father, a destiny that he was reluctant to follow. Becoming a man like him also implied becoming a horrible man; therefore he could not fully accept his father's double-edged virile gift. Hence, he felt unable to become a great artist, because he thought that nobody could be greater than his father. His father was seen as "the" exception to the rule; he fantasized that his father was not encumbered by any limitation and was as such able to enjoy greatness. Becoming a woman thus provided a solution to the problem, even though it was a solution that tortured him. In the end, being a good husband became his singular creative solution. However, he was a husband who remained very dependent on his wife and also on the heritage of the father of her name. Generalizing from similar cases, Juliet Mitchell has reflected on a possible widespread "normal" tend: the absence of the castration complex in men whose heterosexuality is negotiated not via castration, but by identifying with the woman they love.[20]

[20] Juliet Mitchell, "Sexuality, Psychoanalysis, and Social Changes." In: Anthony Molino and Christine Ware (Eds.), *Where Id Was: Challenging Normalization in Psychoanalysis* (Middletown: Wesleyan University Press, 2001), 96–108.

Reparatory Symptoms

Sergei was responding to an instance of severe anxiety. Taking his wife's name as a solution proves that certain symptoms are comparable to an emergency repair kit, in this case by lending a spare name just when the Name-of-the-Father faltered. His solution made up for the deficiencies in the Name-of-the-Father, albeit provisionally. However, while Sergei was being overwhelmed by the conviction that he was going to become a woman, the extreme anxiety he experienced in response was a sort of masculine protest, even in the face of a destiny that he felt was unavoidable. This anxiety inscribed a sort of sexual difference. Schreber initially experienced his transformation into God's bride with protestation, but later on he accepted it, even experiencing occasional states of bliss. For Schreber, feminization was a fate that had a pacifying effect.

Sergei's is not a case of a gender transition since all along he refused the idea of becoming a woman. His rejection of feminization was a way to inscribe a first trait of difference, a limit, some sort of a father function. Creatively, Sergei found a sexual positioning neither as a woman, nor as a man, but rather as a husband. Always prone to speculations, Sergei evolved a complex theory about the huge benefits of having adopted his wife's last name. Nevertheless, this solution might fail should they decide to have children, as this would imply his assuming of a position as a father in the usual sense, an event that might again bring up questions about his sexual positioning. So far, he seems to have found an acceptable compromise.

Beyond Oedipus, Woman

The "push-towards-Woman" is not an Oedipal phenomenon (it is not a push-towards-mother).[21] Lacan uses the notion of "push-towards-Woman," not as correlated with the Oedipal model, but instead related to the modes of enjoyment proposed in his sexuation formulas. Schreber's imposed feminization was a way to write the enjoyment of the Other (feminine). The "push-towards-Woman" is a specific way by which the subject relates to the Other (feminine), an Other of sensual pleasure, in other words, what Lacan calls jouissance. The push-towards-Woman is

[21] Marie-Hélène Brousse, "The-Push-to-the-Woman: A Universal in Psychosis?," *Psychoanalytical Notebooks* 11 (2003), 79–98, here 83.

thus a construction that expresses an interpretation of jouissance in terms of its very feminization. Indeed, Schreber's transsexual delusion was triggered by a speculation about women's sexual enjoyment, "that after all it really must be rather beautiful to be a woman submitting to the act of copulation."[22]

Lacan contended that Schreber's paranoia was to become "the" woman that was needed to grant the jouissance of the Other. Thus, Lacan writes that, because Schreber was "unable to be the phallus the mother is missing, there remained the solution of being the woman that men are missing."[23] One may introduce variations in this logic such as "being the phallus that the mother lacks," "being 'the' woman men lack," "being the woman God lacks." These inscribe several strategies to stabilize a psychosis, to support jouissance while securing a sexual rapport that does not exist. Luis Izcovich describes Schreber's process of feminization, with its logical consequence of his transformation into a woman, as a structural point of completion with stabilizing effects.[24]

Schreber's feminization, described by Lacan in 1958 as only imaginary, must be understood more generally as granting him a "transsexualist jouissance" in which we can see the real manifestation of jouissance in his body. The effects take place at the level of the three registers of the symbolic, the real, and the imaginary.[25] His feminization has an imaginary function, as it reenacts the mirror stage, that dialectical progression when children identify with their mirror image, a stage marked by jubilatory laughter, as witnessed by Schreber's bliss in looking at his feminized image in the mirror. It has also a symbolic reference: the woman as an exception, "the" woman, who will copulate with God and create a new world order by providing a new generation, is a Name-of-the-Father in disguise, as we shall see. The "push-to-Woman" functions for Schreber as a creative solution (a "sinthome").[26] Later in his illness, he knows that he will not fully

[22] Freud, "The Case of Schreber," 36.

[23] Lacan, "On a Question Preliminary to any Possible Treatment of Psychosis," 472.

[24] Luis Izcovich, "Identification féminine et pousse-à-la-femme dans la psychose," *L'Évolution Psychiatrique* 69 (2004): 291–301.

[25] Lacan, "On a Question Preliminary to any Possible Treatment of Psychosis," 476.

[26] Lacan's late notion of the *sinthome* refers to a "symptom" that does not need to be eliminated or cured but that rather becomes a creative solution, a supplement to make up for the father's deficiencies. See Lacan, *The Sinthome: The Seminar of Jacques Lacan,* Book XXIII, tr. Luke Thurston, ed. Miller (Cambridge UK: Polity Press, 2016), 147. The *sinthome* is a strategy of survival that makes life livable.

become a woman in this life, but the potential of a future transformation in the afterlife sustains him because it makes up for the deficiencies in the Name-of-the-Father and is a correlate of his transsexual jouissance. For Schreber and Sergei, Woman is the excess represented by the mythical primordial father. Both the father of the primal horde and Woman are mythical starting points of unbridled fullness whose "primordial repression" constitutes the symbolic order subtending the paternal function. Woman functions as an ideal image, someone who has access to unlimited jouissance, a jouissance beyond the phallus, the jouissance of the Other. Woman becomes a solution to the problem of a jouissance that—like trauma—resists any imaginary or symbolic assimilation. This led Catherine Millot, who followed the thread of "the" Woman, to argue that all transsexuals are psychotic. Given this structure, "the transsexual symptom appears to function as a substitution of the Name-of-the-Father inasmuch as the transsexual aims to incarnate the Woman. Not *one* woman in the sense of 'not-all,' implying that no one could claim to represent All women—the transsexual position consists of wanting to be All, all woman, more woman than all woman, and representing them all."[27] As I have suggested elsewhere, my general thesis is somewhat different and at least more nuanced.[28] Some revealing nuances are provided by gender nonconforming people themselves. American drag queen, actor, model, singer, songwriter, and television personality RuPaul explained the difference between impersonating *a* woman or Woman: "I do not impersonate females! How many women do you know who wear seven-inch heels, four-foot wigs, and skintight dresses?" adding, "I don't dress like a woman; I dress like a drag queen!"[29]

In Gilles Deleuze and Félix Guattari's *Anti-Oedipus* (1972) a text published in France in the same year that Lacan coined the "push-towards-Woman," Schreber's is portrayed as a trans subject: "He is not simply bisexual, or between the two, or intersexual. He is transsexual. He is

[27] Catherine Millot, *Horsexe: Essays on Transsexualism*, tr. K. Hylton (New York: Autonomedia, 1990), 42. See also Millot, "Un cas de transsexualisme feminine" et "Transsexualisme et homosexualité," *Ornicar?* (1981): 167–176.

[28] Patricia Gherovici, *Please Select Your Gender* (New York: Routledge, 2010), 181–182; and Gherovici, *Transgender Psychoanalysis*, (New York: Routledge, 2017), 13, 32–33, 90–92.

[29] Susan Corso, "Drag Queen Theology"; https://www.huffpost.com/entry/drag-queen-theology_b_175120 (access March 2021).

trans-alivedead, trans-parentchild,"[30] President Schreber is placed simultaneously as child and parent in a spectral lineage for which there is no difference between generations. He comes in a dead and alive genealogy, trans-alive-dead, both child and a parent, trans-parent-child. Are Schreber's struggles over the Freudian father-complex or rather, might not his transformation be a strategy of survival? Could he be trying to find a way to be alive rather than be dead by becoming a father unlike his own, which would allow him to find his place in the world of the living as a trans-parent?

A Trans-Parent

Before concluding, I want to illustrate this structure with the brief example of Stanley, a trans man in his early forties.[31] He was raised in Chicago's Polish-American community by a grandmother who, he told me, was the only person who loved him. Stanley's grandmother had rejected her daughter—Stanley's mother—because she "only loved boys." Nevertheless, when, as a child, Stanley was sent to live with his grandmother, she warmly embraced the little "tomboyish" girl.

Stanley's mother, Marika, left home as a young teenager to marry Robert, who was fifteen then. Marika was already pregnant when she moved out. Stanley's father, Robert, was the sort of a muscular, fun-loving, heavy-drinking man Marika's mother, Gilda—who was also of Polish descent—preferred. When Marika moved in with Robert's family, she became very close with her new husband's family. They were all very poor. Stanley grew up under very precarious conditions, deprived of material comforts and affection. There was little stability as they moved from home to home, every time to worse conditions, squatting in abandoned houses, with no electricity or heating.

Stanley's mother's teenage marriage had refashioned Claude Lévi-Strauss's formula for exogamy: "I take a wife and give a daughter." His mother gave herself as a daughter to her husband's family and in turn gave her own daughter (Stanley) to her mother. My analysand says his grandmother would always admonish: "Do not get pregnant." Stanley would answer, "I will never be pregnant." Reproduction, or rather, avoiding it,

[30] Gilles Deleuze and Félix Guattari, *Anti-Oedipus*, tr. Robert Hurley, Mark Seem, and Helen R. Lane (Minneapolis: University of Minnesota Press, 1987), 77.

[31] This is a modified version of a case discussed in my book *Transgender Psychoanalysis: A Lacanian Perspective on Sexual Difference* (New York: Routledge, 2017), 112–14.

was where social mobility resided. Stanley believes that being where he is today has a lot to do with not being pregnant as a teenager like his mother was. This has allowed him to not repeat a destiny that he claims most girls from his inner-city school have followed. Today, Stanley is a married trans man, satisfied with his job as a medical assistant. His wife, a nurse, is a heterosexual cis woman who never dated anyone queer before meeting him. They have a daughter conceived by artificial insemination. They are by all measures an ordinary couple whose current problem is that Stanley's wife wants a second child. My analysand fears that he will have a son and opposes the idea quietly. He believes that it would be difficult for him to be the "father of a boy." As he says this, a revealing slip of the tongue follows: "I cannot be a trans father." In fact, Stanley is already a trans father; he has a daughter. He thinks that raising a son will expose an insufficiency—a lack of knowledge about masculinity. Stanley regards himself as a "feminist man," a label that has the other sex—difference—written in its identity.

He is not, he says, like a biological man. He feels at ease among men but also feels different (this is important because he is not psychotic). Recently Stanley mentioned a dream: "*I was making love with a man. He does not know I am trans. I am anxious. I touch his penis but find a weird translucent plastic thing with a red rod in it.*" He added, as if to explain: "*A transparent plastic thing.*" At this point, I stopped him by echoing his words: "trans parent plastic thing." I had let the words return to him and he heard them back anew; he laughed. The "trans-parent thing" was indeed "plastic." Stanley was reinventing the notion of family, a "queer family" as he called it, taking distance from the trauma of the poor conditions and neglect of his upbringing. The word "parent" had been loaded with negative connotations—having had a severely abusive and dysfunctional father and mother. Life had indeed been quite plastic, and Stanley was still looking at his gender transition with some astonishment as if he was still baffled by his own survival.

Ultimately, the most radical discovery of psychoanalysis is that sex is tied to the death drive. Stanley's "castration" has to do with his acceptance of his own mortality, a fact not unrelated to his conflicted desire to become a parent. Reproduction proves the mortality of the individual. One does not "duplicate" in sexual reproduction, as we often think. We do not buy a share of immortality by having children; quite the contrary. As Lacan puts it, sexual reproduction means that "the living being, by being subject to sex, has fallen under the blow of individual death." Reproduction does not guarantee immortality through replication but rather shows the uniqueness (and death) of each individual. In Stanley's case, this is made absolutely clear—his wife will get pregnant using sperm from an anonymous donor. And Stanley is aware of this fact. He is quite relieved that, thanks to the artificial insemination, his offspring will not carry the "defective, addiction-prone" genes in his family. For Stanley, the cut of castration or mortality with which he is struggling to come to terms is also an expression of his singularity as a subject, as a feminist man, as a "trans parent."

For Freud and Lacan, sexual reproduction and death are two sides of the same coin. Sexual reproduction requires more than one individual; one person or partner alone simply cannot produce a new being. In principle, the sexed living being implies the death of the immortal individual. Sexual difference and sexual reproduction account for a constitutive lack in the subject—a lack Lacan ascribes to "reproduction, through the sexual cycle." There is no pre-programmed "biological" dictate in the psyche that determines why somebody will situate herself or himself, independent of her or his body, as a man or woman; further, there is no "biological" dictate that seeks a "fitting" complement.

To occupy a sexual positioning is to accept a primal loss. Sex needs to be symbolized and gender needs to be embodied. The major signifiers at work in Stanley's unconscious—"trans," "parent," "plastic"—may reknot themselves. Stanley often says in session that it is "weird" to be a trans man, that his transition is hard to explain, even to himself, but that he needs to invent something to survive. His transition was a new way of being. In the years preceding his transition, he was drinking heavily and ruminating about suicide. As a "trans-parent," Stanley has assumed the protective function and prohibitive function, tasks that Lacan ascribes in 1938 as defining the role of the father.[32] The father is a position in discourse, a third party at the origin of subjectivity. This feminist man is at ease in the world because he can pass in his masculine persona. His being a man is never questioned. Stanley is tall, lean, muscular, good-looking, and has all the markers of what, in our society, is seen as virile masculinity. Though he is plagued by doubts in many aspects of his life, Stanley is certain that he is a good parent to his daughter: he loves her dearly, is patient, thoughtful, and attentive; he is proud of being a family man. He assumes

[32] Lacan, "La Famille" in *Encyclopédie française* 8, Paris: A. de Monzie, Editor 1938. Reprinted in: Lacan, "Les complexes familiaux dans la formation de l'individu." In: Lacan, *Autres Écrits*, ed. Miller (ser.) Champ Freudien (Paris: Seuil, 2001), 23–84.

his role as a trans-parent, as "the one who lays down the law," and notices that has less trouble than his wife in setting limits for their child. Despite his hesitations, Stanley has reinvented the function of the father by taking distance from the law of reproduction as its only legitimacy. While he understands that "father" is not the opposite of "mother," which would imply that the man/woman divide is demanded by nature, he still likes to be called "dad" by his daughter. He is not duped; he knows that being a father may be, as Joyce once wrote, a legal fiction only.

CHAPTER 9

Blindness and Repair in Institutional Psychoanalysis: A Brief History

John Frank

As a member of the American Psychoanalytic Association (APsaA), the oldest psychoanalytic organization in North America, I have witnessed and been part of a remarkable period in its history, one which parallels and engages an equally remarkable chapter in our country's cultural history; how we as psychoanalysts have understood, felt about, and dealt with homosexuality in our patients, our families, and ourselves.

I still cringe when I see the word "homosexuality" associated with psychoanalysis. As a psychoanalytic candidate in Philadelphia in the early 1970s, I was taught that homosexuality was a sexual deviation and that admitting homosexual candidates for training in our Institutes could erase the important distinction between normality and pathology. In a climate where tribal loyalties to deeply held cultural beliefs encompassed psychoanalytic training, lines drawn to separate minority groups turned out to be grossly misguided and hurtful to people's dignity. It also reflected poorly on APsaA and its practitioners and created a hierarchical atmosphere that some compared to Medieval guilds and religious monasteries.

J. Frank (✉)
Philadelphia, PA, USA

L. Weissberg (ed.), *Psychoanalysis, Fatherhood, and the Modern Family*, https://doi.org/10.1007/978-3-030-82124-1_9

The first part of this chapter will be an insider's history of the changes within the APsaA attitude toward homosexuality—from a pseudo-scientific facade covering irrational and unacknowledged bias to gradual acceptance and advocacy—from blindness to repair. As the central explanatory paradigm of homosexuality equals pathology crumbled, the Oedipus myth's place in psychoanalytic narrative came under further scrutiny. Paralleling the shift in attitude toward homosexuality, a second—and perhaps related paradigmatic institutional shift occurred from a focus on the child's Oedipal fantasies to the realities of adult-child instinctual and power relationships and their actual effect on children.

The second part of the chapter will deal with two other areas of psychoanalytic institutional blindness; the realities of adult sexual, physical, and emotional abuse of children and the boundary violations of analysts who abuse their patients. Is it possible that the strict adherence to Freud's Oedipus model developed at the turn of the century, to the exclusion of the family and child's social world, may have subtly and unintentionally contributed to psychoanalytic patriarchal abuses of authority including ethical boundary crossings? How could such institutional transgressions, with its lack of accountability of the powerful to the powerless have flourished, and how does such accountability become established or avoided? While these questions can't be answered here, they need to be raised in reviewing the darker side of psychoanalysis's institutional history and our wish not to repeat it.

Psychoanalysis and Homosexuality

In 2012, the parent organization of the Psychoanalytic Center of Philadelphia (where I trained), the APsaA, had its one-hundredth birthday. With 3500 members, it is the oldest and most traditional or classical of our national psychoanalytic organizations, and for many, the preeminent psychoanalytic organization in the world. My association with psychoanalysis goes back to my teens in New York City where I was drawn to Sigmund Freud's writings, had the good fortune to be invited into the homes of several analysts, and soaked in some of the psychoanalytic heyday power juices in the 1950s (I have probably attended close to forty annual APsaA meetings).

My first awareness of homosexuality as a distinct sexual orientation wasn't until my Freshman year in college. During my elementary and high-school years, I suspect nearly all queer variant students were completely closeted. At home, my unmarried Aunt Lottie lived with us for a number of years and while she had a close friend, Marge; the idea that they might be gay didn't occur to me until decades later. "Gay" wasn't in vogue and if a reference to homosexuality was made in conversation, it was a rolling of the eyes rather than words. In college in the early 1960s, there were several "out" students but they had no organizations, no voice, and were seen as an isolated oddity on campus. Knowing no "out" medical students or psychiatric residents during my professional training in the late 1960s, I assume they too were closeted.

In the 1990s, having finished my psychoanalytic training and following my son's example of "coming out," I "came out" to my colleagues as the father of a gay son. In those days, being a psychoanalyst and the parent of a gay child was not a slam dunk. A prevailing cultural belief in my own profession was that parental character and behaviors were a likely source of their children's sexual orientation and gender differences, both of which were considered a form of mental illness. Feeling a mixture of anxiety, shame, and fear of exposure over my and my wife's possible role in our son's "deviancy," we began to review our parenting behavior with each other—she a social work specialist in parenting education and I a child psychoanalyst and child psychiatry training director—to see if we could discover how we might have been responsible for our youngest child's homosexuality.

Fortunately, in 1999, at APsaA's annual meeting, a newly created workshop had been formed by David Levi and Susan Rosbrow-Reich as part of the Committee on LGBT issues called "New Perspectives on Homosexuality: When a Son or Daughter is Gay: Special Issues When Psychoanalysts are Parents."[1] Here was a forum that brought together recently "out" analysts, the first crop of APsaA's newly accepted gay candidates, and like me, straight analysts with gay children. During an impromptu lunch with a colleague who I had known from residency days, he mentioned in passing that he had a gay daughter. In addition to relief at discovering an older analyst colleague also had a gay child, I was shocked that he had disclosed such private information in a public setting without obvious feelings of shame. Over the years, I would learn that a majority of psychoanalytic candidates and senior analysts felt the need to hide that they had gay children for fear of the anti-gay stigma and that their

[1] Susan Rosbrow-Reich and John Frank, "When a Family Member is Gay: The Third Generation," *The American Psychoanalyst* 39, 4 (2005): 29.

professional lives would be compromised among colleagues. Many of them rationalized their silence with the notion that they were private people but I believed they would have preferred the freedom to speak openly with friends and family and share the successes and frustrations of not just their heterosexual children with friends and colleagues.

The following year, I volunteered to present my story to the workshop. Even though APsaA workshops still had the professional aura of "scientific discussions," I was very appreciative that I could bring both my wife and gay son to the workshop meetings which turned out to be both supportive and conducive to real working through of several issues related to coming out as an analyst and a family member. Over the next years, the workshop subjects included analysts coming out to parents about themselves or their gay grandchild, and psychoanalytic approaches to diverse gender experiences in children and adolescents, a first foray into transgender issues. In conversation with an analyst teacher about homosexuality, he asked if I had ever come across a father of a gay boy who wasn't narcissistic or overly distant and a mother who wasn't overly close? I told him he was speaking with such a father right now. His jaw dropped as he fumbled apologetically for words telling me he really didn't know.

This is why I still cringe when I see the word homosexuality associated with psychoanalysis; I believe that as psychoanalysts, our blindness to our biases was and continues to be costly. My teachers from an earlier generation claimed their use of the word "deviant" or "perversion" to describe homosexual behavior was not pejorative.[2] They were psychological scientists, they said, engaged in scientific classification and study. In 1973, when my son was 3 years old, Irving Bieber, an influential Psychoanalyst known for attempting to convert gay men to heterosexuality, told an interviewer that "a homosexual is a person whose heterosexual function is crippled, like the legs of a polio victim."[3]

At the beginning of this twenty-first century, Charles Socarides, another leading proponent of homosexuality as illness and credited with "treating more homosexuals than anyone else,"[4] wrote that the male homosexual

[2] Charles Socarides, Abraham Freedman, Kenneth Gould, and Selma Kramer (Eds.), *Objects of Desire; The Sexual Deviations* (New York: International Universities Press, 2002), xvii.

[3] See the interview with Bieber in: "The APA Ruling: The Issue is Subtle, the Debate is Still On," *New York Times* (December 23, 1973): 109.

[4] Bertram J. Cohler and Robert M. Galatzer-Levy, *The Course of Gay and Lesbian Lives; Social and Psychoanalytic Perspectives* (Chicago: University of Chicago Press, 2000), 12, 352.

needs to "defend himself against the ... Oedipus complex."[5] Massive predominantly unconscious childhood fears, Socarides held, could destroy the "standard male-female pattern (of male penetration of the female)" (4). Elaborating on classical Freudian theory, Socarides wrote that a child's identification with the same-sex parent marks the successful resolution of the Oedipus and Electra complexes leading to mature gender and sexual identity. Those failing same-sex identification risked future psychoneurosis, pedophilia, and/or homosexuality. The day after my coming out at the APsaA meetings, Socarides and several of his colleagues had their annual workshop on "The Sexual Deviations." For several years, both the older and new theories/visions of homosexuality were presented back-to-back at APsaA workshops.

The cause of homosexuality in this story is a psychological one, based on a fear of, and defense against, heterosexuality. Scratch the surface of any homosexual man, and you find a frightened straight man. Homosexuality was the pathological shadow of heterosexuality. In the 1968 edition of the holy grail of Psychiatry, the *Diagnostic Manual of Mental Disorders*, homosexuality was listed as a personality disorder; a lifelong deeply ingrained maladaptive behavior pattern in the company of anti-social personality and drug dependence. Under the name of science, the search for causes and cures for homosexuality took up decades of psychoanalytic hours and gay patients' time, money, and emotional pain. Striking was how many gay patients themselves—believing there was no alternative model—bought into these psychoanalytic assumptions about the causes and treatment of homosexuality. It was also a testimony to their longing to be accepted as part of the human family and their willingness to suppress and override their deeper sexual and loving impulses.

Because psychoanalysis in the 1960s had enormous influence on psychiatry, mental health, and American culture, its theories and treatments contributed to the painful silence and closeting of the not yet defined or out gay community. When homosexuality as a "psychiatric illness" became one of the hottest culture war issues in the 1980s and 1990s, institutional psychoanalysis had not yet returned to its humanitarian foundation. As a psychiatric resident at Harvard's Massachusetts Mental Health Center in the late 1960s, I once discussed a young gay man, who had come to the clinic for anxiety and depression, with a distinguished training analyst who was my supervisor. When he discovered that my patient wasn't motivated

[5] Socarides et al. (Eds). *Objects of Desire,* xvii.

to change his orientation, he was no longer interested in the patient and the discussion ended right there. Looking back, I am amazed that my supervisor couldn't see past the homosexuality diagnostic label and how vulnerable and susceptible I was to this demeaning stereotyping of my gay patient.

Two years after the 1969 Stonewall uprising in New York City jump-started the beginning of the modern LGBT movement, gay activists, believing that homoerotic feelings and behavior were an expression of normal human sexuality, disrupted the American Psychiatric Association's annual conventions protesting the pathologizing of homosexuality. John Fryer, a Professor of Psychiatry at Temple University, became the first gay American psychiatrist to speak about his sexuality in a public forum.[6] At a 1972 panel on homosexuality and mental illness, entitled "Psychiatry: Friend or Foe to Homosexuals," he was listed as Dr. H. Anonymous, and Fryer wore a face mask, wig, over-size tuxedo, and used a special microphone to disguise his voice. "I am a homosexual. I am a psychiatrist," Fryer said.[7] He compared the struggles of homosexuals to that of African-Americans and described the lives of gay psychiatrists who hid their sexual orientation out of fear of indignity. From behind the mask, Fryer told his colleagues "it is time that real flesh and blood stand up before you and ask to be listened to and understood insofar as that is possible" (126). Fryer didn't acknowledge that he was the psychiatrist behind the mask until the Association's annual meeting 22 years later. In 1973, the entry "Homosexuality" was removed from the *Diagnostic Manual of Mental Disorders*, and Fryer's speech is often cited as having been critical in this decision by organized Psychiatry.

Stephen Mitchell, a psychoanalyst working outside of the APsaA umbrella, critiqued both the equation of homosexuality with pathology and the theoretical basis that analysts used to justify "curing" homosexuality with analytic treatment.[8] This was published after I completed my analytic training. Mitchell's work received little attention or recognition from

[6] Dudley Clendinen, "Dr. John Fryer, 65, Psychiatrist Who Said in 1972 He Was Gay," obituary, *New York Times* (March 5, 2003), section C:13.

[7] Fryer, cited in Dustin Vern Edward Schneider, "The Constitution of Queer Identity in the 1972 APA Panel, 'Psychiatry: Friend or Foe to Homosexuals? A Dialogue.'" Thesis (University of Montana, 2013), Appendix B, 126; https://scholarworks.umt.edu/cgi/viewcontent.cgi?article=5198&context=etd (access March 2021).

[8] See Stephen Mitchell, "Psychodynamics, Homosexuality, and the Question of Pathology," *Psychiatry* 41 (1978): 254–263; and Mitchell, "The Psychoanalytic Treatment of

mainstream psychoanalytic journals,[9] a sure sign in retrospect of psychological blindness in need of processing. He described and explained abuses of influence and authority in traditional psychoanalysis. He saw the substitution of compliance to received wisdom for true independent thinking in psychoanalytic education and curriculum and how institutional illusions created an official story as if it were universal preventing unofficial stories from being heard. Nancy Chodorow and Jack Dresher underscored that Mitchell's inquiry into standard analytic thinking about homosexuality became the central critique taking on the entrenched anti-homosexual bias in the psychoanalytic world.[10]

In 1987, Richard Isay, whose training analysis was focused on trying to convert him to heterosexual, became the first openly gay psychoanalyst to advocate anti-discriminatory policies for APsaA including threatening an ACLU law-suit when the then president of APsaA asked that the Committee on Social Issues not bring up a resolution to de-pathologize homosexuality to the Board on Professional Standards.[11] Isay believed that "American Psychoanalysis created the developmental deviation theory of homosexuality between 1940 and 1980 in order to enhance its own acceptability within mainstream American culture in which analysts were raised, trained, and worked and provided the rationalization for keeping lesbian and gay people from being trained in APsaA institutions" (150).

Out of disappointment and frustration, Isay distanced himself from APsaA but many who came after him had the support of more progressive officers and a society more sympathetic to gay rights. There is no way of knowing how much the pain and rage caused by APsaA's closed doors to those who wanted to be analysts and the creative talent lost to the organization because of its discriminatory policy hurt the reputation of

Homosexuality; Some Technical Considerations," *International Review of Psychoanalysis* 8 (2002): 63–80.

[9] Roughton, Ralph. "Opportunities Missed," *Studies in Gender and Sexuality* 3 (2002): 73–82.

[10] Nancy J. Chodorow, "Prejudice Exposed: On Stephen Mitchell's Pioneering Investigations of the Psychoanalytic Treatment and Mistreatment of Homosexuality," *Studies in Gender and Sexuality* 3,1 (2002): 61–72; Jack Dresher, "A History of Homosexuality and Organized Psychoanalysis," *Journal of the American Academy of Psychoanalysis and Dynamic Psychiatry* 36 (2008): 443–460; Dresher, "Don't Ask, Don't Tell: A Gay Man's Perspective on the Psychoanalytic Training Experience Between 1973 and 1991," *Journal of Gay & Lesbian Psychotherapy* 6 (2002): 45–55. See also Dresher, "In Memory of Stephen Mitchell," *Studies in Gender and Sexuality* 3 (2002): 95–110.

[11] Richard Isay, *Becoming Gay* (New York: Pantheon Books, 1996), 157–161.

traditional psychoanalysis. It also sowed the seeds of Stephen Mitchell's important work mentioned above, as well as creating the soil for the Relational School of Psychoanalysis in the 1980s,[12] and a new influential journal, *Psychoanalytic* Dialogues, founded in 1991.

It took two decades for The American Psychoanalytic Association (APsaA) to catch up with the American Psychiatric Association in accepting gay students for psychoanalytic training and to be eligible to become faculty members. It was the same year APsaA opened its doors to non-medical candidates (psychologists, social workers, University academics from Universities) for psychoanalytic training, a change that had been resisted since its founding in 1911. Ralph Roughton, APsaA's first out gay training analyst, was invited to give a Plenary Address to the membership-a first in its history.[13] Just years earlier, Roughton revealed the secret he carefully guarded for close to 60 years fearing disclosure would ruin his family and career. He raised these questions: Why were analysts unable to theorize about homosexuality that was not pathology? Why was psychic maturity defined only as a heterosexual genital achievement? Why were gay and lesbian perspectives on sexuality never sought out and considered? What could we learn about men and women growing up gay with a normal life course? These crucial questions contributed to a gradual but major sea change in attitudes within APsaA with regard to theory making about homosexuality, gender, and sexuality in general.

In 1997, in an about face, APsaA turned from the blindness that gripped it to become the first mainstream mental health organization to endorse gay marriage and in 2002 supported gay and lesbian parenting, including adoption, visitation, and custody; "the child requires committed, nurturing, and competent parents without prejudice regarding sexual orientation. ... Gay and lesbian individuals and couples are capable of meeting the best interest of children and should be afforded the same rights and ... responsibilities as heterosexual parents."[14] One can't help but look at the dramatic change in institutional psychoanalysis in light of the breath-taking cultural changes culminating in the 2015 Supreme

[12] Jay A. Greenberg and Mitchell, Object Relations in Psychoanalytic Theory (Cambridge: Harvard University Press, 1983).

[13] Roughton, "Rethinking Homosexuality: What it Teaches us about Psychoanalysis," *Journal of the American Psychoanalytic Association* (*JAPA*) 50 (2002): 733–763.

[14] American Psychoanalytic Association (APsaA), "Position Statement on Parenting" (2012); https://apsa.org/sites/default/files/2012%20%20Position%20Statement%20on%20Parenting.pdf (access March 2021).

Court decision in support of gay marriage; the increasing visibility of out-celebrities, responsiveness to the civil rights and woman's movements, and gay rights advocacy within and outside of psychoanalysis.

Responding to the decision, President Barack Obama referred to "countless small acts of courage of millions of people across decades who stood up, who came out, who talked to parents—parents who loved their children no matter what."[15] "Gay" entered the psychoanalytic lexicon as an identity embraced by people who could accept their bodies, voice, self-image, rights, creativity, longings, and conflicts. The term "homosexuality"—which described sexual desire and behavior associated with oedipal and pre-Oedipal pathology is now rarely seen in mainstream psychoanalytic curricula or in panels and workshops within APsaA. The previously named Committee on LGBT issues became the Committee on Gender and Sexuality; a new generation of young analysts—both gay and straight—no longer committed to binary gender categories now theorize and write about heterosexual and homosexual development and gender. Perhaps a small minority within APsaA believe this change was a nod to political correctness rather than reflecting more genuine social and psychological realities.

Psychoanalysis and the Abuse of Power: Parents, Children, Clinicians, and Patients

If one topic of debate stirred the most feeling among my teachers when I was in training, it was whether a patient's emotional difficulties were better understood through an Oedipal or pre-Oedipal childhood conflict model; 3–6 years or 0–3 years. But much more was at stake for psychoanalysis than a competing developmental time period. "Pre-Oedipal" was about the importance of the parent-child attachment relationship, a foundational dyad at the heart of the child's capacity to self-regulate through internalizing a "good enough mother."[16] It was about how a child acquires social language, cognitive skills, a positive self-image, and the achievement

[15] Administration of Barack Obama, 2015, "Remarks on the United States Supreme Court Ruling on Same-Sex Marriage" (June 26, 1015); https://www.govinfo.gov/content/pkg/DCPD-201500463/html/DCPD-201500463.htm (access March 2021).

[16] Donald W. Winnicott, *The Maturational Processes and the Facilitating Environment: Studies in the Theory of Emotional Development* (New York: International Universities Press, 1965), 57.

of emotional well-being. Suddenly, the mental life of the child's parents during its early years loomed in importance. As D.H. Winnicott said, "There is no such thing as an infant, only the mother-infant unit."[17] Raising serious questions about the influence of parents' mental life on their children marked the beginning of the pre-Oedipal lens as a psychoanalytic tool from which analysts could return to Freud's previously discarded adult seduction/abuse theory to re-consider adult desires and conflicting feelings toward children.

For many analysts, the early care-taking environment became as etiologically significant across a wide range of mental health and public health problems as the previously more exclusive intrapsychic focus. Many dropped the term "pre-Oedipal" altogether as the parent-child relationship was sufficiently important in its own right to no longer shadow its historical antecedent, the Oedipus complex. Including the parents' mental life in a "two-person" rather than a "one person" psychology required a changing view of the mind as interpersonal and intersubjective and became an important psychoanalytic paradigm shift.[18] This change quickly extended as well to the emotional life, values, and biases (countertransference) of the clinician in the therapeutic dyad. The newer emphasis on care-taking in early development was readily embraced by the relational school, but was concerning to traditional analysts who worried about the loss of the intrapsychic focus.

The recurrent debate over the centrality of Oedipus in mental illness has been an important part of psychoanalytic history. In the 1940s, in addition to personality factors, a main issue underlying institutional splits, described by Karen Horney, Erich Fromm, and Harry Sullivan, was the degree of attention to social and cultural over intrapsychic factors.[19] Freud's discovery of the Oedipus complex cannot be separated from his earlier seduction theory—that adult seduction/abuse of a child was at the

[17] Winnicott, "The Theory of the Parent-Infant Relationship," *International Journal Psychoanalysis* 41 (1960): 585–595, here 39.

[18] Hans W. Loewald, "Transference-Countertransference," *JAPA* 34 (1986): 275–287; Theodore J. Jacobs, "The Corrective Emotional Experience—Its Place in Current Technique," *Psychoanalytic Inquiry* 10 (1990): 433–454; Charles Spezzano, "The three faces of two-person psychology development, ontology, and epistemology." *Psychoanalytic Dialogues* 6,5 (1996): 599–622.

[19] Sanford Gifford, "Psychoanalysis in North America from 1895 to the Present." In: Ethel S. Person, Arnold M. Cooper, and Glenn O. Gabbard (Eds.), *Textbook of Psychoanalysis*. 1st Edition (Washington, DC: American Psychiatric Publishing Inc., 2005), 387–406.

root of the hysterical-neurosis—a theory he abandoned in the summer of 1897.[20] Almost simultaneously, from his self-analysis, Freud discovered the Oedipus complex, infantile sexuality, and the repressed unconscious. Freed from the realities of adult seduction, Freud and many of his followers substituted primarily an intrapsychic process and model of dynamic mental functioning, the heart of which is the child's defense against unwelcome desire and fantasy as the source of psychoneurosis. True, Freud left room for the role of environmental forces to shape early mental life. But for generations of Freud's followers, social and cultural forces were minimized because of how easily they could be used to deflect and detract from the highly defended inner world of instinctual conflicts.

It was momentous for Freud and psychoanalytic history to create an Oedipal lens from which to reflect on pervasive "self-induced" emotional suffering. From nineteenth-century Victorian European society, Oedipus crossed geographical, historical, and cultural boundaries. After the Copernican and Darwinian revolutions, some considered the Oedipal unconscious the third great blow to twentieth-century man's illusionary, privileged place in creation. Yet on turning his back on parental abuse and exploitation, an idealization of parenthood crept into his thinking. Freud's mothers often appear in his writings as a generic breed of similarly minted coins, assumed to be loving, knowledgeable about child care, engaged in untroubled attachments, and constant as the K in a scientific formula. This may have been Freud's way of helping us pay attention to the unfolding of the child's infantile sexuality and defensive repression without having to simultaneously consider the complications of parental desire and behavior directed toward the child.

The separation of the child's mental life from that of its parents trickled down to the training of child psychiatrists in the 1970s where social workers were assigned to work with the child's parents while the psychiatrist met individually with the child. The social worker and the child psychiatrist conferred about the family but the child psychiatrist rarely met with the parents directly. One purpose of this split was to ensure that the child psychiatrist's scientific field; the child's mind and behavior, would not be diluted by unwanted parental input and distortion. In my first decade of private practice, I learned the hard way that parents need to be engaged and participate in the treatment with their child not only because they are

[20] Ernest Jones, *The Life and Work of Sigmund Freud*. 3 vols. *(New York:* Basic Books), I: 265–267.

so needed, but also to prevent unbearable feelings of isolation and exclusion. It is true that attention to the child in the individual interview is a key building block of clinical child psychiatry and child analysis but both fields increasingly work in tandem with parents, even encouraging joint sessions with child and parents.

The actual seduction versus Oedipal fantasy debate goes back to Sandor Ferenczi's writings in the 1930s. Ferenczi countered Freud's emphasis on children's Oedipal fantasy by describing how parental hypocrisy and distortion of the truth along with actual seduction and the demand for silent collusion affected children.[21] Parents' behavior with their children as a reflection of parental desire, affects, and conflicts in this scenario were of central importance. Until recently, Ferenczi's name was rarely found in mainstream psychoanalytic curriculum. The avoidance of parental realities in psychoanalysis lasted for decades in post-WW II mental health circles as long as Oedipus reigned supreme. Hans W. Loewald, a highly credentialed classical analyst described a declining interest among analysts in the Oedipal triad paradigm in favor of the mother-child pre-Oedipal dyad, especially whether and how the caregiver was meeting the child's emotional needs.[22]

While Freud's drive theory began with childhood sexuality and aggression, Ferenczi began with adult aggression and incest—which preceded the Oedipus' complex; before Oedipus' triadic involvement with his parents, his father Laius tried to murder him. Motivated by an urge to thwart a prophecy of his own death at the hands of his son, Laius abandoned Oedipus as an infant on a mountain side. Adult sexual and physical abuse of children—consistent with Freud's aggressive and sexual instinct theory—begin in the adult's, not in the child's, mind. This view from the adult perch has not been an easy switch for a Freudian because parental sexuality and aggression toward children have been out of focus since the discovery of Oedipus. From 1900 to 1975, actual incest and seduction were rarely dealt with in psychoanalytic books or articles and when it was, the child's sexuality was highlighted. Bennett Simon refers to aspects of institutional psychoanalysis that make the recognition and undoing of

[21] Sandor Ferenczi, "The Confusion of Tongues Between Adults and Children: *The Language of Tenderness and of Passion*," tr. Michael Balint, *The International Journal of Psycho-Analysis* 30 (1949): 225–230. The paper was first presented at the Twelfth International Psycho-analytical Congress in Wiesbaden in 1932.

[22] Hans W. Loewald, "The Waning of the Oedipus Complex," *JAPA*. 27 (1979): 751–775.

"errors" such as including incest under the Oedipal umbrella as taking decades.[23] Simon's interest in actual trauma came about because of an earlier interest in the similar defense mechanisms used by patients abused by parents and patients abused by therapists.

In the last half of the twentieth century, psychoanalytic developmental and clinical theory focused on the biological and social foundations of human relationships where the risks of failures in parental empathy, and the intergenerational transmission of trauma were being documented. New routes of discourse untraveled by Freud;[24] object relations, self-psychology, and relational psychoanalytic schools incorporated findings from attachment and infant research, pediatrics, neuroscience, feminist and critical social theory—uncommon source materials in classical analytic circles.

Looking at parenting vulnerabilities in this way can induce our own feelings of shame related to personal defenses against old demons, and emotionally crippling parental conflicts—those of our own parents or of ourselves as parents—uncomfortable subjects for the most experienced clinicians. Physical and sexual abuse, parental deprivation, failures of attunement, and disorganized attachment[25] led social critic and psychoanalyst Elizabeth Young-Bruehl to coin the term "childism" comparing it to racism, sexism, and homophobia.[26] She hoped we could acknowledge and understand prejudice against children as a major social priority. Oedipus blinded himself as punishment for his blindness to his own incest and patricide. As analysts, what are the implications of awakening to our own childism?

As a young faculty member at Hahnemann Medical College in the 1970s with a joint appointment in the Departments of Child Psychiatry and Pediatrics, I was a liaison between the two Departments around clinical care and consultation to staff. While teaching analytic candidates Freud's Oedipal and drive theory at the Psychoanalytic Center, I witnessed daily on the pediatric floor the physical and psychological effects on

[23] Bennett Simon, "Incest—See Under Oedipus Complex: The History of an Error in Psychoanalysis," *JAPA* 40,4 (1992): 955–988.

[24] See Peter Fonagy, *Attachment Theory and Psychoanalysis*. New York: Other Press, 2001.

[25] John Bowlby, "The Nature of the Child's Tie to Its Mother," *International Journal of Psychoanalysis*, 39 (1958): 350–373; Heinz Kohut, *The Analysis of the Self*. New York (New York: International Universities Press, 1971); Donald W. Winnicott, "Transitional Objects and Transitional Phenomena," *International Journal of Psychoanalysis* 34 (1953): 89–97.

[26] Elisabeth Young-Bruehl, *Childism*, New Haven: Yale University Press, 2012.

children of their parents profound social, economic, and psychological struggles, including many forms of negligence and abuse from adults with limited resources, supports, or understanding of child development.[27] Their children suffered malnutrition, developmental delays, multiple types of emotional trauma and scarring, and even Munchhausen by proxy where a parent would induce an illness in their child in order to receive hospital staff attention. At the time, I did not find my psychoanalytic training to be helpful in understanding and counseling these families nor to aiding the pediatric staff with their overwhelming emotions trying to care for them.

By the mid-1970s, the so-called psychoneurotic patient whose Oedipal conflicts Freud hoped to alleviate by the talking cure were becoming less common in analysts' offices.[28] In their place were patients referred to as narcissistic, borderline, and other character problems with alarming histories of physical, sexual, and emotional trauma. "Soul Murder" was the term Leonard Shengold coined for brutal acts against children resulting in psychic and spiritual annihilation.[29] "Developmental trauma" was Philip Bromberg's term for harmful parenting practices and non-recognition of the child.[30] Gradually psychoanalysis has sought to rebalance Freud's original weighting of fantasy and reality, imagination and fact so that inner demons could be understood along with experiential demons passed down from parents and other adults to offer a more nuanced and balanced clinical narrative.[31]

Two papers exemplify the shift from Freud's Oedipal origin to an appreciation of how dyadic parent-child interaction contributes to symptom formation. They also look at gender and sexuality from a newer psychoanalytic perspective inclusive of family and social forces. Ken Corbett's paper, written on the 100th anniversary of Freud's "Little Hans"-essay, depicts a boy whose (pre-Oedipal) needs for attunement and recognition

[27] C. Henry Kempe, Frederic N. Silverman, Brandt F. Steele, William Droegemueller, and Henry K. Silver, "The Battered-Child Syndrome," *Child Abuse & Neglect* 9 (1985): 143–154.

[28] Gifford, "Psychoanalysis in North America from 1895 to the Present."

[29] Leonard Shengold, *Soul Murder*, New Haven: Yale University Press, 1989.

[30] Philip M. Bromberg, *Awakening the Dreamer, Clinical Journeys* (New York: Routledge, 2006), 6–8.

[31] Theodore Jacobs "Commentary," *The Psychoanalytic Quarterly 89* (2020): 831–847, here 837–839.

went unnoticed by his parents and by Freud.[32] Corbett believes Freud's first Oedipal child essay, transmits culture-bound theories and pervasive gender binary posing as universal mental health norms. Hans' horse phobia became Freud's archetype for normal oedipal boyhood masculinity, with its phallic drive, desire for mother, rivalry with father, and castration anxiety. Freud's heteronormative and homorepudiating authority merge with that of Hans' father as "Oedipal" interpretations are passed down to Hans through his father.

The particulars of Hans' father and mother, Corbett writes, were submerged by Freud's gender stereotyping. Interviews with Herbert Graf (the real "Little Hans") and his father contrast Freud's depiction of Hans' mother as excellent and devoted with that of a very troubled family (745);[33] parental unhappiness, a deteriorating marriage, child beatings of Hans' sister, and multiple other traumas. After reading Corbett on Little Hans, and thinking feminist theory, I imagined Little Hans' penis containing a psychological "homunculus" destined to grow into the normal male gender and heterosexuality; boy to man-adventurous-aggressive-bread winning. Likewise, the girls' genital "femunculus" determines her gender dynamics; straight, submissive, home-bound, nurturing, and concerned with relationships. Corbett views traditional psychoanalysis for most of its history as reinforcing the view that homosexuality was a deficit pathology. He refers to a "regulatory anxiety" which the social milieu supports,[34] contributing to a person's perceived failure to measure up to the specific normative expectation around binary gender or heterosexual orientation.

The second paper by Avgi Saketopoulou is about six-year-old Jenny who came to treatment because of violent acting out and inability to be comforted by her parents.[35] She couldn't stand the fact that she had a penis. As central as penis envy was to past analysts, Jenny was miserable that she had a penis. She wore dresses and told others she was a girl. She insisted that no one refers to her penis. She tried to hide her male genitals from her analyst until ready to discuss this terrible reality. When finally

[32] Ken Corbett, "Masculinity Foretold," *The Psychoanalytic Quarterly,* 78 (2009): 733–764.

[33] See also Kurt Eissler, Box Ri (1955), Sigmund Freud Papers, Library of Congress, Washington.

[34] Corbett, "Boyhood Femininity, Gender Identity Disorder, Masculine Presuppositions, and the Anxiety of Regulation," *Psychoanalytic Dialogues* 19 (2009): 353–370, here 354.

[35] Avgi Saketopoulou, "Mourning the Body as Bedrock; Developmental considerations in treating Transsexual patients analytically," *JAPA* 62,5 (2014): 773–806.

comfortable, she confessed to her therapist: "There's something I haven't told you. Daddy thinks I'm a boy!" Then she added sadly, "Sometimes I wear boy clothes so his heart doesn't keep breaking!" (796). At 6, Jenny was worried about disappointing her Daddy that she loved so much. Eventually she did accept "her unthinkable penis" (794), and the fact that she had a history of having been a boy. Jenny and her father—like most of us—believed that anatomy is bedrock when it comes to gender and sexual orientation. A hard lesson to unlearn.

Similar to failed psychoanalytic treatments of homosexuality, Saketopoulou reminds us that attempts to eliminate gender variance through treatment can damage children's self-esteem. That the body can now be aligned with subjective gender has new meanings for trans patients, their families, and society. Contemporary psychoanalysis is becoming a safe place to theorize non-normative gender and to consider how institutional biases kept transgender experience-like gay experience outside of empathetic inquiry.

As more gay, and now trans as well, personal stories are told, a new generation of psychoanalysts listens differently to painful narratives about pressures to conform to social expectations and to deny so-called unacceptable differences. Rather than automatically assuming unconscious defenses against oedipal pathology, analysts can attend to the distress of children whose gender experience doesn't match their assigned biological sex. Our broader developmental lens helps us appreciate the anguish in our gay and trans patients when trying to cope with rejecting family and cultural responses to their feelings of difference. We are also more aware of the need for education and advocacy on behalf of those gay and trans patients who come from marginalized parts of our society and have not had a supportive family and or community attend to their special needs.

Viewing the plasticity and variability of gender, "masculine traits" are as likely to be transferred from mother and "feminine traits" from father to their child as vice versa. As Kyle Pruett has shown, fathers who spend more time with their children begin to resemble our idea of a maternal nurturing figure.[36] Neither the gender and sexual orientation of parents nor a child's biological sex at birth can predict that child's gender, sexual orientation, or self-worth.

[36] Kyle D. Pruett "The Nurturing Male." In: Stanley H. Cath, Alan Gurwitt and Linda Gunsberg (Eds.), *Fathers and Their Families* (Hillsdale: Analytic Press, 1989), 309–408.

What correlates best with a child's emotional well-being is the caregiver's responsiveness to that child's uniqueness while providing loving relationships in a supportive family and community. Newer psychoanalytic views about gender and sexual orientation in the modern family are in their infancy. While no longer seeking psychological origins of differences, people with diverse gender and sexual expressions are subject to the same inner conflicts as their less diverse-seeming peers. Like everyone else, they can be their own worst enemies and to the same degree can benefit from "talk therapy."

I will end my foray into the history of Oedipal/pre-Oedipal shifts in the psychoanalytic community by mentioning one more highly charged matter related to the Oedipal/incest imbalance; that of psychoanalysts' sexual boundary violations enacted with their patients. After avoidance and denial paralleling the silence surrounding sexual exploitation of children in families, sexual boundary violations by analysts and other therapists have found their way into our journals and public forums. Glenn Gabbard refers to such catastrophic breaches as a "professional form of incest"[37]—something which concerned Freud as soon as he discovered transference and counter-transference.

While the "resolution" of the Oedipal complex is now more psychoanalytic lore than a realistic goal, we have not really worked through our communal failures to accept the professional incest barrier and better understand its boundary violations. Our institutions, practitioners, and those we train must feel that psychoanalysis has a secure ethical conscience rooted in the agreed-upon standards of practice that patient safety always comes first. Psychoanalytic institutions must create whatever policies and procedures will maximize participation of members around prevention, continuing education, and accountability to the professional community.

Conclusion

Our psychoanalytic legacy is revolutionary in its liberating understanding of the self and its techniques for dealing with the darkest corners of our emotional life. It is the only sustained mental health approach to freeing unacknowledged human potential underlying repeated human failure and self-sabotage. But what may not have been recognized about this very same legacy?

[37] Glenn Gabbord, cited in Gifford, "Psychoanalysis in North America from 1895 to the Present," 379.

Did our analytic heritage blind us to the actual hurts and trauma occurring in unequal power relationships between straights and gays, parent and child, clinician and patient? Did the Oedipus' complex blind us to Laius's infanticide, to gay normalcy hiding under homosexual pathology, to adult abuse hidden by childhood sexual fantasies, and to clinician's unethical behavior while focusing on patient sexual dynamics? Was an unintended consequence of Freud's discoveries a pass for powerful adults to continue hurtful behaviors while many of us remained silent behind our scientific neutrality and studies?

Finally, what can we learn from the misuse of the Oedipus complex to explain homosexuality and from the enormous role parents' own early experiences have in their children's emotional and behavioral lives? The misuse of Oedipus left a theoretical gap in our understanding of gender, sexuality, their normal variations, and the limitations of our treatments. This has been a humbling experience for many of us. Analysts must live with their own incomplete Oedipal resolutions and lingering biases,[38] a reminder of the continuing work we all need to do on ourselves. Confronting the realities of sexual abuse and violence toward children as well as more subtle parental failures of attunement and attachment has led to a re-evaluation of Oedipal and pre-Oedipal paradigms in our educational programs. Confronting the realities of analyst sexual boundary violations has hopefully awakened analysts' greater accountability to their patients and their colleagues and the need for ongoing courses in ethics and counter-transference enactments.

While offering an insider's historical slice of institutional psychoanalysis, I have also been remembering, repeating, and working through my own relationship to my parent organization which has nurtured my professional identity and provided me with collegiality, and an endless source of rich intellectual stimulation. While psychoanalysts—even the best analyzed—will never be free of old stereotypes and unconscious biases, our progress over the last decades has been rapid and continuous with inclusivity replacing exclusivity on several fronts. Psychological blindness needn't be permanent. We need and welcome thoughtful and curious young people who seek to deepen their own and the relationships of others and are passionate about picking up the clinical challenges Freud and his descendants left for us all.

[38] Muriel Dimen, "Both Given and Made: Commentary on Sakeopoulou," *JAPA* 62, 5 (2014): 807–814.

CHAPTER 10

A Fatherless Nation: Alexander Mitscherlich Analyzes Post-War Germany

Liliane Weissberg

The Living Room Set

In 1980, Herlinde Koelbl published a book of photographs, *Das deutsche Wohnzimmer* (*The German Living Room*). Koelbl would focus in later years on the human face and publish portraits of German Jews, of German women, or of German politicians.[1] But in 1980, she was less interested in the human figure. The black-and-white images were portraits of another kind, namely pictures of the interiors of post-war, West German houses and apartments (Fig. 10.1).[2] People were not exactly absent here; they were placed in their living rooms and seemed to show them off to a wider

[1] See for example Hildegard Koelbl, *Jüdische Portraits. Photographien und Interviews.* Frankfurt/M: S. Fischer, 1989; *Starke Frauen.* Munich: Knesebeck, 1996; or *Spuren der Macht: Die Verwandlung des Menschen durch das Amt. Eine Langzeitstudie.* Munich: Knesebeck, 1999.

[2] Koelbl, Manfred Sack, *Das deutsche Wohnzimmer.* With a contribution by Alexander Mitscherlich. Munich: C.J. Bucher, 1980.

L. Weissberg (✉)
University of Pennsylvania, Philadelphia, PA, USA
e-mail: lweissbe@sas.upenn.edu

L. Weissberg (ed.), *Psychoanalysis, Fatherhood, and the Modern Family*, https://doi.org/10.1007/978-3-030-82124-1_10

Fig. 10.1 "Walter L." (Photo: Herlinde Koelbl). From: Herlinde Koelbl and Manfred Sack, *Das deutsche Wohnzimmer* (*The German Living Room*), Munich: C.J. Bucher, 1980

public—some proudly, some hesitantly, and some with nonchalance. These rooms took center stage, however, and offered a peculiar testimony of the economic miracle to the post-war years, and the dreams and ambitions of their inhabitants.

The living rooms spoke eloquently of their inhabitants' taste, their class affiliations, and their social ambitions. The photographs' titles identified their inhabitants by their professions only, or by their first names, or by the initial of their family name. Some of the people depicted could be easily identified, however, as they were prominent personalities, such as the writer Martin Walser or the Bavarian politician Hermann Höcherl. The book itself was divided into four chapters that produced groupings of professions and social classes and followed a model already employed by August Sander in his famous collection *Menschen des 20. Jahrhunderts*

(People of the 20th Century), a project that Sander had begun in 1911, and that would extend to the period of WWII.[3]

Understood as a "face," the West German living room could offer certain national characteristics. In its middle-class version, it was defined by a set of a couch and two matching chairs, a so-called Garnitur, and sported often an oriental carpet, and a wall unit that would consist of bookshelves, a space for a television set, and perhaps a glass vitrine with a built-in bar. Above the couch, there would be a painting of a landscape, for example, the alps, or a forest scene with deer. In its lower-class version, the living room. Chairs might not always be coordinated, and possibly less comfortable, and oil paintings could be replaced by prints. Everywhere, however, a sense of aspiration was palpable. Just like the inhabitants of these rooms, the objects that they contained expressed upward mobility; they wanted to appear exclusive and expensive. There were signs of superfluous consumption: glasses, placed on shelves, served as decoration only; useless lace doilies were placed on tables and chairs, and some walls sported antlers, even though these rooms were not occupied by hunters. There was a general rejection of modernist design.[4] The inhabitants of these living rooms longed for the historicism of the foundational years of the German Empire, the *Gründerjahre* of the late nineteenth century, and seemed to ignore Germany's more immediate past. In these living rooms, historicism served as an instrument of historical amnesia.

At the center of all these living rooms was the couch. This piece of furniture predates the decoration of these living rooms, of course, as well as the historicist period. French artisans conceived of the modern living room couch in the seventeenth century, to serve the upper class, aristocratic market.[5] These early pieces followed the design of a Turkish sofa and were viewed as exotic; they were expensive as well. Sitters had to assume a new bodily position, moreover, and sit less stiffly than they would on a chair; women adapted to the new furniture with dresses that would allow more comfort. But one could not only sit on a couch, one could also rest on it too. In contemporary literature and arts, the couch became primarily a seating option for women, often underlining their desirability. Needless

[3] See the new edition, August Sander, *Menschen des 20. Jahrhunderts*. Munich: Schirmer-Mosel, 2010. The large editions of Sander's photographs were all published posthumously.

[4] See Manfred Sack, "Das deutsche Wohnzimmer," in: Koelbl and Sack, *Das deutsche Wohnzimmer*, 7–21, here 11.

[5] See Joan DeJean, *The Age of Comfort: When Paris Discovered Casual--and the Modern Home Began* (New York: Bloomsbury, 2009), 102–164.

to say, it could also promote a reputation of immoral behavior for the sitter.[6]

By the late nineteenth century, however, couches were mass produced by furniture factories and had become popular items for middle-class living rooms. As firmly upholstered day beds, they turned into the regular equipment of medical offices, too.[7] A patient was not to sit or lie down to relax, but to assume the appropriate position to be examined by the doctor, or to receive treatments such as massages. Female patients who suffered from hysteria were homebound and unable to move easily. For them, domestic furniture like the couch turned into a kind of hospital bed. Sigmund Freud would conduct home visits to such patients, already by 1886, he had introduced a couch in his own medical office, to encourage his patients to lay down and relax. At first, the couch aided his early experiments with hypnosis. Soon, however, Freud would abandon hypnosis, and concentrate on "the talking cure."[8] Once again, the couch turned into a medical stretcher, but into an instrument that aimed to heal the mind and inner life rather than the body. Freud's couch received an oriental carpet as a cover, and as his practice took on the semblance of an upper bourgeois living room, the couch became once again a domestic piece of furniture.[9] His patients would rest comfortably on the couch, while the doctor seated himself at its head, and remained invisible for his patients. They just had to concentrate on their associations and flow of words.

Did Koelbl's photographs simply offer a series of portraits of post-war West German living rooms, spaces filled with objects and human extras? Or was she functioning as a psychoanalyst of sorts as well; one who could offer a cumulative image of the psyche of the young Federal Republic of Germany? A preface to Koelbl's volume, entitled "Confession to Proximity: What Turns an Apartment into a *Heimat*?," seems to suggest the latter. Its

[6] Juliane Vogel, "Die Couch im Raum: Positionen," in: Lydia Marinelli (Ed.), *Die Couch. Vom Denken im Liegen* (Munich: Prestel/Sigmund Freud Privatstiftung, 2006), 144.

[7] Lydia Marinelli, *Tricks der Evidenz. Zur Geschichte psychoanalytischer Medien*, ed. Andreas Mayer (Vienna: Turia + Kant, 2009), 245–266, esp. 247, and Claudia Guderian, *Die Couch in der Psychoanalyse*, Stuttgart: Kohlhammer, 2004.

[8] "The Talking Cure" is a term coined by Bertha Pappenheim, Freud and Breuer's patient "Anna O." in the *Studies on Hysteria* (1895); see John Lauer, "Anna O and the 'talking cure,'" *QJM: An International Journal of Medicine* 98 (2005): 465–466.

[9] In regard to Freud's couch, see Marinelli, "Die Couch," esp. 248–251, and Liliane Weissberg, "Ariadne's Thread: Sigmund Freud, the Textile Industry, and Early Psychoanalysis." *MLN* 125 (2010): 661–681.

author was the psychoanalyst, Alexander Mitscherlich. The text itself was an excerpt from his book, *Die Unwirtlichkeit der Städte. Anstiftung zum Unfrieden* (Our Inhospitable Cities: An Incitement to Unrest), which had been published in 1965, and widely received in Germany.[10]

While Koelbl directed her gaze to the arrangement of furniture and the habitus of the inhabitants of these spaces, who seemed to freeze in front of the camera, Mitscherlich focused on the term "*Heimat*" instead. He was looking for the idea of a home expressed in these post-war dwellings:

> What turns an apartment into a *Heimat*? I would like to propose that this question cannot be answered first and foremost by the choice of beautiful furniture or carpets, by big rooms or sunny windows, not even by its very location or the art of its architect. All of this I have seen already in ideal combination, and have not been convinced that such a house or apartment had become a *Heimat* for anybody. Instead, I would like to insist on human relationships that are in some ways bound up with a specific place.[11]

To regard these rooms as homes may offer their "human natural history" as Mitscherlich proposes (140), and attach a higher meaning to them. He is less interested in the representational function of the objects depicted than in the social relations that these objects reflect and imply. Theodor W. Adorno wrote about the "random gossip of a mother-in-law" that took place on the divan, and that had turned into the talking cure performed on the analyst's couch.[12] Mitscherlich was not interested in the transition from social chatter to the monologue of the "talking cure," however, and he did not view the psychoanalytic process as empty. But in moving the interpersonal discourse into the foreground, he transformed the loneliness of the patient into a question of his or her human relationships and membership in a social network. Mitscherlich returned the couch to a social context. If Freud in the late nineteenth century had moved the couch from the living room to his medical office by pretending it was a living room, Mitscherlich changed the direction of this move. For the sake of psychoanalysis, he returned it to the living room.

[10] Alexander Mitscherlich, "Konfession zur Nahwelt. Was macht eine Wohnung zur Heimat?," in: Koelbl and Sack, *Das deutsche Wohnzimmer*, 135–143. Siehe Mitscherlich, *Die Unwirtlichkeit der Städte. Anstiftung zum Unfrieden*. Frankfurt/M: Suhrkamp Verlag, 1965.

[11] Mitscherlich, "Konfession zur Nahwelt," 135. Further reference in the text.

[12] Theodor W. Adorno, *Minima Moralia. Reflections on a Damaged Life*, tr. E.F.N. Jephcott (ser.) Radical Thinkers (London: Verso, 2005), 43.

A Post-War Career

Alexander Mitscherlich did not set out to become a psychoanalyst or even a physician. Before WWII, he studied history, philosophy, and history of art in Munich. Under the influence of Ernst Jünger, he then moved to Berlin and befriended Ernst Niekisch who was active in the national-revolutionary movement. Mitscherlich became a publisher and bookseller. As such, he distributed the journal *Der Widerstand: Zeitschrift für national revolutionäre Politik* (Resistance: A Journal for National Revolutionary Politics) that was edited by Niekisch. The journal did not please the new German government, and in 1933, the SA arrested Mitscherlich for a brief period of time. In 1935, he moved to Switzerland, and there he began his studies of medicine. In 1937, he returned to Germany briefly, to find a lawyer for Niekisch who had legal troubles, and was once again arrested. During his arraignment, the Gestapo showed Mitscherlich letters in which Niekisch as well as Jünger expressed reservations about him. Consequently, Mitscherlich decided to break with both.[13] Once released, he decided to remain in Germany, however. In Switzerland, he had become interested in psychosomatic medicine and had been influenced by the Swiss psychoanalyst Gustav Bally. But he had read Victor von Weizäcker's work in medical anthropology as well. He chose to continue his studies with Weizäcker, and in 1941, he completed his dissertation under Weizäcker's supervision in Heidelberg.

After the war, Mitscherlich found himself in a remarkable position. Although his early interest in Jünger and his cooperation with Nickisch could not possibly be construed as a true critique of the Nazi regime, and although he completed his studies in Heidelberg, a place that had served as a center of the National Socialist movement, Mitscherlich construed his arrests by the SA and the Gestapo as evidence of his status as a victim of the Nazi regime. He downplayed the complex political position of Weizäcker, whose professional career had flourished in the Third Reich; Weizäcker had served as Mitscherlich's adviser, and Mitscherlich was employed by him. As Martin Dehli argues in his account of Mitscherlich's early career, he was eager to obscure the reasons for his arrests and chose not to reflect on his own political position in the pre-war and war years.[14]

[13] Martin Dehli, *Leben als Konflikt. Zur Biographie Alexander Mitscherlichs* (Göttingen: Wallstein Verlag, 2007), 72–80.

[14] Martin Dehli, *Leben als Konflikt*, esp. 80–82.

Mitscherlich's political position after the war cannot be described as simply democratic, either. In 1948, he published a study, "Freiheit und Unfreiheit in der Krankheit. Das Bild des Menschen in der Psychotherapie" (Freedom and Lack of Freedom in Illness. The Image of the Human Being in Psychotherapy), in which he asked whether all lives were worthy of being saved, much as Weizäcker did. He had already penned an early version of this text in 1943.[15]

In 1941, Weizäcker had moved to the University of Breslau, and in 1945 he returned to Heidelberg. In 1949, the Department of Psychosomatic Medicine, of which he would become the director, was founded. Mitscherlich started his career as a physician in that Department and hoped for a permanent position there, but any professorship proved to be an elusive goal. He was an unpopular colleague, feared by many and—as he would see it—persecuted by many as well. The University had been deeply supportive of the National Socialist Regime, and many of its faculty members held onto their beliefs into the post-war years, or tried to hide their political past, or were simply very conservative. Mitscherlich appeared—and claimed to be—to be a man beyond reproach. In 1947, he contacted a person in the Hessian education office as he lobbied for a professorship, and he described his situation at the University of Heidelberg's Medical School as follows: "I had to interrupt my university career in this country just shortly after I began it 14 years ago; I left this country out of reasons of conscience; I was put into prison in this country in which my friends were murdered—it is not much that I ask for."[16]

But by the end of WWII, Mitscherlich had not really decided at all whether he wanted to continue working as a medical doctor, or become a writer instead; he even considered a political career.[17] The American allies appointed him to the provincial government Mittelrhein-Saar, where he was in charge of the division of public health. This position did not extend beyond two months, but Mitscherlich was able to serve as a political adviser afterward as he participated in the Denazification process of the Heidelberg faculty, and hence was also helpful in re-establishing the University. In his evaluations of individual professors, Mitscherlich often

[15] See Dehli, *Leben als Konflikt*, 116–118.

[16] Mitscherlich, letter to a government official, Ministerialrat im Landesdirektorium für Erziehung und Unterricht, March 19, 1947. Cited in Dehli, *Leben als Konflikt*, 225.

[17] See Dehli's detailed study, *Leben als Konflikt*, and Tobias Freimüller, *Alexander Mitscherlich. Gesellschaftsdiagnosen und Psychoanalyse nach Hitler* (Göttingen: Wallstein Verlag,) 2007.

noted the mutual silence about the events of the past, as former University faculty tried to aid one another to gain a reappointment. The fact that Mitscherlich issued these evaluations confirmed his outsider status in Heidelberg which would continue to characterize his professional standing in the field of medicine—an outsider position and reputation that he began to cherish as well. In future years, Mitscherlich would appear dressed in a white coat that mostly was meant to reflect on his medical profession. But it was also made to stand for his political record, as his *weisse Weste* (white coat/clean record) marked him to be innocent and morally beyond reproach, just as he began to describe himself as a victim of the National Socialist regime.

Soon after the end of WWII, Mitscherlich had the opportunity to combine his medical education with his political and journalistic interests. On December 9, 1946, the Allies staged a trial against twenty doctors and three NS functionaries in Nuremberg; they were charged with "Crimes against Humanity." Mitscherlich was sent to Nuremberg as an observer on behalf of the German Association of Physicians. Together with Fred Mielke, he published a report, *Das Diktat der Menschenverachtung* (The Dictate of Contempt for Humanity: A Documentation) in 1947.[18] The authors did not only condemn the particular doctors charged, but they strongly criticized German physicians who had practiced during the Third Reich more generally. While the German Association of Physicians tried to focus on a few perpetrators only, Mitscherlich addressed the profession at large. He was concerned with a doctor's ethical stance and the meaning of the Hippocratic oath which each physician would have had to follow. "What people in our midst have done, or chose not to do, can only be worked out believably from us if we investigate the real situation carefully, and accept that the horrible aspects belong to us as well," Mitscherlich wrote in his preface and chose a rhetorical formulation that would stress two points.[19] First, he appealed to conscience and called for a judgment based on evidence; secondly, he also turned himself into an object of research by including himself. When writing about the doctors,

[18] Alexander Mitscherlich and Fred Mielke, *Das Diktat der Menschenverachtung*, Heidelberg: Lambert Schneider, 1947; Alexander Mitscherlich and Fred Mielke, *Doctors of Infamy: The Story of the Nazi Medical Crimes*, tr. Heinz Norden. With statements of 3 American authorities identified with the Nuremberg medical trial and a note on medical ethics by Albert Deutsch; with 16 pages of photographs. New York: Henry Schuman, 1949.

[19] The preface is reprinted in: Mitscherlich, *Gesammelte Schriften* VI, ed. Herbert Weigandt (Frankfurt am Main: Suhrkamp Verlag, 1983), 151–154, here S. 153.

Mitscherlich used a "we," and he insisted on the fact that he was studying general human behavior. Mitscherlich was an anthropologist and remained one until the end of his life. In 1960, he published a new edition of *Das Diktat der Menschenverachtung* under the new title *Medizin ohne Menschlichkeit: Dokumente des Nürnberger Ärzteprozesses* (Medicine Without Humanity: Documents of the Nuremberg Doctors Trial). The book sold well and was widely reviewed. Robert Jay Lifton referred to it in his international best-seller *The Nazi Doctors: Medical Killing and the Psychology of Genocide.*[20] Mitscherlich's new book confirmed the general perception that he was an outsider to the medical profession, not only at the University of Heidelberg but in Germany at large. Some accused him of befouling his own nest.[21] It now seemed even more impossible for him now to assume a professorship at the psychosomatic clinic in Heidelberg.

Together with Felix Schottlaender and Hans Kunz, Mitscherlich founded a publication in 1949, entitled *Psyche: Ein Jahrbuch für die Tiefenpsychologie und Menschenkunde in Forschung und Praxis* (Psyche: A Yearbook for Depth Psychology and Anthropology in Research and Practice). One year later, he assumed the sole editorship, and the journal continued to flourish, and widen its scope, and establish itself as the leading psychoanalytic journal in Germany.[22] Increasingly, Mitscherlich relied on professional connections abroad. With the support of the Rockefeller Foundation, he was able to visit the United States in 1951 and to meet with American psychoanalysts, primarily Franz Alexander.

Mitscherlich's decision to work with the American allied forces in Heidelberg and to look to America in terms of his own career as a scholar as well had important consequences. He was able to forge contacts to German and Austrian emigrants. Alexander himself, for example, had been educated at the Berlin Institute and provided a link to pre-WWII German psychoanalytic practice. At his home institution in Heidelberg

[20] Robert Jay Lifton, *The Nazi Doctors: Medical Killing and the Psychology of Genocide* (New York: Basic Books, 1986). Lifton wrote the preface to the American edition of Alexander and Margarete Mitscherlich's *Die Unfähigkeit zu trauern* (1967): *The Inability to Mourn. Principles of Collective Behavior.* Tr. Beverly R. Placzek (New York: Grove Press, 1975), vii–xiii.

[21] See Mitscherlich and Mielke, *Medizin ohne Menschlichkeit. Dokumente d. Nürnberger Ärzteprozesses*, Frankfurt/M: Fischer Bücherei, 1960.

[22] The journal *Psyche* changed its name in 1966 to: *Zeitschrift für Psychoanalyse und ihre Anwendungen* (Journal of Psychoanalysis and its Applications), and appears more frequently now.

where he held a minor appointment, this involvement was not appreciated, and Mitscherlich tried to fend off professional hostilities by individual professors or the University administration with a steady stream of complaints and legal charges. For the younger generation of German doctors in Heidelberg and elsewhere, however, Mitscherlich's connections proved to be a boon. He proceeded to invite as many emigrants as possible to lecture or offer seminars in Heidelberg, and thus, he could also promote early contacts and conversations between the leading representatives of the field who practiced abroad and were instrumental in the establishment of the psychoanalytic profession, and German students who were just completing their medical education.

But it was not only with American psychoanalysts that Mitscherlich forged contacts. He met, too, with emigrants who had left for England, and later on, with those from other countries as well. Many of the visitors whom Mitscherlich invited were emigrants who would return to Germany for the first time after WWII. Soon, Mitscherlich would view himself as a spokesperson for those former victims, implicitly comparing himself to those formerly persecuted colleagues; he aligned his position as an outsider in the medical profession with that of the survivors who had to flee Germany. Thus, Mitscherlich's "we" began to fluctuate between an identification with the people who shaped the profession of psychoanalysis and were often Jewish on the one hand, and with post-war Germans on the other. In many of his conversations with members from the administration of the University in Heidelberg, he threatened to leave Germany, too, and emigrate to Switzerland or the United States.

Mitscherlich's many contacts with scholars and therapists abroad helped shape the discipline of psychoanalysis in Germany. He was able to internationalize the field, and he helped connect German doctors with the American psychoanalytic community. Largely because of Mitscherlich's initiative, the German Psychoanalytical Association (*Deutsche Psychoanalytische Vereinigung*, DPV) was able to join the International Psychoanalytic Association (IPA). For psychoanalysts in Germany, it was now possible to receive advanced education and an international certification and to promote further research in the field. But the exchanges with scholars working abroad changed Mitscherlich's own scholarly direction as well. In the early years as a physician, he had supported Weizäcker and the field of medical anthropology and had wanted to promote psychosomatic medicine along these lines. Now, he turned toward Freudian ideas.

But there was a problem. While Mitscherlich became the most recognized German psychoanalyst internationally, he could not become a member of the DPV. He did not have the training analysis which was, and still is, a precondition for any psychoanalyst who wants to practice. In 1958, Mitscherlich entered a training analysis with Paula Heimann, a German émigré who lived and practiced in London. This happened quite late in his career and was largely pro forma; he was in analysis for one year only.[23] A provisional membership period followed, after which he was finally able to join the organization that he had helped shape, and that was recognized internationally in 1959.

Once members of the DPV could gain access to the international psychoanalytic organization, the impact of German psychoanalytic practice and thought could reach beyond the country's boundaries. Mitscherlich saw himself as a person who had re-established the discipline of psychoanalysis in Germany, and this was certainly in the interest of the post-war German practitioners. Mitscherlich did not want only the DPV to be recognized, and to shape its reputation, however. He was also involved with the rivaling Deutsche Psychoanalytische Gesellschaft (DPG). The DPG had been founded Karl Abraham, incidentally Franz Alexander's mentor, in 1920 as the Berlin Psychoanalytic Institute, and had the longer tradition. The DPV had separated from the DPG in 1950 under the leadership of Carl Müller-Braunschweig who pursued a more orthodox Freudian direction. Most importantly, however, the new DPV wanted to split from the DPG to leave the institution's troubled past behind, as Karen Brecht has argued convincingly.[24] The DPG was founded by Freud's student and friend Abraham, but it had continued to exist during the Third Reich, and during that time, psychoanalytic treatment—and the DPG—were politically brought in line with National Socialist ideology. Matthias Göring, the Director of the Berlin institute during that period, was a cousin of Hermann Göring, the powerful political and military leader. A physician and psychotherapist, he had joined the NSDAP in 1933 already, as well as the SA and the NSDAP doctors' federation. In 1936, he established the Deutsches Institut für psychologisch Foschung und Psychotherapie

[23] See Freimüller, *Alexander Mitscherlich*, 188.

[24] Karen Brecht, "In the Aftermath of Nazi-Germany: Alexander Mitscherlich and Psychoanalysis—Legend and Legacy," *American Imago* 52 (1995), 291–312, and Anson Rabinbach, "Response to Karen Brecht, "In the Aftermath of Nazi-Germany: Alexander Mitscherlich und Psychoanalysis—Legend and Legacy, *American Imago* 52 (1995), 313–328. See also Dehli, Leben als Konflikt, 176–216.

(German Institute of Psychological Research and Psychotherapy) that replaced the Berlin Psychoanalytic. Göring's Institute, and the DPG, were made to represent a "Deutsche Seelenlehre" (German Study of the Soul) that was to turn against "Jewish" psychoanalysis and adopt the racial science of the Third Reich.[25] In 1936, Göring founded the *Zeitschrift für Psychotherapie und ihre Grenzgebiete* (*Journal of Psychotherapy and Related Fields*) that he co-edited with Carl Gustav Jung, the well-known Swiss analyst and former student and colleague of Freud with right-wing sympathies. After Germany's annexation of Austria in 1938, the Institute was active in Vienna as well. Roughly 200 former members of the Göring Institute were still practicing in post-war Germany, a situation that Mitscherlich chose not to comment on. Rather, he wanted to represent the continuation of tradition for psychoanalytic thought and practice in Germany that led back to Freud, and to do so, he had to skip over the Third Reich period and keep silent about the DPG's members' former political affiliations. In addition, the number of psychoanalysts he could work with increased dramatically. For the international association, he presented a sizable, united, and politically untainted association.[26]

While Mitscherlich was unable to attain a professorship in Heidelberg in these early years, he was still dreaming of expanding Heidelberg's clinic of psychosomatic medicine. But from the late 1950s on, he sought contact with the University in Frankfurt/M. Already in 1951, he was in contact with Max Horkheimer at the Institut für Sozialforschung (Institute for Social Research) who had been impressed with Mitscherlich's work about the Nuremberg Doctors' Trial. Horkheimer suggested that Mitscherlich contribute to the Institute that he and Adorno had just re-established in Frankfurt after they returned from emigration. At the same time, however, Horkheimer seemed to have had doubts about Mitscherlich's possible

[25] See Geoffrey Cocks, Psychotherapy in the Third Reich: The Göring Institute, second expanded edition. Piscataway, N.J.: Transaction Publishers, 1997. See also Veronika Füchtner, *Berlin Psychoanalytic: Psychoanalysis and Culture in Weimar Republic Germany and Beyond* (ser.) Weimar and Now: German Cultural Criticism. Berkeley: University of California Press, 2011.

[26] Edith Kurtzweil, "Legitimationsprobleme der Nachkriegs-Psychoanalyse in der Bundesrepublik," in: Herbert Bareuther, Hans-Joachim Busch, Dieter Ohlmeier and Tomas Plänkers (Eds.), *Forschen und Heilen. Auf dem Weg zu einer psychoanalytischen Hochschule* (Frankfurt/M: Suhrkamp Verlag, 1989), 165.

contributions to a theory of psychoanalysis or sociology.[27] Mitscherlich did not become a member of the Institute, but both Horkheimer and Adorno joined Mitscherlich's planning committee for a lecture series organized to mark the hundred-year anniversary of Sigmund Freud's birthday that should take place in Frankfurt in May 1956.

The event received much attention from local politicians. The Hessian head of state, Ministerpräsident Georg August Zinn, supported Mitscherlich's wish for a professorship and tried to lobby for such a position at the University of Frankfurt. Frankfurt University was, after all, a public institution. Zinn was also in favor for the establishment of an institute for psychoanalysis in Frankfurt. For him, such an institute would gesture toward the liberal pre-war culture of Frankfurt that had largely been shaped by its Jewish inhabitants. It would be a political act of reconciliation and establish further commitment to democratic life and Germany's postwar "normalization."[28]

The Institut und Ausbildungszentrum für Psychoanalyse und Psychosomatik (Institute for Psychoanalysis and Psychosomatic Medicine) was founded in Frankfurt in 1959, three years after the Freud celebration, and on April 27, 1960, it inaugurated its new building with a festive event. Mitscherlich was in charge of the Institute, and at first, he worked both in Frankfurt and in Heidelberg. Only in 1967, and after rather protracted negotiations, he finally obtained a professorship in Frankfurt. Mitscherlich was he was already 59 years old. Zinn had established a chair in psychoanalysis at the University after the Freud anniversary celebration, but the medical faculty rejected Mitscherlich's appointment, and his professorship had to be established in the Humanities. The Institute itself took up its work in provisional quarters and moved to a new and modest, functional building in Frankfurt's Westend. Five years after its founding, it received a name and became the Sigmund-Freud-Institut (SFI). Mitscherlich directed the SFI until 1976.

[27] See Dehli, *Leben als Konflikt*, 233. See also Rolf Wiggershaus, *The Frankfurt School: Its History, Theories, and Political Significance*, tr. Michael Robertson (ser.) Studies in Contemporary German Social Thought. (Cambridge, MA: MIT Press, 1994) 544.

[28] As a lawyer and politician, Georg August Zinn had helped to shape the Grundgesetz (Basic Law, Constitution) of the Federal Republic of Germany. Zinn also supported the work of Fritz Bauer, a Frankfurt judge largely responsible for the Auschwitz Trial and the capture of Adolf Eichmann in Argentina; see, for example, Fritz Backhaus, Monika Boll, Raphael Gross et al. (Eds.), *Fritz Bauer. Der Staatsanwalt: NS-Verbrechen vor Gericht*. Frankfurt/M: Campus Verlag, 2014.

Fig. 10.2 Memorial Plaque to honor Karl Landauer, co-founder of the first Frankfurt Psychoanalytic Institute, 1929–1933, at the entrance of the Sigmund-Freud-Institute, Frankfurt/M. (Photo: Frank Behnsen, 2010)

To connect the new building with the early history of psychoanalysis in Frankfurt, Mitscherlich placed a plaque at the building's entrance, reminding of an earlier institute's founding pre-WWII, and connecting it to the psychoanalytic "Südwestdeutsche Arbeitsgemeinschaft" (South West German Working Group) was founded in Frankfurt already in 1926 (Fig. 10.2). That group had counted Erich Fromm, Frieda Fromm-Reichmann, and Karl Landauer among its members and established the

Psychoanalytic Institute in 1928. Some of its members, including Fromm, were involved with the Institut für Sozialforschung as well. The highlight of the history of psychoanalysis in Frankfurt was not connected with this institute, however, but the city's Goethe Prize. In 1930, it was offered to Freud, and his daughter Anna traveled to Frankfurt to receive it, as Freud felt physically too fragile for the travel.[29]

The pre-WWII institute was already disbanded in 1933, but when Mitscherlich established his new institute, Anna Freud was invited to return to Frankfurt. She did not travel in person, but sent a message, and lauded the "new psychoanalytic era in Germany."[30] Nobody of the old leadership was left. Landauer had perished in a concentration camp; Fromm emigrated to Switzerland first, then to the United States and Mexico; he never returned to Frankfurt. Fromm-Reichmann fled to the United States. But like Zinn perhaps, Mitscherlich did not want a new institute, but a re-establishment of the old one, as if to mend a broken tradition—and forge a genealogical line with the profession's early practitioners. Psychoanalysis was to exist in familial lines, with founding fathers, and student sons. In the search of symbolic ancestry, Mitscherlich followed Landauer. Already earlier, he had established a position for himself as a victim. Now, he would more clearly put himself into a Jewish lineage.

The Place of Psychoanalysis

The above-mentioned anniversary celebration of Freud's birthday in May 1956 focused on the lecture series that was jointly sponsored by the Universities of Frankfurt and Heidelberg. Mitscherlich represented the Medical Faculty in Heidelberg, and Horkheimer the Faculty of Philosophy at Frankfurt. Mitscherlich was able to attract important scholars from abroad to participate in this event, including Erik H. Erikson, René Spitz, Michael Balint, Herbert Marcuse, and his own teachers Franz Alexander and Gustav Bally. The lectures were published in a volume entitled *Freud in der Gegenwart* (Freud in the Present Time) and published in the series Frankfurter Beiträge zur Soziologie (Frankfurt Contributions to

[29] See Weissberg, "Sehnsucht nach Goethe. Sigmund Freud und der Sommer 1931." In: Stephan Braese and Daniel Weidner (Eds.), *Deutsche Sprachkultur von Juden und die Geisteswissenschaften* (Berlin: Kadmos Verlag, 2015), 201–214.

[30] Anna Freud, cited in the web page of the Sigmund-Freud-Institute, http://www.sigmund-freud-institut.de/index.php/institut/die-geschichte/ (access March 2021).

Sociology) issued by Adorno and Walter Dirks for the Institut for Sozialforschung. Mitscherlich wanted to address a wider audience with these lectures. In his own introductory remarks, he stressed the resistance that psychoanalysis had to face as a discipline and the inclusivity of its subject. After all, psychoanalysis deals with "a human being who has to say 'I': i.e. we ourselves."[31] Zinn added words of greetings as well. He was eager to support the missionary drive behind the project; he hoped psychoanalysis would have a great pedagogical value for the German youth.[32] Horkheimer and Adorno argued more cautiously for a stronger interest in Freud. At the event, Horkheimer seemed to agree with Zinn and stressed the timeliness of psychoanalysis in regard to the German youth: "From the stress on the economic side of being, which has been established after National Socialism and in the face of new prescient danger, without looking to the right or left, young people in Germany are suffering under great spiritual difficulties."[33]

But in the "Vorrede" (introduction) to the conference publication, Horkheimer and Adorno offered a much more differentiated argument. They pointed to the inclusion of Freudian psychoanalysis in the early years of the Institute for Social Research, and explained that Landauer's Institute was founded as nothing else but the psychoanalytic division of the Institut für Sozialforschung: "The interaction of social authority and psychic resistance was for many years in the foreground of the empirical studies of the Institute."[34] Horkheimer cited a programmatic contribution to analytic social psychology that appeared in the first edition of the *Zeitschrift für Sozialforschung* in 1932, and indeed, there were two essays authored by a member of the Frankfurt Psychoanalytisches Institut, Fromm.[35] Horkheimer and Adorno viewed the importance of Freudian psychoanaly-

[31] Mitscherlich, "Geleitwort," in: anon., *Freud in der Gegenwart. Ein Vortragszyklus der Universitäten Frankfurt und Heidelberg zum hundertsten Geburtstag* (ser.) Frankfurter Beiträge zur Soziologie 6, Frankfurt: Europäische Verlagsanstalt, 1957, XI.

[32] Georg August Zinn, "Ansprache," in: anon., *Freud in der Gegenwart*, 7–9, esp. 8.

[33] Max Horkheimer, "Ansprache im Namen der Philosophischen Fakultät der Universität Frankfurt am Main," in: anon., *Freud in der Gegenwart*, 31.

[34] Adorno and Horkheimer, "Vorrede," in: anon., *Freud in der Gegenwart*, ix.

[35] Erich Fromm, "Über Methode und Aufgabe einer analytischen Sozialpsychologie," *Zeitschrift für Sozialforschung* 1 (1932): 28–54; and Fromm, "Die psychoanalytische Charakterologie und ihre Bedeutung für die Sozialpsychologie," *Zeitschrift für Sozialforschung* 1 (1932): 253–277. Both essays are included in English translation in: Fromm, *The Crisis of Psychoanalysis. Essays on Freud, Marx, and Social Psychology*. New York: Holt, Rinehart, Winston, [1970].

sis for the own work as an "impulse" only: "If Freud declared sociology to be nothing but applied psychology, however, he may have overlooked that the Laws governing society are not those of pure human interiority."[36] Even if social research could and should benefit from psychoanalytic insights, sociology and psychology have to follow their own different paths:

> We therefore do not support a synthesis of sociology and psychology today, but the insistent, and separate, work in both realms. This would also touch some of Freud's lessons. In his later years, he tended to stress the spiritual being much more than the material conditions of human existence. His positive version of the "reality principle" may suggest that the adjustment to the blind social pressure can be sanctioned by rejecting it, which would thus justify the continuation of pressure. However, this intention is only one side of Freudian thought. It cannot be separated from the other, his very series experience of the burden that human beings have to carry—an experience that marks the unreconcilable depth of Freudian theory, and his substantive importance. (x)

This separation of psychoanalysis from social science was certainly not in the interest of Mitscherlich. In an essay published in 1966, "Die Krankheiten der Gesellschaft und die psychosomatische Medizin" (The Illness of Society and Psychosomatic Medicine), he responded to this in the form of series of questions:

> We recognize sick individuals, we can define illnesses that people have in common, and we can say, that certain illnesses appear often, or rarely, in a population. But are there illnesses that define such a population as a whole, namely as a "social body," does something like that exist? Do we expand the idea of an illness to much here, and become vague and elusive? Are we too easily tempted into analogies when we define certain deficits in society, what Freud had called "Unbehagen in der Kultur" (Civilization and Its Discontents), to easily with the term "illness"? Are we mistaken if we transfer a term that was defined diagnostically as a set of symptoms in regard to a certain illness to the only vaguely formulated situations of human beings in general, i.e. society?[37]

[36] Adorno and Horkheimer, "Vorrede," in: anon., *Freud in der Gegenwart*, x. Further Reference in the text.

[37] Mitscherlich, "Die Krankheiten der Gesellschaft und die psychosomatische Medizin" (1966), in: Mitscherlich, *Gesammelte Schriften* II, ed. Tilman Allert (Frankfurt/M: Suhrkamp Verlag, 1983), 427–428.

And although Mitscherlich would describe such questions as doubtlessly "serious considerations," he continued:

> The term "social illness" is not just an analogous term for me, however. We have to consider that experiences are invariably, and immediately, connected with changes in our physical performance. The conditions of life that society offers have a substantial impact on the formation of our experience.[38]

At the time when Mitscherlich wrote these lines, he was already the author of *Auf dem Weg zur vaterlosen Gesellschaft. Ideen zur Sozialpsychologie* (*Society without the Father: A Contribution to Social Psychology*), a book published in 1963.[39] There, Mitscherlich had offered a general analysis of German post-war society. He did so both as a scholar and as a moral voice. The idea of a "fatherless society" became immediately popular. But Mitscherlich was not the person who coined this expression. It was Paul Federn who gave his essay of 1919 the title: "Die vaterlose Gesellschaft. Psychologie der Revolution" (The fatherless Society: A Psychology of Revolution).[40] The psychoanalyst Federn had written and published this piece shortly after the end of WWI, and the failed German revolutions. Mitscherlich adapted the expression of a "fatherless society" to describe Germany after 1945.

Freud's Oedipal theory focused on the (imaginary) murder of the father by the son who wanted to free himself from a rival to be able to enter a relationship with his mother. In Mitscherlich's study, fathers were killed and murdered as well, but in a rather different context. He did not draw a picture of the desires of an individual, but of a country that was lacking real fathers, thousands of whom had been victims of WWII: a whole generation of men killed or wounded in battle, or returned late from captivity. For Mitscherlich, Germany was a country devoid of father figures. Male role models were absent, and their absence left the youth bereft and disillusioned. Mitscherlich combined anthropological observations ("Man comes into the world not adapted to his surroundings, and

[38] Mitscherlich, "Die Krankheit der Gesellschaft," 428. See also Mitscherlich's essays, "Der psychoanalytische Ansatz in der Sozialpsychologie" (1969), and "Über Psychoanalyse und Soziologie" (1970), in: Mitscherlich, *Gesammelte Schriften* V, ed. Helga Haase (Frankfurt/M: Suhrkamp Verlag, 1983), 9–36 and 37–68.

[39] Mitscherlich, *Society without the father, a contribution to social psychology*, tr. Eric Mosbacher. New York: Harcourt Brace & Word, [1969].

[40] See Dehli, *Leben als Konflikt*, 265.

untrained") with a description of social influences ("How much human behavior is innate is unknown; all we can be sure of is that it is far from adequate for the regulation of life among our fellows").[41] But in the end, he was not just writing about Germany. The specifically German situation was emblematic of the situation of the human being in general in modern times. In Germany, however, the general dissolution of established family structures was met with the loss of the political father figure, Adolf Hitler, the *Über*-father of all Germans during the Third Reich.

With his reading of German history, Mitscherlich dramatically altered the Oedipus story. Hitler does not appear as a dictator who was the head of a government that ordered the murder of millions of Jewish victims and sent millions of German soldiers to their death before committing suicide himself. It is not important that the father tried to kill his children, but that the children were unable to cope with the father's death. Did they feel responsible for it? After WWII, they had to remain silent about the father's deeds and about their own deeds as well. Most importantly, they had to remain silent about their affective relationship with him. They may not have killed their father, but they had now to deny him. Mitscherlich here sketches a picture of the inability of mourning, of unconfessed personal guilt, perhaps even of suppressed homosexual desire. It is a story where women have no place.

While Mitscherlich's book focused on this larger socio-political picture, *Auf dem Weg zur vaterlosen Gesellschaft* was also surely a quite personal work as well. Mitscherlich himself had struggled with an authoritarian father from whom he felt alienated. Already in 1950, he published an essay entitled "Ödipus und Kaspar Hauser" (Oedipus and Kaspar Hauser), that focused on the personal experience of an abandoned child.[42] And he himself turned into an absent father as well. Mitscherlich left two of his three wives after only a few years of marriage and was hardly involved in raising five of his children. Intellectually, too, Mitscherlich had taken leave of his former guiding figures such as Ernst Jünger, from whom he tried to

[41] Mitscherlich, *Society without the Father*, 1. Mitscherlich uses the term "ungebildet" (unformed) here, and thus refers to the bourgeois idea of *Bildung*; see *Auf dem Weg zur vaterlosen Gesellschaft. Ideen zur Sozialpsychologie* (1963), in: Mitscherlich, Gesammelte Schriften III, ed. Helga Haase (Frankfurt/M: Suhrkamp Verlag, 1983), 15.

[42] Mitscherlich, "Ödipus und Kaspar Hauser. Tiefenpsychologische Probleme der Gegenwart," *Der Monat* 3,25 (1950): 11–18; reprinted in: Mitscherlich, *Gesammelte Schriften* VII, ed. Herbert Wiegandt (Frankfurt/M: Suhrkamp Verlag, 1983), 151–163.

distance himself polemically after the War,[43] and had adopted new ones whom he found among the emigrée society. Members of the DPG may not have mourned Hitler as much as they did Matthias Göring, who was simply known as "Papi" to them.[44]

For Mitscherlich, however, the problem of a fatherless society was not just the lack of an authority figure. It was the issue of obedience, a characteristic highly valued as a particularly German under Hitler. In *Die vaterlose Gesellschaft*, he approaches the issue in general terms, asking about the difference between an innate and a learned obedience. What kind of obedience should and can one demand, and how much obedience would be too much? Once again, Mitscherlich uses the inclusive "we":

> Are we too obedient, too ready to fall into line with behavior as it is laid down? Are we lacking in civil courage? Or are we too disobedient and, if so, in what respect? What are the historical reasons for the breakdown of social orders based on obedience? What are the social circumstances, the roles, in which we are capable of being too ruthless and destructive, too contemptuous of legality and obedience, and those in which we can be too submissive, too loyal, and too obsessed with obedience? What is socially liberating and what is socially enslaving?[45]

According to Mitscherlich, Germans compensated for the loss of Hitler by busying themselves with reconstruction. They also elected another father figure, the aging Konrad Adenauer, as a person to lead the new Republic. Mitscherlich himself had become one of these Germans who were ceaselessly occupying themselves with building a new life, by founding new institutes and journals. As *Auf dem Weg zur vaterlosen Gesellschaft* became a best-seller in the Federal Republic of Germany, its author was eager to become a public intellectual writing on topics other than medicine or psychoanalysis. In newspapers and journals, he published articles on historical events and figures, and current affairs. Thus, he wrote about the Prussian King Frederick the Great as an "archetypical grand-father" for the journal *Der Spiegel*, and analyze contemporary German politicians on television or in the journal *Die Zeit*, for example Rainer Barzel, whom he did not know

[43] Dehli, *Leben als Konflikt*, 176.
[44] Kurtzweil, "Legitimationsprobleme," 170.
[45] Mitscherlich, *Society without the Father*, 166.

personally.[46] Mitscherlich attested Barzel "political puberty"; he had not worked out the loss of the *Über*-father Hitler.[47] No couch was necessary anymore for this kind of analysis that could be performed from afar. Indeed, Mitscherlich described the psychoanalyst as pursuing the task of an "anthropologist in the field" or social anthropologist in his book. For this kind of anthropology, a personal encounter was not necessary:

> What interests the sociologist in such cases is their general implications and the extent to which the relationship between hope and reality is changed by developments. The field anthropologist—which is what the practising psycho-analyst feels himself to be—is struck by the same processes of alienation that recur with innumerable variation in individual cases.[48]

Mitscherlich's second best-seller, *Die Unfähigkeit zu trauern. Grundlagen kollektiven Verhaltens* (*The Inability to Mourn: Principles of Collective Behavior*), was authored together with his third wife, the physician and psychotherapist Margarete Mitscherlich. It appeared in 1967. "Inability to mourn" turned into a popular term and buzzword as well. Freud had already distinguished between melancholia, a state of mind that could not find termination, and mourning. Now, Mitscherlich wrote about a collective inability to mourn, an inability even to begin the process of mourning, that defined contemporary Germans. In his earlier work, Mitscherlich had written about the general phenomenon of missing a father figure. *Die Unfähigkeit zu trauern* continued along these lines and focused on the Germans' relationship to their National Socialist past and the fact that they had not worked through that history and experience:[49]

[46] Mitscherlich, "Könige sind archetypische Groß-Väter. Zur Psychologie des Preußen Friedrich II," in: *Der Spiegel*, 23, 4 (1969): 100–110; reprinted in: Mitscherlich, *Gesammelte Schriften* VII, 89–106. "Das Porträt von Rainer Barzel. Arrangement statt Opposition. Beitrag in der Fernsehsendung, Report," in: *Die Zeit* (18. 3. 1966), https://www.zeit.de/1966/12/das-portraet-des-rainer-barzel (access March 2021); also in: Mitscherlich, *Gesammelte Schriften* VI, 297–299.

[47] Mitscherlich, "Das Porträt von Rainer Barzel," 298.

[48] Mitscherlich, *Society without the Father*, 158.

[49] See for example Margarete Mitscherlich, *Trauer ist der halbe Trost. Gespräch mit Meinhard Schmidt-Degenhard. "Das Unglück geschah nur mir allein," musikalische Meditation zu den Kindertotenliedern von Gustav Mahler*. Zürich: pendo Verlag, 1995, and Margarete Mitscherlich, *Erinnerungsarbeit. Zur Psychoanalyse der Unfähigkeit zu trauern*. Frankfurt/M: S. Fischer, 1987. See also Eckard Henscheid, "Die Unfähigkeit zu trauern oder so ähnlich. Ein Spezialkapitel zur Kulturgeschichte der Mißverständnisse," *Frankfurter Allgmeine*

> We can now sum up the foregoing as follows: The inability to mourn the loss of the Führer is the result of an intensive defense against guilt, shame, and anxiety, a defense which was achieved by the withdrawal of previously powerful libidinal cathexes. The Nazi past was de-realized, i.e. emptied of reality. The occasion for mourning was not only the death of Adolf Hitler as a *real* person, but above all his disappearance as the representation of the *collective ego-ideal*.[50]

The collective attempt to escape melancholia turned into a "de-realization" of the National Socialist past. After WWII, the German people had entered the realm of pathology.

Mitscherlich's career had begun as a doctor of psychosomatic medicine; he later worked as a psychoanalyst. At this stage of his career, however, he defined his position once again. By the 1960s, Mitscherlich's reputation rested on his role as a "field-anthropologist" and a public intellectual, writing articles and journalistic pieces, commenting on German politics and society for a wider public. He was very much a West German phenomenon, and he styled himself as the moral conscience of the Federal Republic. Indeed, he turned into a father figure himself, describing, or admonishing, others. But he continued to use the "we," and on the surface at least, he was eager to include himself in this society, to put his role as an outsider aside. He was a member of the West German family and was increasingly recognized as its authority figure. He took on the persona of the Good German but one who would confess to his own failings by not excluding himself from German society. His readers, in turn could both realize their failings, and identify with the author. Mitscherlich's own confessions were palatable fare. His readers were perpetrators and victims at once. They were guilty of having enthusiastically followed a Nazi leader,

Zeitung (12. 6. 1993), https://www.genios.de/presse-archiv/artikel/FAZ/19930612/eckhard-henscheid-die-unfaehigkeit-/F19930612TRAUDOK2.html (access March 2021).

[50] Mitscherlich and Mitscherlich, *The Inability to Mourn: Principles of Collective Behavior*, tr. Beverley R. Placzek (New York: Grove Press, 1975), 23. See also *Die Unfähigkeit zu trauern. Grundlagen kollektiven Verhaltens* (1967), in: Mitscherlich, *Gesammelte Schriften* IV, ed. Helga Haase (Frankfurt/M: Suhrkamp Verlag, 1983), 37: "Wir können jetzt also zusammenfassend formulieren: Die Unfähigkeit zur Trauer um den erlittenen Verlust des Führers ist das Ergebnis einer intensiven Abwehr von Schuld, Scham, und Angst; sie gelingt durch den Rückzug bisher starker libidinöser Besetzungen. Die Nazivergangenheit wird derealisiert, entwirklicht. Als Anlaß zur Trauer wirkt übrigens nicht nur der Tod Adolf Hitlers als realer Person, sondern vor allem das Erlöschen seiner Repräsentanz als kollektives Ich-Ideal."

but this could be understood in general terms as a fact of human nature. One could thus confess to one's past, but turn it into something one could live with. Thus, Mitscherlich's works could enter the German living room culture with ease, and they could be easily integrated into these rooms' bookshelves. Mitscherlich did not only analyze the German concept of German *Heimat*, he offered his readers the promise to feel comfortable at home again.

In the early years of the Federal Republic, questions relating to the German past and possible German guilt were largely repressed. Mitscherlich's books put them into the open but in quite general terms. Thus, he was able to achieve an odd position. He became a popular, even if controversial, author who was admired by Germans of different generations; by those, who did not want to put the achievements of the early post-war Republic into question, and by those who engaged in protest against it.[51] He represented the status quo, but at the same time, students who engaged in political protests in the late 1960s viewed him as an ally as well. Already in 1963, Jürgen Habermas had written in support of social psychology as defined by Mitscherlich.[52] For many, Mitscherlich's work was related to the Critical Theory of Adorno and Horkheimer; he was part of the now-famous "Suhrkamp Culture," named after the publishing house that issued the works of many leftist critics. Among those who protested, who asked questions about the political past of their own fathers, and who were identifying traces of the Nazi past in contemporary Germany, Mitscherlich became a leading figure. A new phrase was coined: "Mitscherlich is a paper father."[53] He did not seem to accept authority and a culture of obedience, and demanded the right to disobey, a *Recht auf Ungehorsam*, viewed as a protest against conformity (377–378). In this context, Mitscherlich's peculiar position at the Frankfurt university, where he was neither a member of the Medical School nor the Department of Psychology, turned into something positive. He was viewed as an outsider

[51] See Clemens Albrecht, Günter C. Behrmann, Michael Bock, Harald Homann, and Friedrich H. Tenbruck, *Die intellektuelle Gründung der Bundesrepublik. Eine Wirkungsgeschichte der Frankfurter Schule*. Frankfurt: Campus, 2000.

[52] Jürgen Habermas, "Eine psychoanalytische Konstruktion des Fortschritts," *Merkur* 189 (1963): 112–117, and Habermas, "Arzt und Intellektueller. Alexander Mitscherlich zum 70. Geburtstag, *Die Zeit*"(22.9. 1978), https://www.zeit.de/1978/39/arzt-und-intellektueller (access March 2021). See also Habermas, "Bemerkungen zu Alexander Mitscherlichs analytischer Sozialpsychologie," *Psyche* 37 (1983): 352–262.

[53] Freimüller, *Alexander Mitscherlich*, 377. Further reference in the text.

Fig. 10.3 Alexander Mitscherlich, in a meeting at the Psychosomatische Klinik in Heidelberg, 1962 (Photographer unknown). From: Tomas Plänkers et al. (Ed.), *Psychoanalyse in Frankfurt*. Tübingen: Ed. diskord, 1996, 394. Courtesy Sigmund-Freud-Institut Frankfurt/M

by choice. His classes at the University were overcrowded, and he became a cult figure (Fig. 10.3).

Mitscherlich walked the tightrope between bourgeois culture and anti-bourgeois opposition. In 1969, he received one of Germany's most distinguished awards, the Friedenspreis des Deutschen Buchhandels (Peace Prize of the German Book Trade). In his acceptance speech, he chose to talk not about contemporary German politics, but about the high birth rate in Brazil.[54]

But how did the Sigmund-Freud-Institut fare in the meantime? The interest expressed by the media, and Mitscherlich's popularity, seem to

[54] Mitscherlich, "Über hergestellte Dummheit—Ansprache anläßlich der Verleihung des Friedenspreises des Deutschen Buchhandels 1969," in: Mitscherlich, *Gesammelte Schriften* V, 363–395, esp. 363–4.

assure its existence. The staff and friends of the SFI had edited, or contributed to, various festschriften for the institute's founder.[55] But dealing with patients was work of another kind. While Mitscherlich always used the "we," psychoanalytic patients were treated individually. In the early years, most of its patients were young men; many perhaps too young to have been active soldiers in WWII. Soon, the demographics changed, and the SFI's patients were primarily young women.[56] Mitscherlich himself continued to write about a "battle of memory," however.[57] But after his death in 1982, his figure faded from public discussion, as well as from psychoanalytic literature, despite the ten-volume edition of his collected works that appeared posthumously in 1983. For the SFI, Mitscherlich turned into a historical figure; questions of the integration of research and teaching, or the possibilities of a psychoanalytic university, took center stage in its publications.[58]

Most curiously, however, the terms of a "fatherless society" and the "inability to mourn" survived, and took on a life on their own. While he was cited as their author, the terms had little to do with his works anymore. If Mitscherlich coined the "inability to mourn" as a description related to the loss of a specific father figure, Adolf Hitler, the general reception was quite different. For most, Mitscherlich became the author who wrote about the inability to mourn the victims, the Jews who were murdered and had no graves. In 1993, even his widow, Margarete Mitscherlich, was ready to reinterpret her husband's words. In an essay

[55] Clemens de Boor and Käte Hügel (Eds.), *Psychoanalyse und soziale Verantwortung. Eine Festschrift für Alexander Mitscherlich zu seinem 60. Geburtstag*, Stuttgart: Ernst Klett Verlag, 1968; Peter Brückner, Thomas Leithäuser, Werner Kiesel, *Psychoanalyse: Zum 60. Geburtstag von Alexander Mitscherlich*. Frankfurt/M: Europäische Verlagsanstalt, 1968 (a second edition appeared in 1969); Sibylle Drews, Rolf Klüwer and Angela Köhler-Weisker (Eds.), *Provokation und Toleranz. Festschrift für Alexander Mitscherlich zum 70. Geburtstag*, Frankfurt/M: Suhrkamp Verlag, 1987; Sibylle Drews (Ed.), *Freud in der Gegenwart. Alexander Mitscherlichs Gesellschaftskritik*, Frankfurt/M: Brandes & Apsel, 2006.

[56] See Otto Goldschmidt, "Die Patienten einer psychoanalytischen Großstadtambulanz. Statistische Auswertungen einer Stichprobe von 646 Patienten des Sigmund-Freud-Instituts aus den Jahren 1960–1980," in: Bareuther et al. (Eds.), *Forschen und Heilen*, 344–418.

[57] Mitscherlich, *Der Kampf um die Erinnerung. Psychoanalyse für fortgeschrittene Anfänger* (1975), in: Mitscherlich, *Gesammelte Schriften* VIII, ed. Max Looser (Frankfurt/M: Suhrkamp Verlag, 1983), 387–561.

[58] See Bareuther et al. (Eds.), *Forschen und Heilen*, and Tomas Plänkers, Michael Laier, Hans-Heinrich Otto, Hans-Joachim Rothe und Helmut Siefert, *Psychoanalyse in Frankfurt am Main. Zerstörte Anfänge, Wiederannäherung, Entwicklungen*, Tübingen: edition diskord, 1996.

published in *Psyche*, she not only referred to the discourse of the Holocaust but offered words of comfort as well. In the context of German unification, Germans were in the process of regaining their ability to mourn these victims.[59]

The SFI as an institution changed as well. In 1995, it turned into a foundation with closer association to the Frankfurt University and defined itself primarily as an academic research institution. A newly founded Frankfurt Psychoanalytic Institute offered training analyses, and the name of this new institution echoed that of the early institute of 1928. For the SFI, there was less public attention without Mitscherlich, and its publications did not necessarily seek a large audience anymore. In 2004, the SFI was nearly dissolved because of financial cuts but managed to survive. Psychoanalysis itself became less popular, as a treatment, as well as an instrument of social change.

But not just the institute, also the researchers and patients at the SFI had changed. Today, the SFI once again counts Jewish members among its staff, and at least one project seeks to bind this institution to Frankfurt's Jewish community. Since 2002, the analysts Kurt Grünberg and Isidor Kaminer, have engaged in a project with the Zentralwohlfahrtstelle der Juden in Deutschland (Central Welfare Office for Jews in Germany). They founded a Treffpunkt für Überlebende (Meeting Place for Survivors). This project deals with the Nazi past as well, albeit by focusing on a different group of the German population. Accompanied by two social workers from the Zentralwohlfahrtsstelle, Noemi Staszewski and Ania Hadda, these analysts meet with Jewish survivors of the Holocaust. In the early years, the meetings were conducted in the rooms of the B'nai Brith, the Jewish Honors Society. The Society owned an apartment in the Frankfurt Westend, and the spaces in question were the former wood-paneled living and dining rooms of the upper bourgeois apartment. There was no couch in sight, but coffee and cake were served on long tables (Fig. 10.4).[60]

[59] Margarete Mitscherlich, "Die (Un)Fähigkeit zu trauern in Ost- und Westdeutschland: Was Trauerarbeit heißen könnte," *Psyche* 47.2 (1993): 406–18. See also Anna Parkinson, *An Emotional State: The Politics of Emotion in Postwar West German Culture* (Ann Arbor, MI: University of Michigan Press, 2015), 113.

[60] Weissberg, "Kaffeezeit." *Unser "Treffpunkt" in Frankfurt am Main 2002–2012* (Frankfurt am Main: Zentrale Wohlfahrtsstelle der Jüdischen Gemeinde, 2012), 17–19; and https://www.zwst.org/medialibrary/pdf/10_Jahre_Treffpunkt_Frankfurt.pdf (access March 2021).

Fig. 10.4 *Treffpunkt für Holocaust Überlebende* (Meeting Place for Survivors of the Holocaust), living and dining rooms of the B'nai Brit Loge, Frankfurt/M, 2012. (Photo: Treffpunkt/Michael Bause, Aktion Mensch)

For the visiting survivors, the apartment was not home, but a safe space for conversation. They were not in search of a *Heimat*, but merely a temporary room of their own. In a linguistic mix of German, Polish, Romanian, or Hungarian they defined a talking cure in hopes of being able to face their past, as well as their present life in post-war Germany.

PART IV

Media Matters

CHAPTER 11

The Planetary Father Function

Laurence A. Rickels

Prologue

In the analytic reception of Sigmund Freud's science, the Oedipus complex, the seat of the father, is regularly displaced with regard to a newly emphasized parallel universal in psychic reality. The complex housing life and death with father can then be seen as a hideout for and diversion from this other realm of relations. In lieu of many examples of innovation in analytic theory requiring the alternation with the Oedipus complex to gain traction, consider two: the masochism of the wish to be refused (Edmund Bergler) and the narcissism of the self (Heinz Kohut).[1]

Already in Freud's court, the momentum of alteration through alternation can be observed in the constructions of psychoanalysis, which arise when the transference swaps over in session onto an interpretation and the incomplete substitute produces a complete result. A treatable disturbance

[1] Both examples are dictated by recent work. Edmund Bergler is the supervising analyst of the third volume of my *Critique of Fantasy* subtitled *The Block of Fame*, Santa Barbara: punctum books, 2020. In my contribution to a forthcoming volume on Isabelle Huppert for Edinburgh University Press, I excavate Huppert's performance of Elfriede Jelinek's Erika Kohut via the other Kohut's analysis of narcissistic rage.

L. A. Rickels (✉)
European Graduate School, Saas-Fee, Switzerland

L. Weissberg (ed.), *Psychoanalysis, Fatherhood, and the Modern Family*, https://doi.org/10.1007/978-3-030-82124-1_11

in the paternal relationship to the analyst can thus dislodge a deeper untreatable problem, which it isolates and contains like an inoculation.

That the construction of the analytic relationship to the father might breach impasses in this way has special significance for the theorization of mourning. The unique opportunity of comparing Freud's case study "Notes Upon a Case of Obsessional Neurosis" to the original notes he jotted down following the sessions with the Rat Man shows the upward displacement from the spectral souvenirs of a dead sibling to scenarios of blocked mourning for the father, which in the published version could be worked through. The displacement lingers on in the case study, often in the footnote underworld. This two-timing in the analysis of mourning inspired my book *Aberrations of Mourning*, in which I sought to uncover alongside the Oedipus complex dedicated to the mournable father a spectral underworld admitting the unmournable losses of mother, child, and sibling. I didn't oppose these regions but followed out the time charts of their paralleling under the aegis of a concept, which I modeled on Freud's "uncanny" and named "unmourning."

Not every loss on a scale of mourning or melancholia is embodied in an object relation. That's why the theory of the crypt, which influenced my work of unmourning, turns on secret words.[2] In the meantime, I would go one step further inside the microstructure. Where the international reception says "desire," the original language of Freud's science says "wish." When the dead do return in your night dreams, are they back to confirm a relationship of wanting or to punctuate the end of the sentencing of a wish? If it seems a contradiction to say that the wish is stronger than its fulfilled content, then that's because the death wish happens to come true in time.

Freud's poetics of the daydream followed his signature work on the composition of the night dream like an afterthought or contradiction. It was in *The Interpretation of Dreams* that Freud introduced the Oedipus complex as the lexicon for translating the secret message of the night dream's unconscious wish. The gist of daydreaming, however, isn't

[2] I am referring to the theory set forth in Nicolas Abraham and Maria Torok, *Cryptonymie. Le verbier de l'Homme aux loups*; precede de Fors par Jacques Derrida, Paris: Aubier Flammarion, 1978. In *Aberrations of Mourning: Writing on German Crypts* (Detroit: Wayne State University Press, 1988), I offered only one bona fide cryptonymic analysis, therefore, namely my reading of the magic word in the corpus of Adalbert Stifter.

unconscious and is secretive only on a scale of private versus public. No one wants to share their waking wish fantasies, which are inartistic, to be sure, even at times antisocial, certainly always embarrassingly narcissistic. However, our private daydreaming, which we must own as our second nature beginning in adolescence, flexes omnipotence of thoughts, the word for the creative power that the Rat Man coined in Freud's earshot. By altering his daydreams into the acts of a heroic saga, the first poet was, also for his audience, as Freud underscores, the first hero: he rescued the creative impulse of omnipotence from the privacy and privation of daydreaming.[3]

In his 1907 essay "The Poet and Daydreaming,"[4] Freud makes the counterintuitive move of privileging waking fantasy although the night dream was the readily available analog for aesthetic experience. According to the poetics of fantasy, then, since every night dream is already a perfect composition, if dreaming and waking reality divided up the spoils of psychic life, then the night dream would be enough and art not necessary. There is art because we are always going off alone with fantasying, prematurely flashing on a figment without realization or endurance. There is art, then, to vouchsafe the evolution of the social relation out of the tight spot of wishing.

Since my study of Philip K. Dick, *I Think I Am*, I have allied Freud's reflections on the endopsychic perception inside delusional thought, which affords an inside view of the regular functioning of psychic reality, with Walter Benjamin's discovery of the range and rage of reading in modern allegory.[5] To this end, I had to get past Freud's embargo on philosophy and religion without compromising his Enlightenment stance. In this

[3] "The poet who had taken this step and had in this way set himself free from the group in his imagination, is nevertheless able … to find his way back to it in reality. For he goes and relates to the group his hero's deeds which he has invented. At bottom this hero is no one but himself." In: Sigmund Freud, *Group Psychology and the Analysis of the Ego*. In: Freud, *The Standard Edition of the Complete Psychological Works*, tr. James Strachey, ed. Anna Freud et al., 24 vols. (London: The Hogarth Press, 1953–1974), XVIII: 67–144, here 136 (edition will be abbreviated *SE*).

[4] This is how I prefer to translate Freud's title "Der Dichter und das Phantasieren," which in Strachey's translation in the *SE* goes by the title "The Creative Writer and Daydreaming." See *SE* IX: 141–154.

[5] See my opening chapter, "Endopsychic Allegories," in *I Think I Am: Philip K. Dick*, Minneapolis: University of Minnesota Press, 2011. By "modern" I mean the secular tendency to immerse the everlasting, the transcendent, in finitude, which Benjamin sees occupying center stage in the Baroque "mourning play."

essay I rely therefore on the safety clause Benjamin allows secular allegory: the foregrounding of the intrigue keeps an infernal monopoly on violence from leading allegory into the light of Christianization, the quiescence at the beginning and end of the allegory of reading.

At the same time, also since my study of P.K. Dick, Gotthard Günther's discovery of the new worlds and words of science fiction is a mainstay of my reading with B-genres. The planetary civilization that is a given in science fiction occupying and cathecting Outer Space found the first clearing for arrival or return through the break in metaphysical traditions that the Enlightenment introduced. Günther emphasizes that the Enlightenment, which was quickly neutralized back home, was transferred intact to the new world, which got the break of a cosmically new start. I add to Günther's Enlightenment introject the interlude of Mesmerism, which led to an efflorescence of clairvoyant states triggered in patients undergoing magnetic treatment. More than the treatment itself, the studies that collected and evaluated these liminal states offered a prologue of prep work for the formation of Freud's science. My supplement finds motivation in two related points that Günther does make. One, that what we call superstition is the reverb of return from repression of the first planetary culture, animism, which the regional civilizations couldn't tolerate. And two, that the Enlightenment gave mankind in the new world the all-important outside chance to experience emotionally and fully the demolition derby and clearing house to which traditional metaphysics can be reduced.

From the opening season of psychoanalytic thought demarcated by *The Interpretation of Dreams* and "The Poet and Daydreaming," my essay considers two further works that can be seen as at once liminal and foundational. Freud's "Fragment of an Analysis of a Case of Hysteria" introduced the technical innovation of free association and, in the recoil of Dora's flight from treatment, the theory and therapy of the transference. The first analysis of the symptom picture of literature, "Delusions and Dreams in Jensen's Gradiva," explores the analogs arising from the novella's self-reflection on its origin in daydreaming, which matches archeology and repression, haunting and transference. Based on the literary sentencing of the wish, Freud erected psychoanalysis upon a defective foundation,[6] which he kept shoring up and never replaced. To protect the endopsychic

[6] I am referring to Jacques Derrida's reading of "the defective cornerstone" in: Derrida, *Memoires for Paul de Man*. (ser.) Wellek Library Lectures, New York: Columbia University Press, 1989.

allegory of the wish—and the pageant of relations with the dead turning around the death wish—Freud later swerved from the Devil in the Death Drive and upheld instead the intrigue of advocacy and speculation.[7]

Like in the constellation through which Theodor W. Adorno gave form to his thought the points raised here are also at play in each of the following six sections, ratcheting up in the course of repetition and variation toward a conclusion that's a given. The Oedipal relationship to the father goes out on an update as the planetary father function.

Long derided for Lorenzo Da Ponte's "impertinent" libretto,[8] *Così fan tutte* (1790) was even tampered with in the nineteenth century to let the women in on the intrigue and turn the test around into a comedy of errors. To counter their guilty assumption of a high-fidelity love, the "philosopher" Don Alfonso directs the men to depart, marching as to war, and then enter the stage they left as new suitors of their own betrothed. To win over the steadfast women the disguised men even feign taking poison in despair. But the experiment doesn't begin to yield results until the women's maid, recruited by the philosopher as his assistant, arrives in the guise of a medical practitioner with a brand-new treatment plan: "This is a piece of magnet, the stone the great Dr. Mesmer discovered in Germany and then became so famous in France."[9] By instructing the women to assist in the recovery of the stricken men, the *Magnetiseur* exploits the near-miss between hands-on care and the early mother's ministrations (which is a turn-on for both sexes). The philosopher's trial seduction ultimately leads the men to wed the women as planned but to forswear the testing of their unconditional love. The wife is the father's delegate.

In his account of daydream fantasy, Freud accords each wish fulfillment scenario with a date stamp that belies the apparent escapism.[10] The role of Mesmerism in Wolfgang Amadeus Mozart's opera shows the impression of the Enlightenment. Conceived as a declaration of independence from

[7] In his *La Carte postale* (Paris: Flammarion, 1980), Derrida made book on this tilt that undoes biology as biography and the proper death as the proper name. In Notebook Ten of my *The Devil Notebooks* (Minneapolis: University of Minnesota Press, 2008), I pursue the significance of Freud's self-proclaimed role as Devil's advocate (rather than as another uninhibited client).

[8] Eduard Hanslick, *Die moderne Oper. Kritiken und Studien* (Berlin: A. Hofmann, 1875), 81.

[9] Act 1, Scene 16; See www.operafolio.com (access March 2921).

[10] Freud, "Creative Writers and Day-Dreaming," *SE* IX, 147. Further page references are given in the text.

longstanding metaphysical traditions, the Enlightenment is the historical introject that Gotthard Günther made the defining moment in his genealogy of "the American apocalypse."[11]

In Europe, the Enlightenment was followed by Romanticism, which brought back the metaphysical mother lode. But the Enlightenment was transferred directly to the settlement of the long unacknowledged continent. Günther's reading of the future is based on the conundrum that so many discoveries of the Americas launched from both shores of the regional civilizations prior to Columbus's accidental arrival there (he was, after all, looking for a new way to India) went completely unacknowledged. Acceptance of a new world was the first step toward one world and its de-geo-centering before the final frontier of Outer Space. The Enlightenment supplied the break with the metaphysical basis of regional civilizations, a break that was given the new world. With the how-to encyclopedias of the Enlightenment in hand, the settlers of the new world demarcated a new "West" in contrast to the Faustian West.

Günther, who discovered both cybernetics and science fiction while an émigré in the US, supplemented Oswald Spengler's understanding of a final "Faustian" phase of regional high culture, which was phasing out without the prospect of succession. Günther proposed instead that the prospect was already upon us of a new high culture that would be planetary (i.e., global), but as the staging area for a galactic civilization that would no longer be earth-bound.

Science fiction, according to Günther, is the first understanding of world culture (and beyond) which rejects the civilized past of the civilizations grounded in the East. While primitive culture has always been a planetary phenomenon, the regional civilizations are tied to specific geographically circumscribed areas, which they require, in Spengler's estimation, as their *Mutterboden* (maternal ground). Science fiction via its ungrounded projection of artificial habitats based on reason alone and via its unabashed manipulation of time (as in time travel) was the first platform for Western cultural aspirations unbound by the Eastern past. The spaceship shatters the symbolism of classical metaphysics and thus abandons the classical form of life. The visions of Outer Space presuppose a universal planetary culture—and condition or determine a new non-classical conception of reality.

[11] Gotthard Günther, *Die amerikanische Apokalypse*, ed. Kurt Klagenfurt, Munich: Profil, 2000. Page references are given in the text.

Out West Günther recognized in the wide-open layout of neighborhoods in Southern California, which relied on and reflected the car as the sole means of transport, the address rehearsal for life on foreign planets (184–85). The aloneness and emptiness that cannot but characterize the period of transition, the waiting around for the conquest of Space, must be met as the related challenge of structuring Inner Space as habitable. Borrowed from *Futureworld* (1976) and *Supergirl* (1984), the term "Inner Space" is used here to reset the issue of consolidation or stability, which presses at the outer limits of psychic reality, on Freud's reflections on the destiny of omnipotence in wish fantasy and art.[12]

Mesmerism was the premier therapy fad, the first in the series that circumscribed a concise prehistory of psychoanalysis. Its inaugural role in the settlement of Inner Space was evident in the "social networking" it provided those patients whose own mediumistic talent was triggered by the magnetic treatment. If Mesmerism proved a vehicle for the patient's own clairvoyance, then the patient participated in the assessment and treatment since able to see into bodies. Through the laying on of hands the clairvoyant medium could then also diagnose and treat other patients in the community.

Arthur Schopenhauer's "Essay on Seeing Ghosts and Related Matters"[13] counts as his attempt to update Kant's essay on Swedenborg within the archive of clairvoyant states collected in the trail of Mesmerism. Schopenhauer's reflections (deposited inside the foundation of psychoanalysis) mark at the fork in the road or method that followed the

[12] A legend to this mapping was provided by Melanie Klein, who forwarded the work of mourning to a new address: the "inner world" of identifications, internal objects, or ghosts, which we are forever retrofitting to withstand the impact of each new loss. See Klein, "Mourning and Its Relation to Manic-Depressive States." In: Klein, *Love, Guild and Reparation and Other Works 1921–1945* (New York: The Free Press, 1984), 344–69. In *SPECTRE* (Fort Wayne: Anti-Oedipus Press, 2012), I introduce the inner world (Klein's "modification" of the melancholic crypt) into Ian Fleming's construction of an underworld organization for the world of James Bond in preparation for the crossover into the film medium.

[13] Arthur Schopenhauer, "Versuch über das Geistersehn und was damit zusammenhängt." In: Schopenhauer, *Sämmtliche Werke in fünf Bänden*, Grossherzog Wilhelm Ernst Ausgabe (Leipzig: Insel Verlag, n.d.), IV: 271–369. In Freud's extensive survey of the literature on the dream in *The Interpretation of Dreams*, Schopenhauer's essay is the only philosophical precursor that enters Freud's theorization. The transfer goes through because the will translates as the unconscious in which the wish fantasies that the dream states reflect are on permanent record.

Enlightenment (according to Freud and Günther), a detour that plumbed the empty receiving area of no longer tenable thought systems. Benjamin showed in *The Origin of German Tragic Drama*[14] that legibility was vouchsafed allegorically in the ruinous setting of archival access. At this fork in the method survival in Inner Space had to be addressed and secured in tandem with allegorical exegesis in the funereal archive. In his later media essays Benjamin again treated the basics of survival through psychic reformatting of being at a loss.

Schopenhauer refers five times in the course of his treatise to the documentation of the sessions with Auguste Müller in Karlsruhe.[15] With the onset of puberty Auguste was sorely afflicted, symptomatic, desolate, and alone. Upon contact with magnetic therapy Auguste turned out to be clairvoyant, which meant in her case that she could also discern if anyone in town was calling her gift into question. She rose to the occasion of making room in Inner Space for herself, her omnipotence.

Her clairvoyant knowledge of which cure to prescribe was put through by her recently deceased mother. In the Enlightenment the theocratic conception of the afterlife was exchanged for a more personalized relationship to the dead.[16] From now on you expected to meet up again with the loved ones who had gone on ahead. Because standards of education and improvement continued to apply, the dead were sent to foreign planets for "testing" or "cleansing" (to borrow the terms Daniel Paul Schreber used in his *Memoirs of My Nervous Illness*).[17]

[14] I will be using John Osborne's translation of Walter Benjamin's *Ursprung des deutschen Trauerspiels* throughout this essay (London and New York: Verso, 1998). Page references are given in the text.

[15] Wilhelm Meier, *Höchst merkwürdige Geschichte der magnetisch hellsehenden Auguste Müller in Karlsruhe*, Stuttgart: J. B. Metzler'schen Buchhandlung, 1818. Page references are to this edition and are given in the text.

[16] See the opening chapter of Diethard Sawicki's *Leben mit den Toten. Geisterglauben und die Entstehung des Spiritismus in Deutschland*, Paderborn: Schöningh, 2002. Contact with dead led to the updating of the afterlife as the prospect of continuity across Outer Space. Sawicki also documents the Enlightenment view of the enrollment of the dead in continuing education programs on alien planets.

[17] The date stamp of the Enlightenment in Daniel Paul Schreber's *Denkwürdigkeiten eines Nervenkranken, nebst Nachträgen und einem Anhang über die Frage: "Unter welchen Voraussetzungen darf eine für geisteskrank erachtete Person gegen ihren erklärten Willen in einer Heilanstalt festgehalten werden?"* (Leipzig: Mutze, 1903) lies in the book's affinity with modern Spiritualism. At least the press, which specialized in books dedicated to communication with the other side, recognized Schreber's *Grundsprache* (basic language).

In his preface to Wilhelm Meier's document, Carl Christian Klein calls those who doubt Auguste's art of healing "zero-people" (iv), in other words, without the least tele-capacity, which in this setting means that they lack empathy. But by this blank charge he also projects into them the empty and withdrawn state that the magnetically enriched patient was able to overcome both in herself and for others. Schreber's rights to a shared reality were restored once he could empathically accept the coexistence of zero-people, which, earlier in the course of rebuilding a world from his own ground zero, he took to be "miraculated-up" figments or simulations.

The dead mother occupies the communications hub above, while in her own tele state on Earth (which she passes into through undeath) Auguste must corral her witnesses, collaborators, and detractors into a network (coextensive with the published document). It operates as her father's function, which she tests by her own turbulence and calls to order. When the *Magnetiseur* was unable to keep an appointment, Auguste reclaims the dis-appointment as the very session in which her telecommunications system prescribed the cure for her ailment. But since she is unconscious during these transmissions, only the conversation with the *Magnetiseur* could have secured the content. At the next session after the appointment that wasn't kept, she again enters the magnetic sleep-waking state.

> In this highly unusual state she resembles a marble statue, someone who has just lapsed into lifelessness. All vital coloring is gone. Not the slightest sign, not the least breathing indicates life. ... After some time, in this state, she folded her hands and prayed for 2 minutes. Suddenly there followed a deep and long inhalation, and with it, life, color, and movement returned.
>
> The *Magnetiseur*, who alone can speak to her at this point, addresses several questions to her. ...
>
> Question. Do you know the means for your rehabilitation?
>
> Answer. Now I no longer do. ... If only you had been here! ... My God! Now I have to wait 14 days. (13–15)

Repeated entreaties to find the relief ahead of this schedule Auguste rebuffs. And what is the cause of her illness? Cat whiskers she somehow swallowed. Her therapist calls this possibility into question, but she won't budge: She sees them!

In the season of her clairvoyance Auguste mixes together a recognized therapy, occult knowledge, and fairytale Fantasy. The mix gives her back a controlling interest in her life, which was shattered by bereavement and repression. The interest is upheld by the intrigue she makes of the differences between those who believe (and obey) her and those who doubt her role as medium (or prove lax in keeping to her schedule). The creative interest of omnipotence, which accrues to and through the intrigue that carries it forward, heads withdrawal off at the impasse and supplies the father function.

At the close of *The Origin of German Tragic Drama*, Benjamin covers the arrears of allegory by the intrigue that inheres in the dramatic plotting on stage. But first Benjamin gives the surprise twist that there is a half-life to the allegorical mode of reading, which lies in allegory's origin. Allegory first aimed at revising the evidence of Antiquity: the naked pagan body was transferred to the account of the creature, with the Devil at the front of the line.

> The … most important impulses in the origin of western allegory are non-antique, anti-antique: the gods project into the alien world, they become evil, and they become creatures. The attire of the Olympians is left behind, and in the course of time the emblems collect around it. And this attire is as creaturely as a devil's body. … The living contexts of their birth disappear, so they become the origins of concepts. … The deadness of the figures and the abstraction of the concepts are therefore the precondition for the allegorical metamorphosis of the pantheon into a world of magical, conceptual creatures. This is the basis … for the survival of fabulous creatures like the faun, centaur, siren and harpy as allegorical figures in the circle of Christian hell. (225–26)

Throughout the majority of the Origin book, Benjamin addresses modern allegory, which carries legibility forward among the ruins of Christianity's decline. Now, however, through the original allegory's poster boy, the Devil, Benjamin projects a turn or return that, by restoring the Christian context, would extinguish in the light of redemption the finite recording surface of remembrance. Transience, which is not so much signified as displayed in allegory, swings around this return into the allegory of resurrection (232). "Allegory, of course, thereby loses everything that was most peculiar to it; the secret, privileged knowledge, the arbitrary rule in the realm of dead objects, the supposed infinity of a world without hope. All this vanishes with this *one* about-turn" (ibid.). It is the abyssal contemplation of evil that triggers the return. A contemporary example of this stimulus package is the interpretation of psychopathic violence in the wake of WWII. In the realm of horror B-pictures the reception of Hitchcock's *Psycho* in the form and forum of slasher and splatter movies amounted to film therapy, which began to reach its termination phase once survival could be pried loose from its equation with murder.[18]

The jumpstarting of psycho horror at the end of the 1990s through the import of infernal instruction (notably in the *Saw* franchise), adumbrated the contemplation of evil not as a turn away from the secular figuration of violence on the screen of psycho horror but as another station in the mourning process awaiting integration. This B-picture vantage is syntonic with Benjamin's own emendation of his sense of a Christian ending of modern allegory in the closing evocation of the German *Trauerspiel* as a ruin that tells all you need to know about the complete edifice.

"The inadequacy of the German *Trauerspiel* is rooted in the deficient development of the intrigue," at which Calderón excelled on the Baroque stage. The Spanish dramatist's deployment of intrigue circumscribes the German *Trauerspiel*'s status as an incomplete substitute or ruin that supplies the allegorical caption to a complete result.

> The intrigue alone would have been able to bring about that allegorical totality of scenic organization, thanks to which one of the images of the sequence stands out, in the image of the apotheosis, as different in kind, and gives mourning at one and the same time the cue for its entry and its exit. The powerful design of this form should be thought through to its conclusion; only under this condition is it possible to discuss the idea of the German *Trauerspiel*. (235)

The German exponent extrapolates from the setting of its failure the prospect of successful mourning looping through simultaneity to vouchsafe the intricate innovations of survival.

When vampiric undeath reached the new world via Todd Browning's *Dracula* it began traveling in American letters through Outer Space (A.E. van Vogt's "Asylum") and, ultimately, underwent science fictionalization as an epidemic outbreak of living death (Richard Matheson's *I Am Legend*).[19] This massified condition of the new-world vampire came to be

[18] See my study *The Psycho Records*, New York: Wallflower Press/Columbia University Press, 2016.

[19] I give a more complete account of this transvaluation in Chapter 3 of the first volume of my *Critique of Fantasy* (subtitled *Between a Crypt and a Datemark*).

reclassified as the zombie's Heimat, and the deferral position of undeath between first and second deaths gave way to target practice with zombies improving the aim of putting the goner to the second death. The vampire is the ruin for reading the complete thrill-a-kill theater of zombieism.

In *The American Apocalypse*, Günther saw the zombie as the harbinger of the onset of a new metaphysical suffering that could supply a restart of consciousness to match the prospect of Outer Space (250). Günther added that the mechanical brains under construction in the United States, which were taking the double formerly lurking in the Gothic milieu of the vampire out on an update, could be seen as the technological equivalent of the idea of the zombie (251).

Andrzej Żulawski's 1981 film *Possession* follows the rise and fall of allegory in infernal precincts, but then, just the same, via the intrigue of Cold War secret agency, pulls up short before allegory's damnation to redemption.[20] Mark returns from a secret mission to his wife Anna and young son in West Berlin. But the marriage doesn't live there anymore. Anna (as played by Isabelle Adjani) is a classic collectible hysteric; once the curtains closed on the theater of hysteria, however, she would be more readily identified on the streets as psychotic. At the same time, she exhibits symptoms of infernal possession.

We know that in the recent past there were intermediary stages to the marriage crisis, like Anna's affair with Heinrich, a yogic sex mystic who is the prosthesis of his mother. But if her dissatisfaction with her marriage leads Anna into environs of a maternal relationship, she is only spinning circles inside the Oedipal foundation of the sacrament. In the meantime, however, she has moved on and entered a relationship with a seemingly infernal creature. Anna announces that she has two sisters, Chance and Faith. In an underground passage Anna undergoes a hysterical-psychotic paroxysm she calls a miscarriage: the death of Sister Faith. But she must care for and carry her forward—unto extinction and preservation. The underworld pageant supplies an allegorical caption to her creaturely relationship. Heinrich ends up the third victim of the tentacled gastrointestinal creature Anna keeps and protects in an apartment right up against the Berlin wall (the split-off living end of Faustian Europe). Heinrich's mother tells Mark that she is looking for Heinrich, not for his body, which she

[20] Hazal Bayar introduced me to Zulawski's film while I was advising her European Graduate School dissertation, which offered a feminist analysis of horror in cinema and theory centered on a close reading of *Possession*.

already identified at the police station, but for his soul. Her suicide upholds the nihilistically transvalued sacrament of the *Liebestod.*

At the start of the film, Mark announced that he was leaving the secret service. But by the end we know it didn't let go. The intrigue that is greater than the two of them catches up with him and Anna. But before they conclude what looks in the Cold War crossfire like another *Liebestod*, Anna introduces Mark to the fully metamorphosed creature. It is his *Doppelgänger*, who survives (together with their son's teacher, a double of Anna, though no one seems to know it). In the final scene the boy back home in the teacher's care begs her not to answer the door. The *Doppelgänger* is knocking. The reminder of reproduction and death cannot prevent the unwitting reincarnation from opening the household wide to doubling.

In Romanticism, doubling was the uncanny harbinger of suicide because the wish for replication (on the human side) could not be fulfilled. Instead, the close of *Possession* is science fiction, occupying and cathecting a new Inner Space that can skip the negative theology of *Liebestod* and let doubling go through. In Günther's assessment, the double as an achievement was unthinkable in the regional civilizations, an impasse that the Berlin wall's division symptomatizes. This, then, is the new idea in science fiction that Günther finds most fundamental: that of a soul, psyche, or self as something that stands in interchangeable relationship to its own content. Via the artificial distribution of processes of reflection across man and machine, human I and human you can be pushed together on one side. The man-made mechanism takes up the other side as the new *Doppelgänger*. The double formerly known as the unacknowledged in oneself heralds at the close of *Possession* a multiplicity like all the iterations of the same moment in the science fiction of time travel, each one unique and binding.

The Postscript in "Fragment of an Analysis of a Case of Hysteria"[21] offers an early consolidation of the insights Freud pursued upon exiting the hypnotic theater of dissociation elaborated in Josef Breuer's case study of Anna O.[22] Although he arrives after the fact at the import of the transference, the other bookend of the analytic session, the importance of free association, is already part of the case study. Free association steers the wish clear of the fleeting fixity of daydreaming, which the technique only

[21] Freud, "Fragment of an Analysis of a Case of Hysteria," *SE* VII: 1–122. Page references are given in the text.

[22] In Josef Breuer and Freud, *Studies on Hysteria*, *SE* II: 21–47.

resembles to the extent that a container bears a resemblance. Applied in the course of interpreting Dora's night dream, free association brings up the debt to the death wish.

Freud admits in the Postscript that Dora walked out on the analysis because he had not attended to a transference that bound him to Herr K. and the rebound of her revenge against them both (117–18). Freud wagered that the negative transferential aspect that Herr K. triggered, also in Dora's relationship to him and to the analysis, most likely turned on money (119).

Money supplies the allegory of dream development Freud introduced earlier (and cited from *The Interpretation of Dreams*):

> A daytime thought may very well play the part of *entrepreneur* for a dream; but the *entrepreneur*, who, as people say, has the idea and the initiative to carry it out, can do nothing without capital; he needs a *capitalist* who can afford the outlay, and the capitalist who provides the psychical outlay for the dream is invariably and indisputably, whatever may be the thoughts of the previous day, a wish from the unconscious. (87)

What underlies the analogy is the wish for free money, which might be called typical. Its foundation in the death wish is masked by its free-floating fulfillment. The fulfillment of the wish for free money in the form of inheritance from the dead steps closer to what is at the same time manically denied. It is the other's death that splits the omnipotence of wishing into shares. According to Freud, the omnipotence of thoughts hiding out in wish fantasy is first applied in the death wish, which, on the rebound, commits a share of the omnipotence to the goner, who can thus return. When the other goes first, then, a departure we inevitably wished upon, there is a ghostly remainder or return—the goner's share in the omnipotence that the death wish flexed—on which we speculate.

Freud comes to recognize in the somatic symptoms he earlier dismissed as history his patient's susceptibility to melancholic identification. The death of Dora's aunt triggered a series of identifications (notably with two cousins), which in the light of her second dream illuminate the foundation of her subsequent hysterical symptoms.

In Dora's second dream, her father is gone, though not yet in her waking lifetime. He goes back to her earliest wish that he get out of the way of her infantile sex. A multi-layered topography of wishing opens up around the dream news of the father's death. A dream, as Freud advises, circumvents repression to give representation to wishes that, in Dora's case, the dreamer in her waking state must actively unfulfill in relation to Herr K., to her father in prehistory, and to the analyst.

The footnotes Freud added to the transcript of Dora's dream are addenda that came up in the course of free association in session. The second addendum concerns the out-of-placement of a question mark. In Dora's telling of her dream what follows the news imparted by her mother in a letter, "Now he is dead," is the fragment-phrase, "and if you like you can come." A question mark cut short the phrase and gave emphasis to "like" (95). Every increment in the lexicon of what the English and French reception of psychoanalysis might call "desire," is marked in the original language by willing and wishing: "Und wenn Du willst?"[23] She recalls the question mark upon recognizing that her mother's dream sentence cites a note she received from Frau K.: "If you would like to come?" This was the note she followed to the lakeside setting where the breakdown of her relations with the K. couple led to her sessions with Freud. As Freud notes, the analysis was subsequently broken off in connection with the content of this dream (95), which, aggravated by his own inattention to the transference, triggered his patient's acting out.

As he underscores in the Postscript, however, Freud came to an appreciation of the transference in order to render intelligible the timing of the benefits the analysis did bestow on the patient despite the botched termination. Transference was party to the intrigue over which Dora obsessed. What survives the failed therapy is the patient's stabilization via an intrigue with which Freud's transference interpretation could still catch up.

Does the intrigue that rescues allegory at the close of *The Origin of German Tragic Drama* enter the "encapsulation" Benjamin attributed to Schreber's delusional system?[24] Yes. Freud identified as method basic to Schreber's recovery of a relational world within the delusion of intrigue the working of endopsychic insight.[25] Freud earlier accorded a closer look at this endopsychic lining in delusion via his reading of Wilhelm Jensen's

[23] Sigmund Freud, "Bruchstück einer Hysterie-Analyse," *Gesammelte Werke*, ed. Anna Freud et al. (London: Hogarth Press, 1942–) V: 256, 261.

[24] Benjamin, "Bücher von Geisteskranken: Aus meiner Sammlung." In: Benjamin, *Gesammelte Schriften*, ed. Rolf Tiedemann and Hermann Schweppenhäuser (Frankfurt am Main: Suhrkamp Verlag, 1972–1989) IV: 615–619; here 616.

[25] Freud, *Psychoanalytic Notes on an Autobiographical Account of a Case of Paranoia (Dementia Paranoides)*, *SE* XII: 1–84; here 79.

Gradiva, which he commenced within a year of publication of the case of Dora.[26]

The archeological setting of protagonist Norbert Hanold's delusion is endopsychic. There is no better analogy for repression than the volcanic burial and preservation of the precincts and populace of Pompeii. When he extends the analogy in session with the Rat Man, however, namely by indicating that the unearthing of long-buried relics tends to release rapid decay, Freud must rush to reassure his stunned patient that everything was being done to reverse this side effect.[27]

The novella Gradiva, which draws on Jensen's own attachment to a lost childhood sweetheart, was retold in terms of untreatable psychopathology in Pierre Boileau and Thomas Narcejac's 1954 novel *D'entre les morts*, which Alfred Hitchcock adapted in *Vertigo* (1958). The torment of Hitchcock's Judy while grief-stuck Scotty tries to remake her into the double of the lost object, Madeleine, finds a vestigial rehearsal between two photographs that Jensen cherished. The first one is the only image that was left of Jensen's sweetheart who died in childhood; the second one he composed like the first, thus setting the image of the other girl he (re) found later in life on the doubling and haunting of a dead ringer.[28] If the second girl's lookalike status was in the eyes of the beholder, then that only underscores that Jensen was seeing double. When Scotty recognizes that there is no ghostly double, it's too late. The melancholic story will have none of it—and accidentally on purpose Madeleine or Judy plummets from the bell tower to die a second death, which is the murder. Jensen proposed another way out of the encryptment, one that didn't pass through the murder in successful mourning, by introducing into the delusion of contact with the ghost of Gradiva the living "lost" object Zoë Bertgang.

In the case of Norbert Hanold, the opposition between eros and repression gives rise to his crisis. His delusion doesn't admit a stabilizing difference between the forces, as did Schreber's delusional system in regard to the zero-people. Hence the author recruits Norbert's repressed love object as his assistant to complete the fantasy of the intrigue. Following

[26] Freud, *Delusions and Dreams in Jensen's "Gradiva," SE* IX: 1–96; here 51. Further page references are given in the text. His treatment of Dora was in 1900 and most of the 1905 publication was written already in 1901. The Postscript, however, bears the date mark of proximity to the *Gradiva* reading.

[27] Freud, *Notes upon a Case of Obsessional Neurosis, SE* X: 155–249; here 176–77.

[28] The biographical information and the two photographs can be found online.

the foot fetish through the crack in oblivion Zoë enters the shaken delusion by identifying herself as the ghost of a Pompeian girl, whose brilliant gait or *Bert-Gang* is her own. She steps in as a therapist: she can enlighten, illuminate (these are the "Enlightenment" images Freud uses in lieu of mere "explanation") the dark spots in the narrative. The narrative as a whole partakes of the coherence her intrigue introduces into Norbert's delusion.

Freud states outright that fantasizing is the harbinger of delusion (58). And yet Norbert's unscientific tendency to fantasize, which culminated in the delusion, also offered a corrective to the repression. Zoë entertains the fantasy coupling as the ghost, declaring the ghost clear. Through her "Enlightenment" the wife-to-be rescues Norbert (and his proposal) from the depths of mother earth and brings reality or realization to the coupling (at once analytic and spousal) under the aegis of the father function. "Aufklärung und Heilung," enlightenment and treatment,[29] coincide in Zoë's therapy, leading to the awakening of affect. Norbert regains "respect" for the couples in the Italian honeymoon setting, whereas before he discerned in them only zero-people like flies to swat (26). In analysis the love that returns finds its "first" object in the treating analyst, which opens up another chapter of work on the transference (90). It amounts to a fantastic reversal of the analytic setting that in Gradiva the repressed love object is the treating analyst. But the patient's ultimate delusion counts in the court of his therapist as auto-analysis.

Zoë metabolizes what she introjects: a failed or maternalized father. The zoologist father gave her the name of his science, which monopolized his libidinal interest. The balancing act of conflict also yielded delusion in the father's case, although a more stable one than Norbert's because he still related to his daughter via the differences leading to compromise that Freud distinguishes from the protagonist's struggle or opposition between eros and repression.

The differences Zoë introduces into Norbert's delusional overvaluation of his science she delivers from her loving relationship to a failed father. Freud underscores that Zoë first fell in love with Norbert when he withdrew from her in adolescence and embarked on his own all-consuming career as an archeologist. That love for him and for her father underwent amalgamation is evident in the belittling caricature she finds for Norbert

[29] Freud, *Der Wahn und die Träume in W. Jensens "Gradiva," Gesammelte Werke* VII: 31–125; here 118.

as an “archaeopteryx,” a bird-creature belonging equally to archeology and zoology (33). Like Dora, Zoë was available for a new release of life from the incestuous milieu of neglect and unfulfillment. That she enlightens Norbert like a father is a benefit that also accrues to her.

Freud considers the discursive preponderance of double meanings (“zweideutige Reden”)[30] an instance of apparent absurdity, which however covers the twofold determination of Hanold’s symptoms (85). Ambiguity matches the double register in the delusion, through which Zoë works the cure. Freud points out that in the analytic session double meaning often discloses the underlying wish by taking a spin through free association. He goes on to address apparent absurdity not only in the formation of a delusion but also in certain dreams (73). In dreams, absurdity is the favorite testimony submitted by those who resist the notion that the dream has the status of a psychic act or function (ibid.). Freud could show, however, that in dreams absurdity covers up ill will, but only barely. In the *Interpretation of Dreams*, he analyzes a son’s dream of his dead father who is still around because he doesn’t know that he is dead. What he doesn’t know and the son can’t acknowledge, Freud drives the point home, is that the son wished him dead.[31]

Zoë learns through her intrigue with and within Hanold’s delusion to accept the death wish as fact of life and love. She hadn’t known going into it that one must first die to come alive, to be loved (37). The integration of the death wish belongs to the foundation of modern science fiction. The culmination of H.G. Wells’s *War of the Worlds* is the protagonist’s closing reflection upon reuniting with his wife that the innovation of their survival lies in the fact that during the invasion each had thought the other dead.

Arguing that the acceptance of absurd content means that strongly charged wishes thus come to be satisfied, Freud gives the example of scientists who, just like Hanold, were able to combine their academic allegiance to reason with their relationship to modern Spiritualism (71). But the opening season of the allegiance to reason, the Enlightenment, allotted more than one lifetime for the fulfillment of the Kantian duty of perfectibility. Extended finitude, however, can never equal everlasting life. Unlike the philosophical spiritualism that Kant, Schopenhauer, and Freud rejected for postulating material versus spiritual lifelines, modern

[30] Freud, *Der Wahn und die Träume in W. Jensens “Grradiva,”* 111–14.

[31] Freud, “Absurd Dreams,” *The Interpretation of Dreams*, *SE* I: 430.

Spiritualism, even if certain adherents sought to reconcile it with Christianity, was constitutively a secular mediatic enterprise that kept to a span of extended finitude, lodged between the recent past and the near future. Heir to the Enlightenment, modern Spiritualism science-fictionalized the afterlife in much the same way the mechanical brain, in Günther's argument, updated the double.

John Bock's *Creaturely Innocence* (*Kreatürliche Unschuld*) (2012/2015) looks like the digital inheritance of the allegorical tableaux of *Possession*. But Bock had not seen the film and was thinking of Pier Paolo Pasolini's allegory *Teorema* (1968). The role of the Visitor went to the maid, Rebecca, the third person rocking the couple in Bock's story.[32] *Creaturely Innocence* (both as film and as performance) is scatter-shot throughout with precise and exaggerated references, associations, ideas, which the artist promotes through heightened cinematography, special effects, and improvisation. The film illuminates a writer screenplay composed in a language Bock devised in the manner of the patois in Stanley Kubrick's *A Clockwork Orange* (1971), only using Northern German dialects that were raised in the course of the nineteenth century to the power of literature, for example by Theodor Storm and Theodor Fontane.

Creaturely Innocence was filmed in the Hindelooper Room, an exhibit in the Fries Museum (in Leeuwarden, Holland)—in alternation with one other space identified as the maid's chamber. The special-effects stage for a cite-specific phantasmagoria of filmic references, Rebecca's room opens upon Inner Space. For our purposes, this Space reaches back to Auguste Müller, whose sessions could be imagined taking place in the Fries Museum's period room. The jump cutting between historical dialects and the idiom-conceit of dystopic science fiction also characterizes Bock's deregulated treatment of the period in a room.

[32] In conversation with my former colleague John Bock, I obtained the information. On another occasion I asked him about the painting on glass that transpired in a performance installation I visited in a New York gallery. I was riveted to my souvenir of films that showed Picasso painting. He rejected this melancholic conceit. In the meantime I recalled that in *Teorema* the son in the household the Visitor enters and exits is inspired to pursue a breakthrough for his painting by swapping his former canvas for glass. The maid in the Pasolini household follows out the withdrawal of the Visitor into a phantasmagoria of miracles and self-immolation. Since Rebecca can be seen to follow her this is a good place to note that the innocent lightness of touch in Bock's performance art and art cinema doesn't belie the suffering but divests it of opposition (and the attendant symptoms of melancholic inhibition and nihilism).

When the head of the household in full period costume pulls out a typewriter from his antique desk the scene is not entirely site-nonspecific. The Hindelooper Room was originally one of many display cases comprising a vaster historical exhibition that in 1878 fit the new format of the world's fair. A reconstruction of what counted as a typical local interior dating back to the seventeenth century, it continued on as "typically Dutch," even to this day. In its current setting it is the portal to an eclectic documentation of the history of Friesland.

But first the Hindelooper Room had to be delivered from the condemned site of its first address. Because it had been assembled it could be disassembled and reassembled—it was transportable like a commodity or, as the Fries Museum's website puts it, like promotional material. The original imitation room, which was a huge success at the Paris World's Fair before it reopened in the first Fries Museum in 1881, is hard to locate.

Two years earlier, this room—almost identical in every way—had been exhibited in Paris, where it was so well received that other cities and even collectors too wanted a similar room: Hindeloopen (1881), Amsterdam (1883), Düsseldorf (1885), Dordrecht (1896), Berlin (1898), Nuremberg (1902) and Arnhem (1919). The Hindelooper Room in the Fries Museum is, in effect, the mother of all Hindelooper rooms, even those that can be seen in Hindeloopen! The room that was installed temporarily in Hindeloopen in 1881 is the same as the one in Berlin in 1898. The room that has been installed in Museum Hindeloopen since 1964 is the same room that was made for Düsseldorf in 1885.[33]

Early in Bock's film the husband enters the maid's room and stereotypes her as the other woman or mother.[34] During their prolonged embrace the camera circles repeatedly over and above them. Folding excess in to access the camera exhausts a recognizable convention and conceit of cinema. Rebecca finds her calling not with the husband but in concert with a creaturely, parasitic mutation organ. Like Odradek, the care or concern of the father of the house in Kafka's story, the organ-creature is introduced into the household by its head, a surgeon. In the Hindelooper Room he unpacks and manipulates the "summary mutation organ" or

[33] https://www.friesmuseum.nl/en/collection/icons/the-hindelooper-room (access March 2021). Benjamin shifted the setting and sense of modern allegory from the corpses on the Baroque stage to the commodities crowding the capital of the nineteenth century.

[34] Down the hall from the Hindelooper Room in the museum is the exhibit dedicated to the life of Mata Hari, dancer and spy, who was born in 1876 in Leeuwarden (as Margarethe Zelle).

"nanogenic mutation" to make it regular, keep the blood circulating, and get it ready to bite.[35] Like a demonic curse it cannot be fixed but only passed on. Rebecca adopts and adapts the creature until it fills out her room and gives her entry into Inner Space: "it crawls inside you and fills you fully" (1125). In time she seduces the wife, who follows her. Rebecca instructs her that "the overturning of the great mother ground" must follow (1128): "My flesh is a fallow field. It must be prepared ripe-fruitful for the planting" (1127).

Rebecca animates the organ-creature and presses its link inside her. The climax of infernal film images that the depressed link released stops short of redemption or damnation. What's left, her inert body, the surgeon deposits in a box (one of the props of Rebecca's big scene). He is reassured that with her removal the household has been restored. But when he restarts their interrupted status quo his wife is elsewhere: "I am in the body ... in nothingness" (1130). To be in the body and in nothingness circumscribes a transition from *Mutterboden* to the planetary father function, the position the wife now holds.

Bock stitches child's play into the borders of the scenes of transgression, horror, and ecstasy. In the domestic space Rebecca sews grapes upon the stockings of her lady. In the "crucifixion" scene the wife in turn inserts playful variations on bodily violation. She attaches edibles to Rebecca's Passion and accompanies the height of the performance on a diminutive scale with hand puppets. Bock mixes the relationship to a creature beckoning from the dark side of adolescence with the innocence or open display of child's play.

According to Freud, daydreaming is heir to the child playing at being big or grownup. But unlike this acceptable content of playing in childhood, which remains out in the open, the antisocial daydream, which picks up in adolescence where child's play left off, goes for a Big Time that can't be admitted in public. Freud even gives the burgeoning industry of analytic publications credit for checking the private horror of individuals who once felt alone with their daydream fantasies, needing a poet without knowing it.[36]

Another way to identify the vantage point for mixing what Freud kept separate in "The Poet and Daydreaming" is that the momentum of fantasy

[35] The screenplay was included in Bock, *Meechfieber* (Cologne: Walter König, 2013): 1119–1130; here 1122–23. Subsequent page references are given in the text.

[36] Freud, "Creative Writers and Day-Dreaming," 145–6.

gathering in the digital relation overshoots the opposition that sets adolescence apart as the living proof of Fallen Man[37]—an opposition buoying up the outer limits of psychic reality. "All the names in history" is no longer the cry before the psychotic break at the end of the world but describes the digital archive's best offer. Every entry is a returning return divested of the former setting on opposition. Simultaneity, Benjamin advised in *The Origin of German Tragic Drama*, is the secularization of time, making it present in space (194). And if we no longer transport a period made to fit a room then—just as we saw happen with the Romantic *Doppelgänger*—let's make a science fiction of it.

That we can feel at home in Bock's Hinder-loop we owe to the prep work of the clairvoyant subjects of Mesmerism and the hysterical patients in the opening season of psychoanalysis. Two cases from the world of performance add degrees of transition to this jump cut. On the list of contemporary artistic practices that Yayoi Kusama began checking off in 1957 there were performances and happenings (including "Walking Piece" and "Grand Orgy to Awaken the Dead" in 1966 and 1969 respectively). She followed the bouncing polka dot from her hallucinations already in childhood to her signature style.[38] The dotting of the phallic I is the extinction of distinction before the prospect of the cosmos. In science fiction we are regularly given to understand that the Outer Space to be colonized for the survival of the species is psychosis, which must be delivered from its status as outer-limit condition and concept and opened up instead for frontier or "borderline" settlement. To become part of the environment, as Kusama underscored, one's own body had first to be obliterated/liberated by polka dots. And yet the orgy of polka dots keeps a wake for the dead.

Kusama returned to Japan following the death of her partner Joseph Cornell and, following her father's death, consolidated her long history of intermittent treatment by taking up permanent residence in Seiwa Hospital for the Mentally Ill. The hospital environment provided the best conditions for her to work. That it was a transportable setting that allowed her on occasion to travel puts through the performance connection with the therapeutic immersion in or micromanagement of a new world.

[37] This is how J.R.R. Tolkien puts it in regard to unwholesome fantasy in his essay christening the Fantasy genre. Tolkien, "On Fairy-Stories," *Tree and Leaf/Smith of Wootton Major/The Homecoming of Beorhtnoth* (London: Unwin Books, 1975): 11–79; here 28.

[38] See Grady Turner's 1999 interview with Kusama in Kristine Stiles and Peter Selz (Eds.), *Theories and Documents of Contemporary Art* (Berkeley: University of California Press, 2012): 111–13.

Brian Wilson, the lead Beach Boy, hated the beach and was afraid of the ocean.[39] He broke down in an airplane during a tight tour schedule. As a client of Eugene Landy's 24-hour milieu therapy, which he entered following his father's death in 1973, Wilson was later able to travel through his abyssal fear of flying (en route to another containment of his stage fright) in a section of the plane set aside for his treatment apparatus and its administrators. The abuse charge Landy landed for his boundary-blending with Wilson misses the point (at which point family interests reasserted control but without, thanks to Landy's treatment, incapacitating the identified patient). On the sliding scale of psychopathology, a point is reached where only something bigger than the two of us applies. Three is a crowd but also the father.

The normal-to-neurotic Everyman in psychoanalysis and psychotherapy is, then, an afterthought, a byproduct of the stabilization of the psychotic borderline at the outset of modern therapy. D.W. Winnicott overturned the central construct of normalcy or neurosis and returned to the original momentum of treatment. But he was also overlooking (in both senses) Freud's introduction of the second system upon contact with the shell shock epidemic of WWI. To illustrate the repetition compulsion, he diagnosed in the serial dreaming of shell-shocked soldiers, Freud cited, for example, the case of a woman who was over and again the very widow of each new husband. Winnicott's famous line that the fear of going insane was a roundabout way of admitting that a breakdown had already occurred was also the long way round for recognizing that mental illness can go out of itself, casting out borderlines that net a structure on the outside for fatality or stability.[40] By its own serial momentum, the repetition compulsion, according to Freud, not only grows into the outside world a protuberance of its disordering but can also fold out a new preparedness for the

[39] To prepare for my stint as talking head in Christopher Dreher's documentary *Pop Odyssee – Die Beach Boys und der Satan* (1997), I did a great deal of research on the Beach Boys, on which I base my account.

[40] D.H. Winnicott, "Fear of Breakdown," *International Review of Psychoanalysis* 1 (1974): 103–07. The horror theater of Grand Guignol in Paris, which opened and shut its doors in sync with the history of psychoanalysis this essay traverses, kept elaborating the fear of going mad even as it is happening, even as it closes in on you and closes you in. Add to this the other focus of Grand Guignol's horror entertainment, our forced adaptation to the latest in technologization, not only the mediatic extensions of the senses but also the latest interventions of surgery, and you have the archive of confirmation of Winnicott's insight. That this insight was Roland Barthes's favorite citational prop closes the loop.

shocks of the new. This is one of the openly admitted mainstays of Benjamin's reading of media in "On Some Motifs in Baudelaire." The other psychoanalytic mainstay, which he didn't identify, was the discovery of dissociation in fetishism, which showed Freud the way past the limiting concept of psychosis.

Freud referred to two non-sexological cases of sons who didn't know that their fathers were dead but who were not, as he would have expected, psychotic.[41] Like fetishists in regard to the makeup of their libidinal objects, the sons both knew and did not know that the father was missing. The dissociation in fetishism showed Freud the way past the impasse in shell shock, which he attributed to the ego's conflict with its "parasitic double."[42] Dissociation, which oscillated at the border between neurosis and psychosis, was the transvaluation of doubling, a new alternative to the death-wish rapport that splits the shares of omnipotent fantasy and summons the father's vengeful ghost.

Along this borderline, Benjamin established the niche market of gadget love, the buffer zone defending against the pathogenic impact of technologization and mass-psychologization. Sitting before the console of switches and pushbuttons, Benjamin's gadget lover could already stagger and calibrate the dosing of shocks and shots boosting his immunity against psychotic shutdown. There is even a time travel feature to this comfort zone: with a click the camera gives the moment shot a "posthumous shock."[43]

By the extrapolations of science fiction, the gadget miniaturizes until its love is a wrap with the occult capacities that Mesmerism reintroduced during the Enlightenment. Like in a true underworld, all the figments and figures of history return but without the former conditioning of opposition. Gadget love opens the Inner-Outer Space for the body's return in surprising continuity with Antiquity, although its intactness is literally the condition of being "in touch."[44] This is where child's play goes in the

[41] Freud, "Fetishism," *SE* XXI: 152–57.

[42] Freud, "Introduction to *Psychoanalysis and the War Neuroses*," *SE* XVII: 207–210; here 209.

[43] Benjamin, "On Some Motifs in Baudelaire," *Illuminations*, tr. Harry Zohn, ed. Hannah Arendt (New York: Schocken Books, 1969), 155–194; here 175.

[44] Following Freud's analysis of Schreber's *Memoirs* and Viktor Tausk's study of Natalija A. and her delusion of the influencing machine, Hanns Sachs gave a strong reading of the primary narcissism of the Ancients, which allowed them to skip the machine age. By advancing to secondary narcissism or by filling a psychotic break with a techno delusion, modern

course of the global expansion of adolescence into both childhood and adulthood. Like the multiverse the universe in *Interstellar* (2014), the father function, regionally decoded and delivered of the setting on opposition or repression, will absorb the mother of memories.

man by contrast seeks to separate the body from itself and thus forestall the crisis of uncanniness. See Sachs, "Delay of the Machine Age," *Psychoanalytic Quarterly* 11, 3–4 (1933): 404–424. I'm suggesting that the digital relation of being in touch gets around the crisis (its last hurrah was the already dated "uncanny valley").

CHAPTER 12

What Is Called Father? (A Fissure in Familialism)

Avital Ronell

The next twenty years? Imagine what may be in store for us, as if we were to make use of a capacity for dreaming-in-common. Let me call up a dreamable future, attuning us to one of its mutating programs. I see the future! (Quoting Friedrich Nietzsche, summoning his philosophers of the future.) Life's misogynist edges will have disappeared entirely, together with the impoverishment of both sexes, opening a vast evolution of gendering spin-offs and affirmative de-authorizations of oppressive strangleholds, lamentable oppressions. Thanks to scientific innovation and the unrelenting rise of social justice, paleonymic family structures will have dissolved into banked memories that come at you only periodically like bats out of historical hell. Remembering the Beatrice Cenci story (she famously went up against a brutal patriarch in the fifteenth century, only to be shot down by Pope Clement VIII, her execution serving as

Sections of this paper have appeared in Ronell, *Loser Sons: Politics and Authority* (2013); published here with permission of the University of Illinois Press.

A. Ronell (✉)
New York University, New York, NY, USA
e-mail: avital.ronell@nyu.edu

L. Weissberg (ed.), *Psychoanalysis, Fatherhood, and the Modern Family*, https://doi.org/10.1007/978-3-030-82124-1_12

inspiration for Caravaggio's martyred St. Matthew)—so, remembering the Beatrices among us, beaten down by the grinding *authority of the father*, as Alexandre Kojève would say, thinking through the mystical foundations of authority, and splicing it together with the mass of programs that it has generated, consciously or unconsciously.[1] The family drama and its attendant violations will have lost its destructive edge. And so, the streaming continues. In twenty years, the scale of world-class aggression and anal-sadistic militaristic strongholds will have fizzled. The State will no longer borrow paternal tropologies to legitimate its incessant incursions—the "State" will move into lower caps and return to the dockets of the nineteenth century. In twenty years, patriarchy as life-form and viability will have gone the way of vinyl records and tape decks. Gender, the first traumatic appointment according to Judith Butler (who argues that the primal instance of psychic scarring occurs early on, when the guardian or parent answers to the prod: "Is it a girl or boy?").[2] In twenty years, the good losers—I am using shorthand—are those whose identities, fissured and complex, receive definition by psychoanalysis and Franz Kafka; in short, those who lean into or assume their castration, mark themselves up by finitude's score. "Women" will look to archival storage clusters to retrieve the files of an oppressive history. They will turn their sights on Sigmund Freud and Kafka who started the countdown, leveling off a particular syntax of violence. Maybe it's worth reviewing what will have disappeared before adding on the laugh track. In twenty years, some of these concerns will have softened, like aggressive nation-states, beating a retreat. *Ach*!

I would like to have said more about my over-determined system of projection and wish-fulfillment, but prudence requires that I keep the focus reasonably narrow. I want to remember what Freud and Kafka had to say about "the victory of patriarchy" and how they struggled with its implications and leakages into imaginary precincts and quotidian effectiveness. Freud, for instance, says that we still have to contend with this victory that for him is not a given or gift.[3] I don't have the kind of expanses

[1] See Alexandre Kojève, *La notion de l'autorité*, Paris: Gallimard, 2004.

[2] Keynote lecture for ACLA, New York University, April, 2014.

[3] Sigmund Freud, *Moses and Monotheism: Three Essays*. In: Freud, *The Standard Edition of the Complete Psychological Works*, tr. James Strachey, ed. Anna Freud et al., 24 vols. (London: The Hogarth Press, 1953–1974), XXIII: 3–140, here 118 (edition will be abbreviated *SE*).

I explore this statement and Kafka's struggle with Father in *Loser Sons: Politics and Authority*, Urbana, Ill.: University of Illinois Press, 2012.

before me to handle all the dreamt-up improvements and historical mutations at once, so I'll keep it short, unlike the patriarchal *Zeitalter*.

* * *

So. Freud, at one point, wonders about the victory of patriarchy—something we still have to contend with. I am contending, but barely. Literature, with its ongoing sense of disaster, helps me along. On this matter of the patriarchal hold, with its inescapable practical edges, I orient myself toward Kafka's work, its starting point and endpoint on the cusp of paternity. An unfinished project of Kafka's, entitled "The Sons," was meant to house the horde of loser sons who could not get up from the incessant destructions suffered at the hands of unwitting fathers. Therein lies a principal quality of tension for Kafka, and we begin to understand why he was one of the most capable, even negatively capable, insurance lawyers of the day, filing on behalf of the losing end of warring parties. But in his literary assignments the paternal commando acts with ambiguous certitude in the way he deals out effects of power. To a certain extent fathers, no matter how persecutory, remain impervious to transferential fantasies that see them as the ruling CEOs of psychic plundering, spoliation, incessant familial, and political defrauding. They readily absorb the transferential hits and deflect them. Pushing back on tyrannical projections, fathers manage these fantasies by upgrading themselves to loving and tender sovereign brutes who have meant little harm and far less damage than they nonetheless prompt. The Kafkan fathers weren't out to get their kids or send them to Kingdom come, as may have been the case when Laius deliberately sought to quell baby Oedipus. Kafkan kids were bound over to another set of lethal circumstances, less calibrated by intention, structural determination, or mere power-play, less mandated by the so-called instinct for survival. Still, they could not avoid getting crushed under the weight of powerful language assaults and the expanding girth of the paternal body, no matter how figurally situated. In the Hermann Kafka family, sexual difference decided whether or not you would be voided. Some girls got away, were somehow stronger, more rebellious, or more compatibly dependent. The boys were either killed off from the start—Kafka refers to two dead brothers who bailed on him, leaving the young Franz to fight off paternal brutishness on a solitary spin—or the boys in the family, divested and chronically put down (Kafka says he didn't have an upbringing, but only a "down bringing"), the boys in any case were prone to failure, subsisting in a kind of power outage, as if switched off, suddenly depleted and emptied of being. Their fate, though responsive to the father's sprawling shadow, was by no means planned or designed by the largely hapless creature who came equipped with special effects and liquidating features that were, Kafka contends, for the most part absolved of guilt or any wrongdoing.

Paternal power surges in the Kafkan world were by some measures inadvertent, innocent. The sons in the world he pulled together thus suffered from, among other things, an exquisite Nietzschean injunction, disallowing any enactment of *ressentiment*. It might have been easier to hate and resent the Persecutor, to push back and mark succession, Ego's winning card, calling upon finitude's vindictive edges. But Kafka plays it otherwise. He scores essential points on the outer limits of Freudian ambivalence, subduing the urge to strike back at the ever-encroaching Debilitator. These tactics, or abolition of tactics, serves to keep Father alive and kicking. (Here a difference can be marked between Freud and Kafka's game of thrones: following Freudian protocols, the father killed off, I'm thinking *Totem and Taboo*, gains in authority, bloats up in the accumulation of harassing qualities when fueled on the sons' *remorse*. Derrida runs with *remorse* by letting it generate *morsels* of paternity, fixing "*mort*" and I would add *moroseness* to the masochistically fated sons—all these "mores" emerge from remorse after having incorporated the father in a feast as one commonly has after a lecture.)

Unlike the anti-patriarchal heroes of Expressionism, Kafka's sons refuse to take up arms against their fathers but instead find themselves strapped into paternal machines that slowly buzz-saw death sentences on their bodies. Among the works that Kafka intended to include in *The Sons* was the famous "Letter to My Father."[4] This work uniquely breaks with the habits of referential discretion to which Kafka committed his writing and in fact resists being assimilated into any stable notion of work. The projected book of *Sons* could neither contain nor deliver the "Letter." Difficult to situate in terms of traditional genre theory, slaloming between imaginary and symbolic poles of address, it undermines the epistolary conventions to which it attaches—unless (but this is not a contradiction) the distress of this letter signals the fate of all epistolary outbreaks. It may be that *every*

[4] Franz Kafka, "Letter to Father." tr. Ernst Kaiser and Eithne Wilkins. In: Kafka, *The Sons: The Judgment, The Stoker, The Metamorphosis, and Letter to His Father*, tr. Kaiser, Wilkins, et al. (New York: Schocken Books, 1989), 113–117.

letter, no matter how radically rerouted or thematically smudged, asks in its own way, "Father, why have you abandoned me?" and participates in the mystagogy that turns paternal into a tyrant, an affiliate of the great Depriver. This version of the paternal lineup reverts to what Jacques Lacan calls—please excuse my French—the father as great Fucker, the obscene libidinal glutton.[5]

Let me however stick to the itinerary of the letter: Every love letter, no matter how purportedly remote from paternal end zones, may involve a similar petition of original privation, whether or not it appears to be dissociated from father's address. I will try to press on with questions raised by this particular non-starter, Kafka's "Letter to My Father," in order to surveil the way it underscores the impossible address, rendering the very notion of "Father" disabling, as something that evades us, holding an impossible position, and, from the point of view of the impossible position alone, invites the father necessarily to be imagined and projected as Depriver. Lacan writes that the notion of the father is scientifically unsustainable, and I think Kafka goes along with this, showing the fantasy of the father as that which is pumped up on a secret store of maternal energy and delivery systems, as in Kafka's story, "The Judgement," to still call the shots. Even when hitching a ride on the phantom mother, the effect of Father rules out his abolition. Georg's father, enfeebled, carries out the work of master agency, managing to break the son and incite a riot of damages to any letter, book, or being that would try to place his son in protective custody. Father, dead or alive, breaks in to make his power grab.

I return to the Letter. Undeliverable and conceptually stalled, the petition to an unaddressable father necessarily bounces. Still, the "Letter" has a personality and psychic currency. Situated between fear and anxiety, it hesitates at every turn between *Mitsein* and the logic of the other—between a world of culpability (where the law is given and fixed) and a world of responsibility (where obligation precedes and exceeds the law—Emmanuel Levinas makes us think of our condition of *liability*, a subtle and pressurizing offshoot of guilty being).

If I state that Kafka situates the *Letter* between fear and anxiety this is because the object is at once known, as in the case of fear, and also points to nothing, as in the case of anxiety. With *Mitsein* meshed into the logic of

[5] The double and split personality of Father has given Slavoj Zizek a rise in many of his lecture performances At N.Y.U., when he asks why we are so astounded to learn about paternal violators in Austria and elsewhere.

the other, the signatory of the letter tries to confront the ordeal of an irrevocable co-primordiality with the father, as would be dictated by Mitsein. But, at the same time, one is tempted by snares in the logic of the other which places a theological horizon on the relatedness, exalting an always nearly transcendental Father. Very little can be taken for granted in Kafka, for his worlds set up so many intricate instances of relatedness that are prone to collapse while at the same time they prove intractable. It is not as though one knew what a father is, what constitutes his—or her, if we accept the Lacanian re-write and Freudian pink slips in terms of the paternal metaphor—essential power, particularly when we recognize that Kafka, an unerring reader of the major downsizers of his era that include Nietzsche, Marx, and Freud, contributed his part to the struggle of relinquishing that which cannot be proven or cognized: namely, from beginning to end, the authority of Father.

Keenly aware of shrinking metaphysical frontiers and the distinct pressure zones of ever de-transcendentalizing effects of power, Kafka sets up shop precisely in the regions flagged by comrades Freud, Marx, and Nietzsche, but without leasing the power tools for establishing something or someone like an Overman; nor does he have the nerves for the appalling complications of neurotic constraints as set out in case studies and their terminal/interminable parameters. (Kafka is possibly equally Marxist and Freudian or Nietzschean in the end as he struggles with the metaphysics of work and the proclivities of the producing subject, refining a sobering recast of the Subject in the age of techno-bureaucracy; still, he offers none of the hypothetical safe landings or promising projections that his fellow doubters, despite significant pessimistic edges, bring into view.)[6] For his part, in step with the incisive group, Kafka sets his sights on the exhausted side of the things, keeping pace with the same class as other metaphysical dropouts and detectors of withering institutions. What does the turf that these language bearers share look like? Coming at the problems they circumscribed from different angles this collective points to a singular facet of the same discovery, working it each according to his own means and idiom, managing the discursive levers of a singular yet shared relatedness to dispossession. Something has happened to the very substance or potentiality of man that led Martin Heidegger to orient his

[6] For an analysis of the Subject, see Philippe Lacoue-Labarthe, "In the Name of…" In: Lacoue-Labarthe and Jean-Luc Nancy (Eds.), *Retreating the Political*, tr. Simon Sparks (London and New York: Routledge, 1997), 78–99.

concerns to Dasein. OK, maybe this is fast-tracking the fate of man without properly accounting for what happened or slowing down to tally up the damages. Let me put it another way and count up the receipts of another bottom line and lineage.

Since Freud, Kafka, and some of the other guys, theoretical points have been scored that downsize the very concept of Man, going as far as to recall and question the Greek ideal of the *anthropos*—this is Jacques Derrida's doing or undoing in a significant essay called "The Ends of Man."[7] The cumulative effect of these seizures has been devastating, allowing as well for a slight liberatory inroad as well. In sum, Man can no longer exult in theoretical bolsters and crowning qualities of being and historicity. No longer appropriable as the "son of God" or the "purpose of nature" or the "subject of history," Man at this point has become divided up and is seen as that who (or *which*) no longer is or has meaning, who no longer can be grasped as the signified of sense. From this point onward "Man" is that being exposed, abandoned, delivered over, subjected. These terms belong to the thought of Jean-Luc Nancy, which has been concerned with modalities of exposition and abandonment. In light of Nancy's work, we might see that, entirely in the manner of his fellow "master discourses," Kafka's text revs up the engine of a distinctive syntax, dealing relentlessly in a displacement of the concept, "Man," which is no longer the substantiality of a pre-given identity or identifiable human according to normative or normalizing scales and determinations. Whether vermin or unrecognizable thingness, man, evermore metamorphosed, has alighted as the being susceptible to exposure, marked for expulsion, yet still in dialogue with the remnants of humanism's principal appointments, figures, and tropological holds. Entangled in familialisms, office spaces, architectural constructs, courtroom drama, and linguistic fails, Kafka's misfits continue to file existential claims, reaching out to the community of the tone deaf. Still, the most minimal communication creaks through. Henceforth,

[7] Jacques Derrida, Margins of Philosophy, tr. Alan Bass, Chicago: University of Chicago Press, 1982. In their introduction to the voluminous tome, *Les fins de l'homme: A partir du travail de Jacques Derrida: colloque de Cerisy, 23 juillet-2 août 1980* (Paris: Galilée, 1981), 13, Nancy and Lacoue-Labarthe write that the destination or *Bestimmung* of man is no longer "a question among others on the subject of man: it is rather man himself who has become a question. For this fundamental reason. … the thinking of man becomes that of finitude—or, more rigorously, the ontotheology of the Subject sees itself shaken up by an analysis of finitude" (tr. mine).

being does not consist apart from the "with"; it exposes itself as the *between* and *with* of singularities.

I cannot be the first to observe that Kafka's texts appear to share core survival issues with those of psychoanalysis. Both modalities of seeing and saying, of seeing insight and resolve, inch toward a nearly Freudian thematics of *Hilflosigkeit* that takes on the facticity of exposed being, eviscerable, undeliverable, and abandoned. Still, there are differences to account for if the alliance is at all to be taken seriously, as, I believe, it must be.

* * *

Very little can be taken for granted in Kafka's world. Though they are cast in their omnipotence, we never know for sure what fathers are nor can we be certain to call down what identifies the son. Kafka makes us start from scratch over and again as he stages the inevitability of sharing what cannot be shared, of discerning between Mitsein on the one hand and the logic of the other on the other hand—fundamental, if intrusive, structures that make continual claims upon his writing. Bound over to the other or to the strictures of being-with, the creatures or "animots"[8] and beings that populate these works show that presence is impossible, signaling only as an offshoot decoy of co-presence. In the "Letter" that has been entrusted to us, the stakes of this "co-" are precisely what Franz tries to negotiate with the elder Mr. Kafka. The son remains confounded by the *between* and *with* that dominate scenes of unbreakable attachment and reveal the strange co-parenting of reciprocally stifling histories. Kafka stands his ground: he subscribes only to that responsibility which thought is. Along with Nietzsche and Nancy he sees his task as doing the labor of the negative, assuring the "not" of certain propositions. Thus, Kafka assumes the responsibility of the *not*, making it an essential part of his writing practice, his ethically intoned praxis: *not* to let oneself be taken by a decisive clench of sense, *not* to identify with it, *not* to assign or embody it definitively, *not* to figure or reify it, and so forth. Instead, he allows for metamorphosis and terrifying cycles of transition. Leaning into them, he risks everything by means of their peculiar articulations, their relentless disarticulations. In each text and his letters, Kafka makes a start from scratch over and again,

[8] The combination of animal and word (*animot*) in French is Derrida's coinage and part of his vast reflection on the place and misplacement of animals in philosophy and other impoverished confinements.

back-peddling toward a region of troubled origins. Neither father nor son is assumed—something that Kafka's works underscore emphatically. Yet, they are shown to co-determine worlds. The abiding complicities of these figural anchors allow the grammars of *politics* to behave as though we all knew what the meaning of these words and their referential radius might stipulate—as if materialities could still be mobilized by the implacability of these paleonyms. If anything, Kafka—precisely by taking recourse to radical disfiguration—was the one to take down the modern family and the burdened assurances of meaning that familialism has continued to exert on political tropologies. *Little can be taken for granted*; even the positioning of the son proves no longer to be reducible to a grant or gift that could be said to originate with what is called Father.

* * *

For his part Freud started us off on the story of an immemorial *Vatermord*, digging deep into the unconscious history of parricidal rage. Kafka, as an avid reader of all the totems and taboos set down by Freud, contributed to the world's irrepressible stories about fathers banishing and destroying their children. Sharing the same insight, both Kafka and Freud start up their search engines in the crime scene of ur-clashes. The effort to determine whose killer impulse started the row is possibly a trivial matter. Which of the posited roles can be charged most convincingly with inversion, projection, aggressive displacement, or with hiding the murder weapon? How has the program of strategic survival techniques been nailed—or rescinded? Something happened in the anahistory of a still gripping psychic heritage that leads one to tap the residual virulence of the paternal metaphor, a Lacanian cipher for Father. The work of disinstalling a lock on the imaginary that holds these figures over the fire of material consequence remains a vivid part of the Kafkan legacy.

Let me close in on a particular feature of the Kafkan dilemma and consider closely the trouble in parricide. Perhaps, rather, I should have clung to the homonymy, parasite, so that I can offer to explore the troubling parasite in Kafka's directory. *I am ready.* This is home turf. *Okay.* In the first place, Kafka gave us the close-up of parasitical existence but only by giving it a paradoxical run: on a fast spin cycle, the parasite turns into a predator, shedding all substantiality before receding back into parasite hell. Unwelcome and excremental, the parasite in Kafka, bloated on guilt and primed on shame, experiences itself as predatory excess. Nonetheless, parasitical vigor proves ever prepared to pounce, to scratch, and to sink back into the system of traces that we understand as writing. Existentially unavoidable, the parasite marks the spot where writing begins and life is sucked out of any internal field of expectation. Kafka, like Jean-François Lyotard after him, teaches that every child arrives on the scene as a parasite, prey to infanticidal phantasms on the part of predator parents—among other things, the starting line of nearly human existence has meant that, in order to avoid this particular scrap of knowledge, we have had to divinize the child and airlift it up into transcendental zones, making it God and angel-like. Kafka shows up right before the dialectical switch is implemented and keeps the child down on an existential ground level. However, if you are still hugging representations of a toughened State or inclined to side with Mr. Kafka, father of Franz, and other authoritarian figures in the crisis, the child (a first immigrant) is powered by the fantasized potentiality to arrive, from the get go, as gruesome predator, invading and parasiting hapless parents. You'd be surprised how many interpreters in literary studies side with the paternal fix of authority and line up with Hermann Kafka and his doubles, setting up a firm if the authoritarian structure of legitimated power plays.

Franz Kafka wants out of the parasite-predator polarity if there might be an outside to such a consistently sticky ordeal. He imagines and posits that becoming a father could spring him from the oppressive quagmire of a predatory parasite. To embrace fatherhood would mean, as Kafka several times indicates, to have arrived, *to have coincided with and nailed a destination*. As Father, he could have coincided even with a proper death—to the extent that destination and death imply each other, as in a "final destination." Literature, no matter how crackled and nonthematic, prescribes a paternal inscription or call in. The address of Father—as phantasm, rhetorical custom or biogenetic prop—is set as literature's telic anxiety, the homecoming for which poets have stood and rhetors posed, from Odysseus's address to Zeus to Saul Bellow's sit down in *Seize the Day*, to appeals made in Dennis Cooper's work to Daddy, to Daddy's appeal in Kathy Acker's Oedipalizations, to Hélène Cixous's counterphobic laugh of the Medusa, and so on. As complicated as locating the father gets in his works, Franz Kafka, for his part, will never have reached the station of Father, just as the letter cannot reach its registered destination, in the end allowing the fiction of paternity to collapse on itself. The failure of the letter to arrive, the failure of Franz to make it past a highly invested boundary, involves a number of deflections that are crucial for the fate of literature. To the extent that Freud has stated that "Fate" and "Father" (*FAThEr*) share the same structure in the unconscious, we can trace their merging itineraries in Kafka.

Now also published as an alone-standing book, the *Brief an den Vater* (*Letter to Father*),[9] which traces a history of traumatic interruptions, is, as Heidegger might but could never have said, a destiny for us.[10] It is a destiny to the extent that it corrupts destinal presumptions and reroutes literature around paternal markers never to be reached or assumed. Fiction shoots out of the wound of unbearable paternity. Among the things that it has going for it are the crucial stalls and breakdowns, the persistent parasitical drainage of which this text remains an unprecedented record. The letter enfolds a destiny that cannot come to pass, if only because the terms of arrival have been withdrawn from its account, strictly delegitimated. The *Letter* tells us of its impossible itinerary in so many ways and sets itself up as a substitute for a type of writing that it serves to erase. Up close and intimate, the *Letter* refuses to disclose its subject or open a historical account. For rhetorically rigorous reasons, Kafka is no longer capable of full-blown biography, though the *Letter* unavoidably gathers up and posts biographical material. History and its satellite narratives have been exhausted as Kafka edges toward a limit of the sayable. Memory, in any case, is always thrown into question, as the attempt at history persistently falls prey to false memory, disruption, aberration, secondary revision, and other transmission problems such as unavoidable static (which the French language designates as "parasites" or "phantoms"). Any trace of a history or development has been crushed by the expropriation of experience that father flags. As in "The Judgment" the patriarch stands up for a hijacked experience of friendship and love when, for instance, he takes away the friend from Russia—a destination crucial to the imaginary mapping and letter-writing of Georg Bendemann. When father shoots down the friend, he cuts off Georg's supply line and escape route, he removes the life-sustaining destination that gave Georg a sense of a possible history, if only in the transmuted form of a geographical remove—the promise of distance. He needed little to get a run on paternal stretches and pernicious

[9] Kafka, *Letter to the Father/Brief an den Vater: Bilingual Edition, tr. Kaiser and Wilkins,* (ser.) The Schocken Kafka Library, New York: Schocken, 2015. The text is cited here from the edition, Kafka, *The Sons.*

[10] I explore the intricacies and micro-folds of the Letter at length in terms of the disappearance of authority and the defeat of politics in Loser Sons.

outreach programs, for remote geographics sufficed to keep him going in a world where tropes of referential plenitude were in any case defunct. Biography and history, which imply an inner transformation and some type of locomotion, are halted by the father's imperious inflations and by the son's corresponding incapacitation, his inability to separate from paternal annexations: the father takes up space and poaches figures that might mark out a separate existence or an independent motor experience. If anything, the *Letter* tells of the drainage of experience, of life flattened out, impoverished and parasited by the paternal predecessor. (The father is not only predecessor, however; he vampirizes the future—he is the *suck-cessor*.) Few things can be translated into experience; it is as if father were the affective correlative of a mall or time stuck in an elevator, or perhaps he evokes the rising rage of idling in traffic, where one is slowly wasted, in a perpetual slump, pretending to move forward or advance in life.

Stuck with Hermann Kafka for a father, Kafka starts up the *herman-n*eutics that keeps Franz running—or creeping, as he often writes—in place. As with the war-weary soldiers that according to Walter Benjamin return from the battle worn down and emptied of experience,[11] unable henceforth to accumulate stories and history, Franz has traded in experience for authority. Authority, though emptied by now of transcendental mooring, props itself up in the space vacated by history, forked over by experience. Deregulated and eerily pervasive, authority cannot be proven or demonstrated or even easily recanted, but is imposed as a force that experience, weakened and rundown, can no longer unhinge. Abandoned by history and bereft of the solidity of experience, the son can offer only testimony, an attestation to his muffled voice and diminished pose in an experience-less space. There is no question of initiating a story, replenishing a world or starting off on an adventure. Even "adventure" implies an overload of agency in terms of possible experience. At best the son can negotiate a position between reactive rage and responsive marginality. Franz chooses to agitate on the margins of a history occupied and closed off to him by Hermann.

* * *

[11] See Giorgio Agamben's treatment of Walter Benjamin's "Der Erzähler" in Agamben, *Enfance et histoire: Dépérissement de l'expérience et origine de l'histoire*, tr. Yves Hersaut, Paris: Editions Payot, 1989), 19–25, and Laurence Rickels vast treatment of the war undead in his oeuvre.

In *Letter to Father*, Franz claims that he would have been able to survive Hermann Kafka had he been known to him as a friend, a boss, an uncle, a grandfather, "even (though more hesitatingly) as a father-in-law."[12] (The irony of the hypothetical marriage that would render Hermann father-in-law, marked with hesitation by Franz, leads to vertiginous interpretive calculations that we'll leave to the side.) Kafka adds, "Only as a father you have been too strong for me" (117). Too close, too powerful, the father's authority is moreover consolidated by the death of two brothers and by the fact that the Kafka sisters were born long after, leaving Franz in early youth to fend for himself. "Only as a father you have been too strong for me, particularly since my brothers died when they were small and my sisters came along only much later, so that I alone had to bear the brunt of it (*ich also den ersten Stoss ganz allein aushalten musste*)—and for that I was much too weak" (117). Franz had to take the first hit all alone, *ganz allein*. Hélène Cixous has offered a reading in her seminar of the hyperbolic doubling of "all alone." Why, she asks in the context of Marcel Proust's "tout seul," does being alone have to be further qualified by the totality of all (*ganz*)? For Kafka the surplus totality indicated by *ganz allein* may work differently than in Proust where "all" inches toward cosmic depletion and doubles the sum of possible aloneness. For Proust, the addition of "all" to qualify "alone" implies a subtraction, an intensification of the experience of being alone. For Kafka, the "all" suggests an add-on. It is as if Kafka, for his part and parties, were arranging a spectral colloquy, an *all*-inclusive gathering of the living and the dead when addressing the father.

If Franz found himself *all* alone in childhood, this is because they were *all* there, crowded in his aloneness: he was not only alone but in the haunting company of dead siblings. Two little ones preceded him but could not make it, leaving Franz at once stronger—he made it—and weakened, a kind of degeneration or parasitical remnant of the perished brothers. Franz does not say how or why they died but he lines up their disappearance with his father's persecutory powers. Nietzsche, another loner who invents free spirits for company, furtively mentions a dead brother in *Ecce Homo,* where the father is positioned as an existential passerby, possessing qualities of a fleeting memory. Here the corpses are stacked up against the father, further numbing the son's chances of viability. It's not clear whether Franz has incorporated the dead brothers: is he now doing their bidding for

[12] Kafka, "Letter to Father," 117. Further page numbers are given in the text.

them, working pro bono for the dead? In terms of now classic theories of mourning disorder or pathology, is he putting in claims for restitution? The unmournable brothers create a blockage in the passageways of the *Letter*. Franz is enfeebled, vampirically seized by the strictures of unmournability. His experience of weakness is linked directly to their demise. Being "*all* alone"—what about this hyperbolic surplus, why are we *all* alone, isn't it hard enough to be just alone?—this predicament of aggravated aloneness appears to mean that he stands in the buffer zone *with* the phantom brothers, *with* the trace of their extinguished existence. His stance up against the paternal wall tethers him to a frayed concept of the *with/without:* he is being-without, arrested at the premature deaths that mark his toppled upbringing, indicating from the start that he was always and ever raised from the dead.

Abandoned and exposed, part of a muffled history of the undead, Franz has to go it alone. He starts out, very young, as a survivor or parasite, paradoxically strong enough—precisely because of his fragility and minimalist life—to crawl past a first marker. The structure of his survival is such that the immemorial fault is equally distributed between his father and himself. Keeping things ambivalent, his sense of who did what to whom remains at times weak. There are no indictments, no witnesses, no subpoenaed evidence, just a structural insinuation: the brothers were killed off/Franz somehow got away. Alive, he's more dead, or at least more vulnerable than the terminated children. At the same time Franz weighs in on the *strength* of his parasitical existence, living off the dead brothers to whom he owes an unpayable debt. The way he settles the narrative account gives a Freudian-Derridian orientation to the matter, as he goes over territory covered by *Totem and Taboo*. Deprived of the fraternal horde, he had no chance of overcoming his father, no primal alliance or secured lineage to support patricidal rites. (To recap: *Totem and Taboo* establishes the law and lay of patricide, the mythic core of any serious reflection on *Vatermord* and is dependent on a notion of vital fraternity, which Derrida follows all the way up to political structures anchored in the orders of *fraternité*, *liberté*, *égalité*.) The sisters were late in coming and the brothers had been dealt a fatal blow. Franz Kafka does not examine the impact of the decimated fraternal horde, the dead weight that thematically holds down the halfway launched letters; he goes only far enough to nail his exposed solitude on the missing brothers. Without the living fraternity, patricide is off the table. If anything, they owe *him* interest and taxes for the exertions he has had to make as the solitary successor, with and without his brothers, going it alone, all alone, as the pretender that father evermore took him to be. One of his brothers, Georg, returns in name, harangued by his father to commit suicide at the end of the story, "The Judgment." The other sibling, Heinrich, leaves less recoverable traces.

Whether pretender to the paternal throne or henceforth lined up with the world of pretense—without the siblings covering his back, he'll have to fake it relentlessly—Franz signs up for the school of make-believe. Pitched against the virile claims of truth and phallus, he sees himself becoming girlie. Father, we are informed time and again, cannot abide the world of pretense. The values of pretense, artifice, parasitism, and language manipulation quickly line up on Franz's side of the line. Allied with and proxy of truth, Father disavows pretense, what Derrida in his essay on this text, translates as *feindre* (to feign or make believe). Other fathers, the argument pressed by Hermann Kafka is quoted as going, feign interest, pretend politeness, they lack the courage to judge or act according to the sometime brutal precepts of honesty. This well-known logic conventionally covers for rude oppressions and pseudo-dialogue ("I was just being honest"). Let us get a close-up of this rhetorical standoff and examine its life-threatening edges. How does the *Letter* drop into the abyss of their relatedness, configuring the paternal as the emissary of law?

Hermann and Franz circumscribe different fields of battle for the purpose of motivating their plaints. In order to fight the father, Franz has to prepare a plan for taking down the father's name, or at least for taking it on for another round. Brought up between the dead brothers and not yet manifest sisters, Franz enters a battle of proper names, unlinking the very sign of survival—the name whose mark is meant to secure surviving beyond the perishability of its bearer. Who truly belongs to the name, Kafka? Who gets to live on in and as this name? On the other hand, who gets cast as a parasitical hitchhiker living off an eminent patronym? The name, apart from any act of subjective volition or eventual agency, is passed on from father to son as untemperable inheritance. But something occurs in the transit.

The young Mr. Kafka wears his father's name uncomfortably, as a fake ID of which he can only expect trouble. This is where pretense and fiction—what his father accuses him of perpetrating—begin to serve him, for his is, he claims, only a pretend-name: It thus turns out that "Kafka" is his *improper* name, truly the name of the Father. "You, on the other hand, a true Kafka in strength, health, appetite, loudness of voice, eloquence, self-satisfaction, worldly dominance, endurance, presence of mind, knowledge of human nature, a certain way of doing things on a grand scale, of course also with all the defects and weaknesses that go with these advantages and into which your temperament and sometimes your hot temper drive you" (117). The signatory does not bear his name fully, to the extent that a truly binding signature is possible. "I, to put it in a very much abbreviated form, a Löwy with a certain Kafka component which, however, is not set in motion by the Kafka will to life, business, and conquest, but by a Löwyish spur that impels more secretly, more diffidently, and in another direction and which often fails to work entirely" (117). Thus, the *Letter*'s hand-delivered scandal: Kafka is *not* a Kafka. What we in the meantime understand as Kafkaesque reverts in reality to the Löwyesque, or that part of Franz that failed to make the Kafka grade. But it is not simply as though Franz could make claims for an original authenticity of the name that would be borne by the father. The defect already emerges in the father's relation to the name, so that the name of the father gets transmitted with a fault line and compromised lineage, offering for each of the contenders only a strained fit. There's no power punching, patriarchal passing on of a name-of-the-father here that wouldn't turn around and bite the paternal bearer. The father himself hasn't fully grown into the name "in so far as I can compare you with Uncle Philipp, Ludwig, and Heinrich. That is odd, and here I don't see quite clear either. After all, they were all more cheerful, fresher, more informal, more easygoing, less severe than you" (117). The essence of "Kafka" comes down to that which escapes the manifest essence of Kafka. Both father and son owe their outstanding features to what fails to meet the Kafkan prerequisites. Where they aberrate from Kafka, the Kafka signature begins. What has by now settled into a registry of sheer Kafkan dispositions—severe father, anxious son, punishing bureaucracies, night sweats, world-emaciation—skids off the history or accumulated substantiality of the name and what it has come to mean in terms of repeatable and recognizable features. Franz can offer the account of the ill-fitting name only in abbreviated form, he writes. Kafka's readers will identify the irony of the abbreviated relation to the name in terms of the K.'s that wander through Kafka's voluminous novels, compressed and deformed, pointing to a never fully knowable name, moving through the sequence of episodes like dissociated letters, partial initials of larger programs. The strength of the name-of-the-father seems to reside in its lapse, its defective and deflected itinerary. Even though Hermann Kafka cannot fully own or live up to the name Kafka it is still a name that he carries off without question while Franz remains clandestine, going about as a stowaway in the father's name.

This hidden and illicit transport offers him his one chance and solid diminishment, the kid's survival kit: Kafka as Löwy is more stealth, timid, more failing. In this sense he sneaks past the name of the father which was posed as his fate. The playing fields uneven, he avoids collision and collusion, diverting the inevitability of a fatal runoff because, as it turns out, the name behind which he hides—the name itself of hiding, secrecy, timidity—is that of the mother, a Löwy, a lioness. Switching names and scrambling the codes of paternity, Franz, the unKafka, can no longer be mowed down by the assumed father, not on these terms and turf anyway. Despite the skirmishes and perpetual standoff, the so-called father's authority has been rigorously impugned. Franz does not say that he is more like his mother but that *he is a Löwy:* "Ich, um es sehr abgekürzt auszudrücken, ein Löwy" (I, to put it in a very much abbreviated form, a Löwy; 117). In terms of rhetorical delivery Franz interrupts the statement, "I, a Löwy" by cutting himself down ("in a very much abbreviated form"), offering the cut and cutting away from the name-of-the-father while retaining a Kafka component—a speck or specter that allows him to hold off on complete disavowal. He cuts himself down to size, saying in abbreviated form his name: "I … a Löwy." The stealth byway supplied by the not-name-of-the-father grants him his peculiar survival skills and password, cutting a new figure in the history of paternal metaphor.

Index[1]

[1] Note: Page numbers followed by 'n' refer to notes.

L. Weissberg (ed.), *Psychoanalysis, Fatherhood, and the Modern Family*, https://doi.org/10.1007/978-3-030-82124-1

The manufacturer's authorised representative in the EU is Springer Nature Customer Service Centre GmbH, Europaplatz 3, 69115 Heidelberg, Germany. If you have any concerns regarding our products, please contact ProductSafety@springernature.com

Printed and bound by CPI Group (UK) Ltd, Croydon, CR0 4YY
30/09/2026
02225457-0010